Out of Balance

OUT OF BALANCE

Scott M. Matheson

With James Edwin Kee

→P

Gibbs M. Smith, Inc.
Peregrine Smith Books
Salt Lake City

This is a Peregrine Smith Book

Copyright 1986 by Scott M. Matheson and James E. Kee

No part of this book may be reproduced without
written permission from the publisher, with the
exception of short passages for review purposes

Published by Gibbs M. Smith, Inc.
P.O. Box 667, Layton, Utah 84041

Financial support provided by Scott M. Matheson Public
Leadership Forum, University of Utah

Designed by Smith & Clarkson
Cover photo by Scott Tanner
Illustrations by Pat Bagley and Calvin Grondahl

Printed and bound in the United States of America

90 89 88 87 86   5 4 3 2 1

FIRST EDITION

Library of Congress Cataloging-in-Publication Data

Matheson, Scott.
  Out of balance.

  Includes index.
  1. Federal government—United States. 2. United
States—Politics and government—1981-   . 3. Utah—
Politics and government. 4. Intergovernmental fiscal
relations—United States. 5. Governors—United States.
I. Kee, James Edwin. II. Title.
JK325.M38 1986   353.9792   86-6760
ISBN 0-87905-256-2

*To Norma Warenski Matheson
and Suzanne Erlon Kee*

MANY institutions and individuals assisted the authors in encouraging and producing this book. We are very grateful for the support of the following, and any others we inadvertently omit.

President Chase Peterson, the University of Utah, its Department of Political Science and the Hinckley Institute provided a home base and academic residencies for the research and interviews associated with this book. Financial support was provided by the Scott M. Matheson Public Leadership Forum at the University.

The Forum was the inspiration of Dr. Robert Huefner. Its aim is to provide an understanding and to encourage the improvement of public leadership, through seminars, lectures, courses and academic residencies of public officials as they leave office. *Out of Balance* is the Forum's first product. We hope it will spawn many other worthwhile efforts. Special recognition is due the Union Pacific Foundation, The Williams Companies and Wang Laboratories for their generous contributions to establish the Forum.

Many associates submitted to lengthy interviews to recapture data and past history, including Larry Lunnen, Maggie Wilde, Mike Youngren, Kent Briggs, Michael Graham, Mike Zimmerman, Jim Butler, Ken Olsen, Dale Carpenter and Dallin Jensen. Marc Young provided early research support and Malin Foster assisted in editing early drafts. Ultimately the final reflection on certain events are the authors.

We appreciate the permissions given to us by Pat Bagley, the *Salt Lake Tribune*, Calvin Grondahl and the *Deseret News* to reprint editorial cartoons. Utah State Archives and the Division of Data Processing were helpful in accessing and working with certain data and files. Special thanks to Liisa Fagerlund, Emilie Charles, Russ Fairless and Joe Leary.

The editors at Peregrine Smith were a source of positive support throughout the editorial stage and we would like to especially thank James Thomas, John Davis and Scott Cairns.

Finally, Linda Waddingham, Wendy Margetts and Doylene Largent worked long hours on innumerable chapter drafts, changes, deletions and revisions. They were dedicated, patient and cheerful throughout.

Out of Balance—
The Role of the States

NOT long ago, governors were considered by many political analysts as the epitome of the glad-handing courthouse politician, the very essence of Good Time Charlie. But during the 1970s, that image faded, and a different breed of activist, forward-looking, intelligent individuals began to aggressively reshape the character and role of governors' offices in many parts of the nation.*

This metamorphosis was not unlike the one Franklin Delano Roosevelt brought to the office of President of the United States. FDR became a new role model for the presidency. His dynamic personality played a role in that transformation, but in large measure, events, both domestic and foreign, forced the change.

Some of the new gubernatorial activism also results from the personality and charisma of the men and women elected to the office, but national and regional events have mainly shaped the transformation. Governors are now much better known and respected in the halls of Congress, in the maze of the federal bureaucracy, in corporate boardrooms and among the general public. They are the emerging force in American politics.

This book is by and about one of those governors, Scott M. Matheson, a man many credit with leading his state from relative obscurity into a leadership position on regional and national issues. Through the words of the former governor, we view a leader balancing the problems of his state with issues of national importance—a governor who deals with state and local leaders and special interest groups, as well as with Department of Defense experts, Interior Department officials, and foreign ambassadors. Scott Matheson exemplifies the new breed of governors who revolutionized the Governor's Office.

The 1950s and 1960s were discouraging years for governors and their states. They were on the defensive. Malapportionment and unjust representation in the legislature led to judicially mandated reapportionment. The states, ignoring basic constitutional rights of their citizens, found themselves on losing ends of federal court and legislative decisions regarding desegregation and protections guaranteed by the Bill of Rights. States were generally considered unresponsive to the problems

---

* The change in the nature of the governors is well documented in Larry Sabato, *Goodbye to Good Time Charlie*, 2nd ed. (Washington, D.C.: CQ Press, 1983).

of the poor, minorities and urban areas. Special interests, vested economic powers and political machines dominated state government politics.

It was during this period that the federal government became involved in more and more of the areas traditionally left to the states, and ironically, these changes came as a result of the forceful leadership of presidents like Franklin D. Roosevelt, Harry S. Truman, John F. Kennedy and particularly Lyndon B. Johnson. Necessity was, indeed, the mother of invention for these men. As the states defaulted, the federal government muscled in on state and local affairs. The gubernatorial response took time, but it came as the nation was reconsidering the dominant federal role.

During the 1970s, the American people became disillusioned with the federal government's ability to solve problems. The war on poverty was largely a failure. The United States, bogged down in the Vietnam war, and faced with growing disenchantment of its foreign policy both at home and abroad, withdrew its combat troops, realizing it could not win. President Johnson's "guns and butter" budget philosophy spurred large deficits and runaway inflation. Our nation's education establishment, once seen as the backbone of America's prosperity and opportunity for its citizens, was crumbling.

Regional conflict was heightened by years of recession and the flight of industry and population from the industrial Midwest and East, to the sunbelt states of the South and West. In the East and Midwest, newly-elected governors were faced with tremendous problems in their urban areas including decay of their basic infrastructure. Highways, housing, water and sewer systems and public buildings were in an alarming state of decay. Industries demanded tax concessions to forego their moving to the sunbelt states. Mounting federal budget deficits in the 1980s brought federal largess to an end, and the nation's mayors began to look to state government for a solution to urban problems.

All was not prosperity and harmony in the West. Western governors were faced with rapid population growth and the contradiction of increased environmental regulations with an increased demand to develop their natural resources. Governors in those states often found themselves walking a tightrope, requiring more political skill, intelligence and insight than previous governors were expected to exhibit.

People began to look to their state governments for solutions to problems, and during the mid-1970s and early 1980s, those problems were many and varied. The failure of state savings and loan institutions recently required the personal involvement of governors in Ohio and Maryland. The potential bankruptcy of a major urban city, the siting of major power plants and educational reform were all issues that demanded the active attention of the nation's governors. The recession of 1981-83 required almost all of the states to raise taxes and reduce budgets, as the federal government attempted to solve its own budget crisis. And President Ronald Reagan is spurring a major domestic revolution – a revolution which will shift additional responsibilities to state government.

Scott M. Matheson is not unique among the strong governors who emerged during this period, but the type of problems that he faced in the intergovernmental arena provided us with an opportunity to examine an extraordinary range of issues and solutions, from the development of the MX missile to negotiating with President Reagan on New Federalism.

Matheson was not a trained political leader. He did not emerge after years of apprenticeship in the legislature or city or county government. Rather, he was a lawyer who believed in the concept of public service as a fundamental prerequisite to good citizenship. So in 1976, when Governor Calvin L. Rampton decided not to run for a fourth term, Matheson became a citizen candidate, pledging to carry on and improve the Rampton tradition of effective and efficient government for Utah.

Events and issues during the Matheson administration required Utah to play against much tougher odds than ever before and forced the state out of the isolation its people and leaders had historically preferred. Those events and Matheson's leadership thrust him into the regional and national spotlight.

During his first campaign, as he developed position papers on major issues such as energy and the environment, taxes, senior citizens, social services, community impact assistance and intergovernmental relations, Matheson emerged as an individual who clearly had a sense of the forces that were shaping Utah. He was determined that Utah was going to control its own destiny through aggressive actions by the executive.

Matheson enjoyed tremendous personal popularity and a following that many believe could have easily led him to reelection in 1984 for a third term. But he chose to step aside, because he felt that it was the duty of the citizen statesman to get in and do the job and then get out. Future historians will have to judge whether or not Matheson, in fact, did get the job done.

This book is not a memoir in the classic sense. I hope that will come later. And the purpose of this book is not to make critical evaluations of his performance. It is an attempt to present major issues and problems from the governor's perspective. The focus is on the governor as an intermediary, or a bridge, between the federal establishment and local officials; between the interest of the state and the national interest, advocating for an effective executive branch against threatened encroachments from the legislative branch.

Matheson does not inject large doses of personal anecdotes or attempt to chronicle every event — that would have detracted from his primary purpose of discussing his role as an advocate for the state at the regional and federal levels. We see someone who makes mistakes and gets angry, but has a commitment and passion for an open process of government that achieves goals for his state.

The book is divided into four major parts. *Part I, Managing Federal-State Relations*, discusses Matheson's views of federalism, the negotiation with Reagan and the impact of the Gramm-Rudman budget debate on states. *Part II, Balancing State Interests Against National Security*, discusses the MX deployment, atomic testing and the movement of nerve gas bombs. *Part III, New Directions in Natural Resource Policy*, analyzes four major topics: public land management, wilderness, water policy, and national resource development and environmental quality. *Part IV, The New Governor*, describes the evolution of Matheson's style of management, his prescription for creating excellence in government, the emergence of regional and national governors' organizations, and the changing nature of the role of governors.

During his eight years in office, Matheson handled an array of problems that would have discouraged and disillusioned a person with less courage and motivation. That he was perceived to be a success, both locally and on the national scene is, in itself, a tribute to his leadership and style. This book is a fascinating statement of the politics and processes that made it all happen, and can serve as an example to other governors and to anyone interested in public management.

James Edwin Kee

PART I

Managing Federal-State Relations

CHAPTER 1

Fiscal Crisis: The Challenge to the States

IN the fall of 1981 I met with House Speaker Thomas P. (Tip) O'Neil, in the company of Governors George Busbee (D., Ga.), Richard Snelling (R., Vt.), James Thompson (R., Ill.), and Lamar Alexander (R., Tenn.). Our purpose was to pledge our firm support for the orderly transfer of federal programs to the states under the banner of President Ronald Reagan's initiative on New Federalism and to request the support of the House in that undertaking.

We were ushered into the Speaker's office and the meeting began with his question, "What do you boys want?" Having set the tone, the Speaker proceeded to lecture the governors on national policy issues. A fruitless discussion followed.

During that same period a breakfast meeting was scheduled between the Democratic senators and governors for the same purposes. Our discussion on New Federalism evoked several unsupportive comments from the senators. Opposition occurred partly because the initiative had been launched by a Republican President and partly because many senators simply opposed the idea of giving any federal powers or programs to the states. Governor Joseph Brennan (D., Ma.) concluded the meeting by observing, "I hope the time comes when senators will begin to trust governors."

What we hoped for in those and other meetings was the forging of a partnership relationship between congressional and other leaders in the field of intergovernmental relations. That hope was never realized.

Nevertheless, during 1981 the National Governors' Association (NGA) worked hard for a thoughtful sorting out of public programs to be returned to the states. Several "block grants" were enacted that year consolidating a number of individual categorical programs. Public hearings before the Congress and open debate on New Federalism captured the country's interest. Governor Snelling, who was chairman of the NGA that year, and I, as chairman-elect, spent countless hours on the Hill testifying on behalf of the states in this major effort. Resistance to change was strong, both among members of Congress and from the innumerable constituency groups who benefitted directly from federal grant programs.

There were exceptions, however. Senate Majority Leader Howard Baker (R., Tenn.) was cooperative and supportive. Senator Dave Durenberger (R., Minn.) responded to a number of the governors' suggestions. But by the end of 1981 the results of the President's New

Federalism initiatives were modest, at best, and in 1982 the national debate shifted to economic and budget concerns.

From the beginning, Reagan had formulated the debate over transferring federal programs to the states in an open, public fashion, in keeping with the traditions of our democratic society. In contrast to that open debate, it is ironic that with no public hearings and little public debate the President signed into law the Balanced Budget and Emergency Deficit Control Act of 1985, setting in motion the most far-reaching change in federal-state relations since the creation of the Republic.

The Gramm-Rudman-Hollings Act (Gramm-Rudman) is a legislative mechanism designed to force a break in the fiscal deadlock over the federal budget which has stymied President Ronald Reagan and the Congress since 1982. It is the new gladiator of federal fiscal policy, and as the saying goes, Gramm-Rudman is "more than meets the eye." Its mission is multipurposed: first, to curtail the growth in defense spending that has doubled during the Reagan build-up; second, to limit or destroy a number of "non-exempt" domestic programs that were federal growth areas in the 1960s and 1970s; and third, to force an accommodation between the President and the Congress in order to produce a balanced budget in five years.

While the Office of Management and Budget and the President will attempt to focus the gladiator's sword only on the domestic side, the politics of the Congress and the budget numbers themselves will inevitably lead to a withering of both defense and domestic programs, unless there is a significant tax increase, an option to date forsworn by the President. Failure by Congress and the President to meet the required annual deficit reductions may trigger the ultimate weapon of the gladiator: across-the-board cuts in all programs not specifically exempted.

The irony of Gramm-Rudman is two-fold. First, it was a rush job and went through none of the normal legislative processes. Congress heard no testimony from those agencies, governments and interested parties most likely affected. Second, although Gramm-Rudman is a federal law aimed at a national problem, the impacts of the legislation may fall the heaviest on state and local government.

New Federalism questions were never raised by the Congress or the President, and the parties who will bear the brunt of the burden, state governors and local officials, were never consulted. They were simply not a part of the process that will likely control their destiny for years to come. So much for the illusion of our open, democratic society.

Gramm-Rudman: Its Roots and Rationale

While Gramm-Rudman was not an inevitable event, there has been a growing realization during the last decade that the federal system was "out of balance." Too much government and responsibility has flowed from states and localities to Congress and an omnipotent federal bureaucracy. Gramm-Rudman marks the end of a quarter century of federal activism in domestic politics. It will lead to a sharp decline in federal grants to state and local government and, inadvertantly, a swing of power and responsibility back to state houses and, to a lesser extent, city halls. While that may not have been the intent of the bill's sponsors, it certainly conforms to the politics of the President.

President Ronald Reagan clearly articulated his domestic fiscal philosophy in his 1981 inaugural message:

> It is my intent to curb the size and influence of the federal establishment and to demand recognition of the distinction between the power granted to the federal government and those reserved to the states or the people.

The President's first strategic move toward reducing federal responsibility was the enactment of a major tax cut, the Economic Recovery Tax Act of 1981 (Kemp-Roth). While enacted as part of a supply-side fiscal policy, the reduction in federal revenue—at the same time the President was committed to a massive defense build-up—placed considerable pressure on domestic programs.

Analysts suggest that the 1981 tax reductions created a permanent mismatch between revenues (at about nineteen percent of GNP) and expenditures (at twenty-four to twenty-five percent of GNP). Perhaps the President believed the impact of his supply-side economics would help close that gap. It did not. The result has been a consistent effort by the President to cut expenditures by reducing the federal role in domestic programs, many of which affect state and local government.

The Omnibus Reconciliation Act of 1981 proved the precursor of future events. That act consolidated a number of categorical programs for state and local government into block grants but reduced aggregate funding by twenty-five percent. The next step came in 1982 when the President proposed a major shift in programs to the states which would have continued the decentralization trend. However, negotiations with the governors failed and Congress balked.

After four years of fiscal gridlock, political rhetoric and $200 billion deficits, the President and the Congress finally concluded that they couldn't have it all—the defense buildup, the tax cuts and a balanced budget. In drafting the budget-balancing amendment to the bill raising the national debt ceiling, Republican Senators Phil Gramm of Texas and Warren Rudman of New Hampshire joined forces with Democratic Senator

Ernest Hollings of South Carolina to respond to the failure of Congress and the administration to effectively grapple with the budget deficit.

Certainly one has to congratulate the political skill of the act's chief sponsor, Senator Phil Gramm. His impact on the 1981 House budget debate, his ability to switch parties (from Democrat to Republican) and the enactment of Gramm-Rudman during his first year as a U.S. senator are a clear signal that we are dealing with a new and formidable force in American politics.

Of the basic priorities set by President Reagan in his first term, economist Alan Greenspan has said, "It's fairly clear that Reagan's priorities were unequivocally defense, tax cuts and a balanced budget, in that order. He wished to have all three. But clearly, he didn't trade off defense for taxes, or deficits for defense or taxes for the deficit. It's a very clear priority structure."[1]

That priority structure is fundamentally changed by Gramm-Rudman, despite the President's verbal commitment to continue the defense buildup. Furthermore, the deficit targets set in Gramm-Rudman support and buttress the process of decentralizing domestic programs which remains the major domestic theme of the Reagan presidency.

Preparation for this imminent decentralization has not, unfortunately, resulted from a thoughtful sorting out of fiscal responsibilities along the lines suggested by the governors in their 1981-1982 negotiations with the President, from the recommendations of the Advisory Commission on Intergovernmental Relations, nor from the 1985 report of the Committee on Federalism and National Purpose, *To Form A More Perfect Union.*[2] These groups argued for a stronger federal fiscal role in basic income security programs (such as welfare and Medicaid) in return for increased state fiscal responsibility for programs which are primarily state concerns (such as education and transportation).

Gramm-Rudman's five-year drive to eliminate the federal budget deficit assures the states of only one-half of the bargain — the shift of programs to the states. It begs the question of greater federal participation in the income security area. While the amendment currently promises no automatic cuts in federal funding for income-security programs, abnormal pressures on defense and domestic programs will ultimately force a shift of a substantial portion of those costs to the states or to the low-income recipients of these programs. I also believe that in the next five years federal budget balancing will lead to the consolidation or elimination of as many as 300 of the 350 grant programs to state and local governments, including significant programs in education, health and human services and capital investment.

David Stockman, former director of the Office of Management and Budget, has missed the point in his recent book, *The Triumph of Politics*. He argues that the Reagan revolution failed because the President lacked the zeal to carry forward Stockman's ideological vision of a "minimalist government — a spare and stingy creature, which offered evenhanded justice, but no more."[3] But Stockman's revolution was never the President's, and it did not find backing in the halls of Congress or in the minds of the public. Reagan's success was to shift the focus of debate from domestic government growth and activism at the federal level to cutbacks and program shifts to the states. Gramm-Rudman is now the current mechanism for that debate.

Gramm-Rudman: Process and Impact

By requiring a balanced federal budget by fiscal year (FY) 1991, Gramm-Rudman essentially rewrites the federal budget process by establishing firm deadlines and new procedures for budget adoption by the President and the Congress. It imposes mandatory ceilings on the federal budget deficit each year beginning in fiscal year 1986 (which began October 1, 1985). The bill requires immediate cuts of $11.7 billion in spending in the fiscal year 1986 budget and requires the President to propose a budget for fiscal year 1987 with a deficit target of $144 billion, or at least $50 billion less than the $200 billion deficit estimated in the current fiscal year. In FY 1988 the deficit target would drop to $108 billion; in FY 1989, to $72 billion; in FY 1990, to $36 billion; in FY 1991 the budget must be balanced.

There are two alternative paths to the Gramm-Rudman deficit targets. Congress can adopt, and the President can sign, revenue and appropriation bills which meet the deficit targets. Alternatively, in the event of inaction or failure by the Congress and the President to reach such accord, the legislation provides mechanisms to force cuts in spending to reach the targets.

On August 20, the Office of Management and Budget (OMB) and the Congressional Budget Office (CBO) will issue a joint report determining whether all appropriated funds when measured against expected revenues results in a budget deficit in excess of the required targets for the upcoming fiscal year (beginning October 1). If the target is not met, OMB and CBO specify program cuts under specific guidelines provided by the Congress in the legislation. This joint report is submitted to the Comptroller General of the General Accounting Office (GAO), who reviews it, reconciles any differences between OMB and CBO estimates and issues his report to the President and Congress on August 25 containing his deficit estimates and budget reduction calculations.

On September 1, the President issues a "sequestration" order containing the budget reductions *as determined by the Comptroller General*. Unless the President and Congress agree to an alternative budget plan during the month of September, that sequestration order takes effect on October 1, the beginning of the fiscal year.

The use of GAO and the Comptroller General spawned a lawsuit by Representative Mike Synar (D., Okla.), who claimed the provision was an unconstitutional delegation of legislative power (to enact spending measures) and that, in any case, Congress could not delegate the power to decide budget cuts to the Comptroller General, its own agent according to Synar. Under an expedited review process (provided for in the legislation), a three-judge panel of the United States Court of Appeals for the District of Columbia Circuit decided on February 7, 1986 that the delegation of legislative power was lawful but only to an appropriate executive branch official (626 F. Supp. 1374). Since the Comptroller General could be removed by a vote of Congress, the Court found that he and the GAO were creatures of the legislative branch. Therefore, the Court held "that since the powers conferred upon the Comptroller General as part of the automatic deficit reduction process are executive powers, which cannot constitutionally be exercised by an officer removable by Congress, those powers cannot be exercised and therefore the automatic reduction process to which they are central cannot be implemented."

At the time this book is coming into print, the U.S. Supreme Court, on July 7, 1986, ruled on the appeal of *Bowsher v. Synar*, essentially agreeing with the lower court decision. In response, Congress may amend Gramm-Rudman to cure its constitutional defects. Barring repeal of Gramm-Rudman, the deficit targets must still be met by Congress and the legislation contains a specific backup mechanism to force the necessary budget reductions.

The fallback procedure requires OMB and CBO to submit their report to a Temporary Joint Committee on Deficit Reduction (constituted of the House and Senate Budget Committees). The Joint Committee *shall* report a joint resolution containing the budget cuts and sequestration authority under an expedited process. While reductions would only occur if the joint resolution was passed by both houses of Congress and signed by the President, there would be considerable pressure to agree to the joint resolution or another alternative which met the deficit targets. Failure to reach an accord would, in effect, repeal Gramm-Rudman. Legislators who voted *for* Gramm-Rudman and *against* its implementation would have a difficult time explaining their votes to their constituents in November.

Of course, the rational approach would be for Congress and the President to agree to a sensible budget compromise, including defense spending restraint, some domestic program reductions and some tax increases. The President, however, has eschewed such compromise, sending to Congress a fiscal year 1987 budget which contains a twelve percent increase in defense (eight percent real growth) and $70 billion of cuts in domestic programs.

If a rational approach fails, Congress can fall back on the automatic spending cuts of Gramm-Rudman. Social Security and a number of anti-poverty programs, as well as interest payments for the national debt and certain defense and other contractual commitments are exempt from these cuts. Medicare and certain other health programs are subject only to limited cuts. All other federal programs are subject to automatic cuts with half the savings coming from defense spending and half from domestic expenditures.

For state and local governments the most significant implication of Gramm-Rudman is the continued erosion of federal domestic programs, which must inevitably lead to a fundamental restructuring of the federal system. The imperatives of the deficit target and accompanying budget mechanisms will make it difficult, if not impossible, to retreat from the direction set by the legislation. And the political decision-making required by large reductions in the deficit with limited areas to cut will compel restructuring.

Although presidential sequestering of funds began in March 1986, the restructuring began with the submission of President Reagan's 1986 budget for the fiscal year 1987 beginning October 1, 1986. The President's budget recommends over $10 billion of major reductions and eliminations of many programs of aid to state and local governments. His proposals include cuts in payments to individuals (Aid to Families with Dependent Children (AFDC), Medicaid, food and housing) of $2.5 billion; reductions in capital spending (highways, community development block grants, mass transit and wastewater construction grants) of $2.5 billion; the elimination of revenue sharing to local government of $4.4 billion; and over $1 billion in program cuts in education and training and social services.[4]

If agreement is not reached between the President and Congress about where the budget cuts take place and the automatic deficit reduction takes effect, fifty percent of the cuts will come from nonexempt domestic programs. Across-the-board cuts would result in budget reductions of twenty to twenty-five percent in those programs including a number of programs important to state and local governments. Estimates of state and local revenue loss under across-the-board cuts *also* exceed $10 billion.[5]

Even if the President's budget is not adopted and the across-the-board cuts of Gramm-Rudman are not triggered, *any* budget compromise that Congress and the President are likely to agree to in 1986 or in future years will include significant cuts in program support to state and local governments; $10 billion in reductions are a likely first-round result. To put that number in perspective, a recent survey of state budget officers revealed that at the end of fiscal year 1985, year-end balances of the fifty states were a modest $5.4 billion, and one-half of that aggregate was held by just four states: California, New Jersey, Minnesota and Wisconsin.

Long-Term Program Impacts on States

The federal budget bottom line becomes more damaging as we approach the end of the decade with a need to make budget cuts totaling $200 billion, or one-fifth of the current federal budget, to achieve a zero deficit. Even after the consolidation of a number of programs into block grants in 1981, we still have approximately 350 specific programs of assistance to state and local governments. Since seventy percent of the budget consists of long-term defense contracts, and programs which Congress has exempted or limited from the automatic cuts of Gramm-Rudman, we must ask the sixty-four-thousand-dollar question: Where are Congress and the President going to find the cuts necessary for putting together a balanced budget package? Unless a significant tax increase is added as part of a balanced budget package, most of the 350 grant-in-aid programs are likely candidates for termination or for devolution back to state and local governments.

There is no fully satisfactory way to categorize federal domestic grant assistance. Nevertheless, for discussion purposes, I have divided them into five broad categories: (1) Basic support to low income families, (2) assistance to other special groups, (3) economic and community development, (4) education, and (5) all others.

Basic support to low income families includes financial aid to families with dependent children (AFDC), medical assistance (Medicaid), supplemental assistance to the elderly (SSI) and various food assistance programs (Food Stamps, Women, Infant and Child Nutrition). Estimated at $64.9 billion in fiscal year 1987, these programs are currently exempt from automatic reductions under Gramm-Rudman and the House of Representatives is committed to maintaining their funding intact. President Reagan, however, has consistently proposed either a reduction in these programs or a shift of their costs to the states.

Assistance to other special groups includes programs of support for community mental health centers, Head Start, block grants to the states for health and social services, low-income energy assistance, subsidized housing (Public Housing and Rent Subsidies), family planning, alcohol and drug abuse prevention, and programs for the developmentally disabled. Estimated at $12.6 billion, most of these programs are targeted by Gramm-Rudman for limited cuts; several undoubtedly will be merged into state block grants with reduced funding and many may get devolved to the states.

Economic and community development programs include job training (Jobs Training Partnership Act and Work Incentive Programs), infrastructure programs for localities (Mass Transit, Wastewater Construction Grants, Federal Highway Aid and Urban Development Action Grants), General Revenue Sharing (now going just to localities) and a number of programs of technical assistance and grants operated by the Departments of Agriculture, Commerce, Labor and Transportation. Totaling $34.5 billion, these programs are likely to be devolved to the states during the next five years.

Federal education programs represent a small share of total education spending, but a number of programs are particularly significant, including Compensatory Education, programs for the Handicapped and programs for Vocational and Adult Education. Presently there are eighty-six federal education programs totaling over $10 billion. Few, if any, will survive the effort to balance the federal budget.

All other federal programs include twelve programs in the Department of Justice, twenty-two in the National Foundation for Arts and Humanities and National Science Foundation, fourteen operated by the Environmental Protection Agency, seven by the Energy Department, fourteen by the Emergency Management Agency, five by the Veterans Administration and a number of miscellaneous. While they total less than $2 billion, most of these programs are likely targets for elimination despite their minimal impact on the $200 billion deficit reductions needed.

Table I summarizes current federal and domestic programs and impacts under the automatic reduction provision of Gramm-Rudman.[6]

TABLE I

Federal Grant Category	Number of Programs	Approx. $ in billions	Gramm-Rudman Impact
(1) Basic Support to Low Income Families	15	$64.9	exempt from cuts
(2) Assistance to Special Groups	62	12.6	limited cuts
(3) Economic and Community Development	108	34.5*	not exempt
(4) Education	86	10.0	not exempt
(5) All Other	82	2.0	not exempt
TOTALS	353	124.0*	

*includes $13.5 billion in Highway Trust Funds

The elimination of three hundred grant programs may seem unrealistic or sheer folly to suggest, but the reality is that the total funding in fiscal year 1985 of every program which Congress did not exempt or subject to limited cuts under Gramm-Rudman was *only* $46.5 billion (including $13.5 billion in the Highway Trust Fund), or twenty-three percent of the budget reductions needed to balance the federal budget by 1991. Many are already proposed for reduction in President Reagan's budget proposals for fiscal year 1987. In addition to these program eliminations, additional cuts are likely to be proposed for the "exempt" programs (AFDC, Women, Infant and Child Nutrition, Food Stamps and Medicaid) and those federal programs targeted to special groups in need.

Thus, it is not unreasonable to assume that the President and Congress will ask state and local governments to bear at least $50 billion of the total budget reduction by 1991. In addition to cuts in their own programs, states can expect increased pressure from local governments and school districts, which will be losing federal funds and seeking to replace those revenues with state dollars. The states will find themselves in the uncomfortable fiscal vise of reduced federal aid for state programs and increased demands from local governments and school districts for more state assistance.

Clearly the states cannot politically afford to substitute new state revenue for the entire $50 billion, which would represent a twenty-five percent across-the-board increase in state taxes. But some combination of tax increases and program reductions at the state and local level is a virtual certainty.

The Consequences of Federal Devolution

Any federal solution of its budget deficit will almost inevitably include a major devolution of federal program responsibility. It will impose extreme short-term fiscal stress on the states; but it will also allow them to reassume primary control over many programs that the federal government initiated during the 1960s and 1970s. Many federal and local officials may fear that state governments will return to the "do nothing" era of the 1950s and early 1960s. Current programs also have strong constituent followings and those constituents will understandably fear that state governments will not adequately meet their needs.

While fear of state inaction is understandable, state governments in the 1980s are much better prepared for these responsibilities than they were in previous decades. I believe that the states are ready for the challenge, *if* the fiscal vise does not close too fast and if the federal regulatory framework provides the states enough latitude to accommodate this tremendous shift of responsibilities. Additional risks to the states include proposed federal "tax reform" measures such as limiting tax-exempt borrowing or eliminating state and local tax deductibility, and a major federal tax increase which might make a state tax increase very difficult. Either of those possibilities could adversely affect state and local ability to raise revenue and assume new responsibilities.

Undoubtedly state and local governments will choose not to pick up all federal programs. But since the early 1960s, reapportionment within the states has created a more balanced and equitable state legislative system. Governors and the state executive agencies have matured and are meeting new challenges. In most cases, the federal grants themselves are administered by states and this has increased the institutional capacity within state agencies to handle additional responsibility. Therefore, there are strong reasons to show, and I believe this book makes the case, that the states are capable and will pick up most of the critical programs now initiated at the federal level.

A major, ongoing problem is the continuing tension among mayors, county officials, and governors. For years many governors have ignored the problems of mayors and county officials. And since the 1960s those officials are used to bypassing the states and going directly to the federal government. That will now change in a dramatic way. Some governors, mindful of this successful end-run approach of local officials, may harbor a grudge. Several of my gubernatorial colleagues have privately expressed their disdain for mayors and county commissioners, while publicly mouthing their support. For example, it took the National Governors' Association (NGA) almost two years to vote in support of local units of government in their fight for legislation to overturn *Community Communications Co. v. City of Boulder* (455 U.S. 40), after the Supreme Court held in 1982 that local units of government do not have the same immunity from antitrust actions that the states enjoy.

The elimination of most federal program support for education, community development and housing will hit school and local jurisdictions first and hardest. However, public interest groups will focus their attentions on state governments in an attempt to replace lost federal revenue for their programs. State support to localities actually grew during the 1970s and 1980s, and as federal aid decreases state governments will either have to pick up some of the slack or, as Illinois has recently done, grant additional taxing authority to local jurisdictions.

I predict a three-way struggle for scarce state resources among educators, local officials and advocates for the poor, all attempting to replace declining federal revenues. Educators are traditionally the strongest lobby at the state level and are likely to be the initial winners in this struggle.

Perhaps this struggle was inevitable. I personally believe that the governors and the President missed a golden opportunity to lead a rational political restructuring when they failed to find a compromise in the New Federalism negotiations of 1981-82.

CHAPTER 2

Changing State Roles in a Federal System

A S a candidate for governor in 1976 and during the first year or two of my first term, I looked upon federal-state relations as a fairly routine part of the daily responsibilities of a state's chief executive. Those matters were resolved strictly on a pragmatic basis. Fortunately, I had an instinctive bias favoring state and local solutions. I soon began to realize, however, that what I was doing was fulfilling the traditional role of a governor in our unique federal-state system.

During a good portion of the past fifty years that system has seen a dramatic shift of fundamental state and local responsibilities to the federal government, primarily because state and local governments defaulted their role or were incapable of providing the public service.

Beginning in the early 60s, however, states began a major modernization and restructuring, particularly in the executive and legislative branches. Today the states have the capacity and the resources to reassume their historical role in the system. That is fortunate, indeed, because in solving the federal budget deficit, Congress may shortly thrust back upon the states the burden and risks of a substantial number of federal domestic programs. If the states take advantage of the opportunity, it is my view that, after a four or five year period of serious adjustment, the federal-state system will be immeasurably strengthened.

Early Federal-State Perceptions

Intergovernmental relations were a concern to me when I ran for governor in 1976 and were the subject of one of my campaign white papers.[1] My focus was on the need for the governor to play a key role in coordinating federal-state-local relations in order to provide responsible and efficient government services. I certainly had no deep philosophical convictions based on a working knowledge of federalism.

In the paper I noted that federal, state and local governments can no longer operate independently of one another. The federal government's expansion into fields which were formerly the primary responsibility of local governments, such as environmental protection and welfare, has effectively converted state and local government into a joint venture with the federal system.

I saw the governor not only as the major actor in coordinating federal-state relations, but also as the person responsible for consolidating the state's position on federal policy as well as playing a strong advocate role before federal agencies and in the courts. I noted the particular problem of two-thirds of the land in Utah being in federal ownership and said, "To prevent the Secretary of the Interior from exercising more authority in this state than the governor, state government must pursue an aggressive effort in all legislative, administrative and legal channels."

In my 1976 position paper, I noted that each level of government had a legitimate, positive role to play in our society. Although I felt authority had become overbalanced on the federal side, I believed this was partly due to the failure of state and local governments to aggressively pursue public responsibilities in those areas where they operate best. "The key to redressing the balance is improving intergovernmental relations," I said, "and the key to improving intergovernmental relations is effective state and local planning, advocacy and cooperation."

Early in my administration, in outlining the long-term goals I had for the state, I indicated that I hoped to create a Washington, D.C. office to assist Utah in presenting its needs and concerns to the federal system and to monitor federal actions that affected the state of Utah.[2]

The Washington office was established early, but only after working out a unique funding mechanism with the Utah Federal Research Committee, which had some discretion in this area, and following a highly partisan refusal of the legislature to fund the office directly.

Each year I waged the funding battle with the legislature and each year we eked out another budget. In the 1984 campaign Norman Bangerter (R., Ut.), vowed to shut down the office, if elected. As governor-elect, however, he was strongly encouraged by a Reagan Administration spokesman to keep that "excellent and outstanding" Utah office open. He did.

In 1976 my major concern was to increase state and local involvement in managing federal programs and federal lands. However, I didn't really appreciate the significance of the federal impact on state government until after I became governor and began to get involved in individual programs. I quickly learned that it was important to spend substantial time back in Washington, D.C. in order to effectively compete for Utah's fair share of available federal resources. That is why I thought a Utah office in Washington, D.C. was so important.

There is a general public attitude that United States senators and congressmen can and do look out for the interests of their state in the distribution of federal monies through the federal executive branch. But, nine times out of ten, they really don't know what's going on in that branch of the federal government. As a matter of fact they rarely track federal legislation in terms of its impact on programs run at the state level. That means it's really up to the governor and other state representatives to make sure that their state's executive branch interests are effectively represented in the federal government.

Several governors, including myself, were criticized for their frequent trips to Washington, D.C. I remember talking to Governor James Thompson (R., Ill.) about this one time. He indicated that he had calculated, on a conservative basis, that each trip to Washington, D.C. had resulted in about $1 million worth of additional federal funding or savings to the state of Illinois.

Management of Federal-State Relations

Initially, my management of federal-state relations was a pragmatic, ad hoc response to specific issues. Frankly, I had no scheme other than basic instinct to guide me. I got involved immediately in federal-state conflicts over the compensation for victims of the 1950s atomic testing in Nevada, the movement of the Weteye nerve gas bombs and the basing of the MX missile. I considered each issue on its own merits and adopted positions which made sense for the state. I didn't coalesce my own philosophical thinking about the proper role of the states and the federal government until later on in my first term.

In addition to the establishment of a Washington, D.C. office, I wanted to increase state involvement in the management of federal programs and of federal lands. Our attempt to increase state participation in federal lands actions led to Project BOLD, discussed in chapter ten. Another area of particular concern to me was the need for the state to assume primacy, or management responsibility, for federal environmental programs.

Primacy is an administrative concept. I always recognized the legitimacy of establishing national programs with respect to clean air, clean water, nuclear waste and land reclamation. Initially, however, I questioned whether or not the federal government should impose all of these environmental standards. I came to recognize that, as a practical and political matter, the states were not willing, in most cases, to enact standards necessary to protect the environment.

Even before I was governor, I was interested in the state assuming administrative responsibility, or primacy, for water discharge permits. As a member of the Utah Water Pollution Control Board in the 1960s, I argued several times before the legislature that the state should adopt statutes necessary for the administration of the applicable federal legislation. To do so, the state had to adopt the federal standard, create an administrative mechanism and provide a part or all of the funding. During that time the Utah legislature simply wasn't willing to listen to that argument. That was also true of many other state legislatures.

In the 1970s, industry became our ally in helping the state gradually assume responsibility for the administration of programs. Industrial leaders learned that dealing with state officials in carrying out federal mandates is both the practical and the economical approach to meeting environmental regulations. State officials are usually better acquainted with the problems of the industries in their own states and, in my experience, are more responsive to the need for finding ways to help solve them. On a number of occasions, industry was willing to support additional fees at the state level to assist the state in carrying the financial burden of the administration of the program.

During the years I was governor, we succeeded in getting the necessary legislation adopted for the state to assume primacy for a whole series of federal environmental regulatory activities including solid waste management, water and air quality, mine land reclamation and the handling of hazardous wastes.

As the nation's environmental program progressed, the states began taking the lead in implementation, issuing permits and enforcement. The federal government provided assistance, oversight and most of the financing. In the 1980s, we have seen the Reagan Administration cut back funding for environmental programs without reducing federal mandates. These events foreshadow what is likely to occur in regard to other programs into the 1990s.

Historic Overview of Federalism

Federalism is neither a partisan issue, nor is it an issue dividing liberals and conservatives. It's a philosophical concept of how the federal governmental system operates, an effort to determine the proper role of state and federal governments. The issue has been debated since the early days of the formation of the U.S. Constitution and was discussed in meticulous detail by Madison, Hamilton and Jay in the *Federalist Papers*. Madison particularly saw an ongoing, important role for the states in the federal system and argued, in *Federalist* number fourteen, that if states were abolished, "the general government would be compelled by the principle of self preservation, to reinstate them in their proper jurisdiction."

What is the value of state government? Why not operate all programs from a central authority? The power of states to decide local affairs was regarded by Adlai Stevenson as "one of the great assets of our free society, making possible democratic participation at the grass roots of our human relations."[3] Thus, one of the essential values of local government is its ability to respond to local concerns. A pluralistic society is best supported by a diversity of governmental policies.

Another value of state government is the diffusion of power that leads to experimentation in policy and law. Judicial scholars such as Louis Brandeis and Oliver Wendell Holmes have stressed in their writings the value of states as laboratories of democracy.[4] Most national-level policy initiatives began as experiments at the state level.

In addition, the states can operate a greater number of programs more efficiently than a central federal body. Perhaps this was not always true, and for certain programs of national scope (such as health research on AIDS), one can still argue for economies of scale, where total program costs are less if the program is conducted at the national level. However, states are no longer cumbersome, outmoded, and incapable political institutions. They are responsive to local concerns, and they operate a wide range of state and federal programs, often more effectively than their federal counterparts. I also believe there is a growing skepticism among political scientists and economists about the extent to which economy of scale is applicable in operating most government programs.

Woodrow Wilson put the matter into proper perspective in 1908 when he stated that the question of the relations to the federal government cannot be "settled by the opinion of any one generation."[5] In other words, the metamorphosis is very slow; experimentation must be lengthy and careful; the separate roles are constantly evolving.

Centralization of Government in the 1960s and 1970s

Federal centralization of power and influence occurred from the 1930s through the 1970s largely because of the failure of state and local governments to solve public problems. Most people believe that the turning point in the ascendancy of the federal government versus the states was during the administration of President Franklin D. Roosevelt. It is true that regulatory reforms dealing with interstate commerce issues and the development of Social Security were significant FDR programs; but the federal involvement with state and local governments by 1960 was only $7 billion, focusing primarily on four functional areas: highways, old-age assistance, aid to dependent children and employment security. No one in the pre-1960 years seriously questioned whether the federal government was taking over functions that ought to remain at the state or local level.

During the 1950s and 1960s, however, most states defaulted on their responsibility in the intergovernmental system. Instead of challenging and solving the new public problems, states retreated to the comfort of the status quo. They refused to meet the growing needs of our minorities and poor, our urban areas and local units of government. Mayors and county commissioners were sinking in a sea of problems. Local units of government could get neither the funding nor legislation from the states authorizing the necessary taxation and other powers to handle their increasing problems.

Locally elected officials went to Washington, D.C. complaining that "governors are ignoring us and state legislators are unwilling to look at our problems. Help!" And Congress helped. It dramatically expanded the system of grants in aid to local units of government. And often, Congress bypassed states and sent funds directly to locals.

Congress also created regional planning and development agencies. Beginning with the Appalachia Commission, it enacted economic development commissions throughout the United States. Full employment became a national goal and the Social Security system was greatly expanded.

At the same time, the states were also under attack from the judicial branch. The Fourteenth Amendment was dramatically extended in desegregation and criminal due process cases. Reapportionment and voting rights cases had tremendous impacts on the states and greatly changed the intergovernmental system. For the most part, the courts and Congress were responding to what they saw as the failure of the states to exert their proper role in the federal system.

During this period, there was a rapid acceleration of federal dollars going to state and local governments as well as a proliferation of the number of federal aid programs. From 1960 to 1980, federal grants accelerated from a modest $7 billion of aid in about two hundred programs to $91.5 billion. This growth occurred during both Democratic and Republican administrations. Two hundred and nine new grant programs were enacted as part of President Johnson's "Great Society," ninety more during the Nixon/Ford administrations and seventy more under President Carter.

By the end of 1980, there were more than five hundred categorical grant programs. This massive expansion of program initiatives included a number of legitimate national concerns, but it also added a list of programs which, in 1960, we would have viewed as wholly state or local in nature, such as support for fire protection, libraries, police, sidewalks, noise control, solid waste disposal and others. Suddenly we found a growing reliance by state and localities on federal funds. As percentages of state-local expenditures, federal grants rose from 14.7 percent in 1960 to 19.4 percent in 1970 and to over twenty-six percent by 1980.

During these years, Congress emerged as the master architect and arbiter of an increasingly dysfunctional intergovernmental system. We experienced a proliferation of congressional committees supervising the various grant-in-aid programs, and an increase in mandates to state and local governments to satisfy special interest needs. By 1980 the federal role had become so dominant that every state, county, city, town, nearly every school district, over half the nation's special districts, twenty multistate economic development groups, fifteen hundred substate regional units, hundreds of nonprofit units and dozens of colleges and universities were all receiving direct federal aid.

A reaction against this phenomenal growth of the federal government was inevitable. It began at the state level, as governors asserted a stronger role for themselves in national policy debates, particularly through regional organizations and a strengthened National Governors' Association. I personally relished the opportunity to be a part of that process.

Growing Capacity of State Governments

During the last twenty-five years a silent revolution has occurred in the states. Governors are serving longer terms in office and have more control over budgets and executive agencies. Legislatures meet annually and have greater staff support. State court systems have become better managed and more efficient. As a result we have better state government, a more equitable tax structure and greater attention being paid to local needs.

In 1967 former Governor Terry Sanford (D., N.C.), in *Storm Over the States,* chronicled the failure of state governments in leadership, management, responsiveness and accountability.[6] By 1986 major reforms had occurred in those areas in every state, and while some have progressed further than others, states generally have made major improvements.

Recent reports, such as the Council of State Governments' *The States: Current Conditions, Future Directions*, document improvements in both management and program areas.[7] For example, the development of professional budget offices reporting directly to the governor, and the creation of legislative fiscal staffs, have made many state budgetary systems more comprehensive and sophisticated than the federal budget. Many states have capital budgets and multi-year budget plans. States have improved their cash management and audit functions to provide greater fiscal accountability. Many legislative branches have created offices similar to the General Accounting Office to provide legislative audits of program efficiency and effectiveness.

CHAPTER 3

Ronald Reagan and New Federalism

AMERICAN federalism — the tripartite system involving shared and separate powers among the federal, state and local levels of government — is in trouble." This warning was issued in 1980 by the Advisory Commission on Intergovernmental Relations (ACIR) following a three-year study of the role of the federal government in the federal system. In a much-quoted follow-up, the ACIR said, "The federal government's influence has become more pervasive, more intrusive, more unmanageable, more ineffective, more costly and, above all, more unaccountable."[1]

The ACIR's findings coincided with the election of Ronald Reagan as the fortieth President of the United States. That election and the following debate thrust the states into a whirlwind of controversy. In his first four years in office, President Reagan initiated four separate federalism proposals that precipitated debate over the proper role of state and local governments vis-à-vis the federal government.

As a member of President Reagan's Advisory Committee on Federalism, as chairman of the National Governors' Association and as a governor committed to appropriate and shared responsibilities between the states and the federal government, I was actively involved in the negotiation and debates that occurred during the first term of the Reagan Administration.

Ronald Reagan took advantage of the states' growing disillusionment with the federal government. While the ACIR and some political commentators were questioning the growth and intrusive behavior of the federal government, Reagan was the first major political figure to make the role of the states in the federal system a major campaign issue.

Despite the enormous increase of federal activity in our lives, people have remained skeptical of the federal government's ability to solve our public problems. Outright failures in the war in Vietnam and the war on poverty, scandals such as Watergate, and continuing stagflation (a combination of static economic growth and high inflation) fueled the skepticism.

In addition, governors, mayors, state legislators and county officials began to advocate a stronger role for themselves. They wanted to say something about the public policies affecting the constituents who elected them. And they wanted a voice in decision making. Commenting on the growing intrusiveness of the federal government, Governor George Busbee

(D., Ga.) declared, "Pothole repair, firefighting, garbage disposal, building codes, jellyfish control are all subjects of solemn deliberation on the Potomac. The Congressional Record sometimes bears an uncanny resemblance to the minutes of a county commission meeting."[2] During the 1970s, there was also an increased awareness that state and local administrative capabilities had improved significantly. The origin of that awareness was widespread executive reorganization, constitutional change and enhanced support to the executive and legislative branches. The emergence of regional and national organizations of governors, mayors and county officials also helped shape the public debate.

Finally, in 1980 public opinion polls showed that the level of support for governmental activities was shifting from the federal to the state and local levels, emphasizing grass roots political efforts. Decentralization efforts attracted both the new left as well as the old right, and the *Wall Street Journal* editorialized that the "revulsion against all intrusive federal government is likely to dominate the next generation of politics no matter which party is in power."[3]

Reagan's Federalism

In his 1981 inaugural address, President Reagan announced eight guiding principles for his federalism initiatives:

1. Substitute state and local government for the federal government in dealing with private institutions that receive federal aid;

2. Where appropriate, cap open-ended federal matching programs;

3. Use block grants to combine and move categorical federal programs to the state and local level;

4. Utilize planning, audit and review functions at the state and local level;

5. Move federal regulatory power, where appropriate, to the state and local government;

6. Remove federally-imposed mandates;

7. Replace federal funding with the movement of revenue sources from federal to state and local governments;

8. Substitute, when appropriate, state government for federal government in dealing with local government.

During his first term in office, the President initiated four different proposals as part of his New Federalism. He created a Presidential Advisory Committee on Federalism, which met sporadically during 1981-1982; he used the Omnibus Budget Reconciliation Act of 1981 to draw out major federalism, tax and spending policies; he initiated a Presidential Task Force on Regulatory Relief chaired by Vice President George Bush, to examine and curtail federal regulatory authority; and he worked with governors, mayors and county commissioners on block grants and other programs. However, he came into the process with some strong personal philosophical views about the appropriate policy role of the federal government, and those views made it difficult for him to compromise with the general views of the Congress and many governors. The rigidness of his anti-New Deal bias in the face of Congress' strong historical support for categorical programs prevented major legislative change.

Reagan Federalism – 1981 – and the Governors' Response

President Reagan's first legislative federalism proposal, made shortly after his inauguration, was to ask Congress to consolidate nearly ninety categorical grants into seven block grants. The governors had supported the concept of block grants in a 1980 resolution and indicated their willingness to accept a ten percent cut in total federal revenues in return for greater flexibility and control over the use of the funds. Block grants would consolidate a number of categorical programs of special assistance into a general purpose grant for use in broad functional areas.

Unfortunately, because of the enormous tax reductions embodied in the Economic Recovery Tax Act of 1981 (Kemp-Roth), the President and Congress were faced with a sizable federal budget gap. One way to help close that gap was to take up the governors' offer by upping the ante from a ten percent reduction to a twenty-five percent reduction, thereby aptly demonstrating the federal axiom, "What's mine is mine, and what's yours is negotiable."

The governors found themselves on the defensive. We were caught up in our own rhetoric about the demonstrated desirability for more block grants but at the same time opposing the significant cuts proposed by the President. In addition to the cuts in the block grants, the President had also proposed capping Medicaid payments to the states, another reduction the governors found unacceptable.

The governors were able to fend off the cap on Medicaid in 1981, and Congress made significant amendments to the President's proposed block grants plan. Ultimately, however, Congress consolidated fifty-seven categorical grants into nine new, or modified, block grants at a budget authority of approximately $7.5 billion. The block grants represented a cut of approximately twenty-five percent (with inflation, almost thirty-three percent) from the previous year's authorizations. The flexibility originally sought by the governors and the President was not granted.

Nevertheless, most governors felt that, despite the problems inherent in the block grants and the cuts, the change represented a significant departure from the heavy hand of federal control. The new block grants were not embraced without reservation. The essence of the categorical grant system is to strengthen the "Iron Triangle" of congressional subcommittees and their staffs, the federal administrators who support the grant and write the regulations, and the interest groups that receive the benefits from the programs. This ongoing coalition sustains the categorical system against broader national and state interests. It has been an ongoing issue of deep concern to governors.

When categoricals are consolidated into block grants, the Iron Triangle weakens. The governor, his budget office, or a state department, immediately gains power and influence over the allocation of federal and state funds. Thus, the generalists gain power at the expense of the professionals representing the special interests.

During the summer of 1981, we also heard rumors that the administration was considering a proposal to convert the Medicaid and AFDC programs into broad block grants. Reacting to those reports, new NGA Chairman Governor Richard Snelling (R., Vt.) stated at the association's August 1981 annual meeting that "Proposals to shift welfare or Medicaid to the states through block grants would be extremely untimely in view of the large budget cuts which states already must absorb within limited flexibility. They also would be inconsistent with our agenda to sort out government responsibilities. The administration has assured us such proposals would follow and not precede consultation. Since there has been no consultation, we cannot believe that this is an administration proposal."[4]

The governors' position at their Atlantic City annual meeting drew general editorial support across the country. The *Washington Post,* on August 12, noted that "Thus far, the governors have given much more than they've gotten — federal grants to the states will drop by as much as one-third in purchasing power next year, while the amount of newly flexible money included in block grants is barely enough to offset last year's $2.3 billion loss in state revenue sharing."

The *Post* went on to say that "The governors are also right that the responsibility for meeting the basic needs of the nation's poor is properly a federal one. States have little control over the number of poor people in their jurisdictions. When they try to control caseloads by limiting benefits, the result is to foster an unhealthy concentration of the needy in more generous, though not necessarily more affluent, areas."

The *New York Times,* on August 15, asked, "What are the proper roles for different levels of government?" They concluded that "despite the administration's evident desire to unload even welfare and food stamps on the states, there are programs that common sense and human decency require to be universal."

The states' budget directors represented by the National Association of State Budget Officers (NASBO) tend to be more conservative and politically cautious than the governors. Thus, despite the promise of increased authority to the governors and state officials, the budget directors saw the massive cuts in the block grants as simply creating additional pressures on limited state funds. In a special meeting in October 1981, NASBO met to discuss the current block grant status and recommend a course of action for the governors.

A fairly bold recommendation of the budget officers was a massive program swap which would have the federal government assume total responsibility for the income maintenance programs such as Medicaid and AFDC (Aid to Families with Dependent Children). The states, in turn, would assume virtually all other categorical grant-in-aid programs. While the immediate net effect was a loss of revenue to the states, assigning income maintenance programs to the federal government would remove the two fastest-growing programs in the state budget and would allow the states to have better long-run control over the other programs. Only the western governors were prepared to support the broad swap suggested.[5]

By the end of 1981, the governors were becoming increasingly cynical about President Reagan's New Federalism. Nevertheless, they remained committed to continued discussions to find a rational sorting out of responsibilities. Some viewed the block grants as an elaborate charade where the governors got hoodwinked because of their supportive rhetoric. Others viewed them as a modest, if inadequate, beginning to sort out the federal-state grant-in-aid system.

My personal concern was that federalism could easily become a euphemism for shirking responsibilities to the state solely as a means of balancing the federal budget. By adopting that approach, the federal government might inadvertently increase friction between the states and the federal government and between the states and localities. As the federal government dropped certain programs and passed their responsibilities on to the states, the states would be confronted by local constituencies who would expect certain programs or services to continue. In many cases, the states are simply not economically able to fulfill such expectations.

During the heat of the debate over the block grants in the summer of 1981, I indicated in a speech on June 10 that "The battle cry of federalism has served as a bludgeon to balance the federal budget, not to balance the federal system. And as Congress now debates the federal cuts in block grants, it appears increasingly reluctant to relinquish its traditional controls and categorical requirements of federal programs." In retrospect, my worst fears were not realized. The block grants did reduce paperwork and helped shift decision making away from the federal government. Although significant federal mandates and restrictions remained, some were lifted, and the Reagan Administration made a conscious effort through variances and waivers to increase flexibility for the states. If domestic programs were destined to be targeted for reduction, the enactment of the block grant plan at least provided state and local officials some ability to target diminishing resources to areas and programs where the local needs were greatest.

Broadening the Federalism Debate

While President Reagan's block grant proposal served as the fuel to drive the federalism debate, the issue soon took on a much broader context. As part of his initiative, the President appointed an Advisory Committee on Federalism, and that committee, of which I was a member, held its first meeting on June 23, 1981. The fifty-two-member committee was made up of federal, state and local governmental officials and representatives from the public. Not surprisingly, there was no unity of opinion as to how the New Federalism should be implemented. Mayor William Hudnut of Indianapolis, Indiana, president of the National League of Cities, expressed the fears of many urban officials that "All the action is going to the states." Other mayors expressed the view that they had not had a happy relationship with governors in the past. The governors, while pleased that they would now have more control over programs, worried that roles and functions were not sufficiently delineated. Georgia Governor George Busbee, chairman of NGA, argued that it was now time to begin a long-term sorting out process. Busbee was always considered by his peers to be a highly capable governor with excellent perspective. In the federalism debate he continued to display his low-keyed but effective leadership style.

Throughout the year, federalism was high on everyone's agenda. Several congressional committees held hearings. Conferences and seminars were sponsored by many interest groups. Governor Richard Snelling, the incoming chairman of NGA, called a convocation on federalism on August 7, 1981 in Vermont – a joint executive and legislative branch effort which was attended by some three hundred people from throughout the state. Snelling was of the same caliber as Busbee, but he utilized a more aggressive leadership style which often generated great controversy. He often found himself at odds with his Republican President; but he served the governors well in the federalism debate.

At a September 24, 1981 meeting with President Reagan, several governors, including myself, presented a list of concerns. In particular, we emphasized that we would vigorously oppose any attempt to shift a greater portion of the Medicaid budget to the states, or to make deeper cuts in the new block grants. We asked the administration to establish an "early warning" mechanism to insure that the states were fully consulted, not only on federal budget cuts but also on the development of any new policies that directly affected state powers and responsibilities.

In a December 4, 1981 letter, Governor Snelling, now NGA chairman, called for the administration to join the governors in a domestic summit to "develop a consensus for achieving the goals we share." Those goals included reducing the federal deficit and devising an equitable distribution of resources and responsibilities among federal, state and local governments. "Under your leadership," Snelling urged the President, "I believe that a domestic summit could significantly aid you in developing a consensus on what will be otherwise intensely divisive issues in the years ahead."[6] Nothing substantive ever resulted from the proposal.

The second meeting of the President's Advisory Committee on Federalism occurred on December 15, 1981. One of the few meritorious presentations came from Senator David Durenberger (R., Minn.), an outspoken proponent of a more rational distribution of program responsibilities. He submitted eight "proposals to redistribute responsibilities in the federal system." The proposals, with a discussion of their advantages and disadvantages, included block grants, sorting out, straight devolution, revenue sharing, megablocks, excise tax returns, income tax returns and combined income tax returns with capacity equalizing grants.

However, state and local government representatives continued their unease about the appropriate role of the states in the sorting out process. Many local governments feared that any program and revenue turnbacks would not trickle down to them. The insecurity of local officials plagued the Advisory Committee, which eventually bogged down because of its size and inability to come to a consensus on fundamental federalism principles. Its final meeting was held on March 22, 1982, and the entire effort ended abruptly, with only a whimper.

The year 1981 had ended with the President telling the Advisory Committee on Federalism that he would not balance the fiscal 1983 budget on the backs of state and local governments, but he was cool to the governors' call for a domestic summit. Richard S. Williamson, assistant to the President for intergovernmental affairs, in a December 16, 1981 colloquy on PBS's "MacNeil-Lehrer Report" with Mayor Hudnut and Governor Snelling, argued that President Reagan had met already with more than seventeen hundred federal, state and local officials during 1981 and claimed there had been substantial consultation. He said the President questioned the value of a domestic summit without a specific agenda. Snelling countered that the governors wanted more than just meetings; they wanted true consultations and would be happy to work with the President in coming up with an acceptable agenda. Snelling also argued that it was essential for such a meeting to occur before the President announced his fiscal year 1983 budget. He pointed out that the potential for further cuts was of great concern to state and local governments already beginning to suffer from the cuts initiated by the President and Congress in 1981. The President ignored Snelling's plea.

The 1982 Reagan Swap Proposal

Faced with mounting fiscal and economic problems, President Reagan chose to use his State of the Union address, on January 26, 1982, to unveil a sweeping proposal for transforming the federal system. "In a single stroke, we will accomplish a realignment that will end cumbersome administration and spiraling costs at the federal level while we assure these programs will be more responsive to both the people they are meant to help and the people who pay for them," said President Reagan in explaining his new federalism proposal.

The President's proposal involved three concepts:

1. *The swap.* Washington would pick up all Medicaid costs, and the states would assume responsibility for all costs of Food Stamps and Aid to Families with Dependent Children (AFDC).

2. *The turnback.* The federal government would abandon 61 grant-in-aid programs, allowing the states to pick them up.

3. *The trust fund.* The states would get the proceeds of a federal fund composed of federal excise and oil "windfall" profit taxes, but after 1990, the federal taxes would be terminated, and the states would fund the programs.

Congress was openly skeptical of the President's program. Some Democrats viewed the federalism proposal as a diversion from the growing deficit problems caused by the Reagan economic and fiscal policies. The reaction of most government officials was generally cautious. "You have to judge whether the glass is half full or half empty. But the President has come a long way," said Governor Snelling.[7]

The swap was viewed as a mixed blessing by most governors. While they had advocated the transfer of Medicaid costs to the federal government as part of a swap, they also viewed the income security programs, such as Food Stamps and AFDC, as continuing federal responsibilities. "Most governors would prefer that the national government took AFDC, Food Stamps and Medicaid and give us an even amount of programs of a more everyday concern, like sewers," said Governor Lamar Alexander (R., Tenn.).[8]

Governors were also concerned about the elements of the trust fund, composed of federal excise taxes, and their eventual phasing out. With fiscal disparities among the states, would the less wealthy states be able to afford to continue the federal programs? "The President's proposal has no chance in getting to first base unless it takes into account the differences between rich and poor states," Governor Alexander said.

Local officials, such as New York City Mayor Ed Koch, described the provisions requiring the states to turn over funds to cities as "inadequate." But a lobbyist for another big city, James Sealy of Los Angeles, was optimistic that his city could receive fair treatment in the distribution of funds by the California legislature. "We're obviously closer to Sacramento than we are to Washington," Sealy said.[9]

Some governors were openly contemptuous of the President's proposal. Governor Hugh Carey (D., N.Y.) called the proposal a "new feudalism," and Governor Jerry Brown (D., Calif.) argued that the proposal would set up "competing colonies" and was a Trojan Horse that was diverting the country from key economic issues.[10]

Other governors were more supportive. Bruce Babbitt (D., Ar.) said that "The President's proposal was a long-overdue attempt to reduce the size and scope of the federal government. The states are fully capable and competent to administer many programs that are now handled at the federal level."[11]

Federalism had risen to a high priority on my own agenda, even before President Reagan had assumed office. In remarks to *U.S. News & World Report,* I noted that my differences with the President's program were philosophical, not political. I repeated my concern that "the heart of the issue is whether the President's program is meant to balance the federal system or the federal budget."[12]

The President dropped the other shoe on February 6, 1982, releasing his budget message urging Congress to "stay the course" by shrinking the social responsibilities of the government while expanding the nation's military strength.

The President's proposed 1983 budget plans drew immediate fire from the nation's governors. NGA chairman Snelling, while applauding both the boldness of the President's federalism plan and his willingness to negotiate on the details, said, "It would be unrealistic to expect the states to support another round of deep budget cuts in 1983 with still greater responsibilities looming in fiscal 1984 and beyond. In part, because of the cuts projected in this budget, it appears that the administration's federalism plan would put an additional $9 billion burden on the states in 1984."[13]

The President's proposal brought a variety of alternative concepts to the table for consideration. Snelling tried to tread a middle ground to preserve NGA options in representing the governors. In a message to all governors on January 28, 1982, he noted that the President's plan had many features incorporating established NGA policy. He argued for a negotiating position which would allow the governors to work with the President and Congress in shaping a plan which the governors felt was good public policy. "If we fail in the negotiations," he argued, "we could always reject the proposal."

His major concern was keeping the negotiations alive, although he recognized that the governors would have to oppose cuts in the 1983 budget which would leave state governments incapable of meeting the requirements of the President's plan.

In a letter to Snelling on February 3, 1982, Governor Babbitt argued that the major problem with the President's proposal was the transfer of entitlement programs, i.e., Food Stamps and AFDC, to the states. "This swap will spark a big fight that could torpedo the entire program, and we should therefore uncouple it from the 'Devolution of the forty-three Categoricals' proposal."[14]

The Income Maintenance Issue

To understand the basic disagreement between the governors and President Reagan over the swap proposal, it is necessary to briefly discuss the nation's basic income maintenance programs which were the critical components of the proposed exchange.

First is AFDC (Aid to Families with Dependent Children), the nation's basic welfare program. In 1981, it provided benefits to 11.1 million individuals at a cost of $6.9 billion to the federal government and $5.8 billion to the states. Each state is free to set its own level of benefits, which in 1981 ranged from a low of $96 a month for a family of three in Mississippi to more than $200 a month for a similar family in New York. Benefits rise with the number of individuals in a family. The federal government matches what the state decides to pay on a formula basis that takes into account state per capita income. The program is administered by state and local governments under federal guidelines.

Second is the Food Stamp program which had 21.7 million recipients in 1981 whose eligibility was determined by federal regulations. Its cost was $11.4 billion, with the federal government picking up the entire tab. Food Stamps are distributed by state and county welfare officials, but the program was designed by Congress and regulated by the Department of Health and Human Services (HHS).

Third is Medicaid, the health program which provides medical care for the poor. Unlike Medicare, which serves the elderly, Medicaid has no age requirement. Medicaid provided assistance to twenty-two million people in 1981, at a cost $30.5 billion. In 1981, the federal government assumed about fifty-five percent of the total cost, and that rate varied slightly from state to state depending upon the services provided. Between 1975 and 1981, Medicaid grew at a fifteen percent compounded rate, far above the rate of inflation. The states were free, at that time, to provide optional services, such as eyeglasses and prescription drugs, with Washington sharing the cost. Thus, benefits and eligibility standards varied from state to state.

One of the major issues in a federalized Medicaid program was whether or not the federal government would provide enough resources to maintain the program at a reasonable level or if a substantial number of individuals receiving services under the existing federal-state program would be denied services under a federal version of the program. If this occurred, those people would likely seek either state or county health aid. In the past, AFDC participants were automatically eligible for Medicaid benefits. Yet, if the AFDC program were turned over to the states, the states would, in effect, dictate the eligibility for the Medicaid program. A number of unresolved questions remained concerning uniform Medicaid standards. For example, would the eligibility include medically-indigent individuals (those with low incomes who do not qualify for AFDC)? Would those currently eligible be covered under a grandfather clause if their programs were phased out? Which, and how many, of the optional services would the federal government pick up? Who would administer the program? And there were several other extremely difficult questions.

It was hard for the states to avoid a computer printout mentality. The President's proposal and every counter-proposal were subjected to intense scrutiny by state budget officials and program deliverers. Net gainers and winners were noted, and there was the ongoing problem of how to be fair to those who won or lost under the swap proposals.

Budget Director David Stockman, while arguing that in the short run, there would be no winners or losers in the President's proposal, admitted that under the Reagan plan, the trust fund would disappear by 1991, and the states would be on their own. He candidly stated that the Reagan plan is simply not designed as a "solution to the fiscal disparities problem." He questioned whether the federal government should even address the disparities issue, saying that such proposals were "a dangerous thing to get into."[15]

I had several meetings with Stockman. My judgment, as I had feared, was that he looked at the federalism initiatives strictly as a means of reaching budget objectives. His comments were always confined to numbers. He never discussed the concepts of federalism or the merits of public programs.

I would have an opportunity to joust with Stockman during the 1982 federalism negotiations. While I respected his intellect, his lack of concern for the substantive policy issues and programs critical to the poor supported the rumor that ice water flowed through his veins.

Reagan's New Federalism agenda was *the* issue for the governors, at their winter meeting, February 21-23, 1982 in Washington, D.C. I was now the chairman-elect of the NGA and would become chairman the following August. I knew that the upcoming debate was a significant window of opportunity for the states, and I was determined to play a major role in it.

CHAPTER 4

The Governors Negotiate

Ihave always felt that income-maintenance was a federal responsibility and that it made little sense to split those programs between the federal and state governments in the manner proposed by the President. Therefore, I entered into the debate over his swap proposal with great skepticism. I was also concerned over the failure of both the governors and the administration to involve Congress in the negotiations. Nevertheless, and in spite of the odds, an opportunity for the states was there, and I decided to make a strong personal commitment to find an acceptable proposal.

Prior to the winter meeting, I developed an alternative federalism proposal which I hoped might receive acceptance of the governors. My key concern was with the President's Medicaid swap for AFDC and Food Stamps. Since the governors had already philosophically taken the policy position that income maintenance programs were a federal responsibility, it was clear that a majority of governors were unwilling to support state assumption of those programs.

My alternative consisted of a more limited swap—federal assumption of total funding for Medicaid in return for state assumption of a set of defined categorical programs utilizing the President's proposed forty-three programs as the starting base for discussions. Any difference in cost between the turnback to the states and the Medicaid pickup would be handled through a trust fund with the same operational characteristics as proposed by the President. There would be no losers as defined in the President's proposal.

While not rejecting the idea of state assumption of AFDC and Food Stamps, I suggested deferring the proposal for further negotiations to allow a "digestion time" for the first swap. This would effectively set aside the issue that was the bone of greatest contention to the states.

In addition to the Utah alternative, Governor Busbee proposed that the Food Stamp program remain under federal financing and that we proceed with a Medicaid/welfare swap, utilizing a smaller trust fund designed to hold states harmless (i.e., make up the lost dollars) during the first year of operation with a gradual phase-out over three years. The turnbacks would be accompanied by a separate trust fund with some permanent source of funding.

Rich Williamson, assistant to the President for intergovernmental affairs, appeared before the NGA executive committee on behalf of the President and urged that the debate not get bogged down with "green eyeshade accountants looking at specific numbers." The President had "guaranteed" there would be no winners or losers. He indicated that

Ronald Reagan, who philosophically believed that the states should assume responsibility for both Medicaid and welfare costs, had compromised on Medicaid, and he hoped the states would compromise on the welfare cost issue. He also urged that federalism issues become separated from the budget issues.

That same theme was echoed by Budget Director David Stockman. "The fiscal year 1983 budget was to be separate from the federalism initiative," Stockman announced. I personally disapproved of that approach, and it was almost unanimously rejected by the governors. Snelling noted that "The 1983 budget is, in the judgment of many governors, tied to the capacity of states to undertake the new federal-state relationship."

I felt that the states were already the losers from the prior years. If we were going to be partners in a federalism initiative, I said, "We can't come into the partnership in an anemic position, and we can't afford another year of state budget hemorrhaging."

The governors were concerned about the deficit numbers the administration was facing and the implications of that deficit for further cuts in programs to the states. In response, Stockman urged that we not hold the federalism agenda hostage to a balanced budget.

Williamson pledged, on behalf of the administration, that their budget numbers were not locked in granite, and both Stockman and Williamson indicated that whatever the final appropriations were for fiscal 1983 for the state programs, those numbers would serve as the basis for the turnbacks versus the trust fund.

While the governors consistently held to their philosophical viewpoint that Medicaid, AFDC and Food Stamps should remain primarily a federal responsibility, Stockman argued that the President's decision to take up Medicaid was not a result of a philosophical view on income-maintenance but, instead, was a concession to pick up a program that had very dynamic growth and match it with a dynamic revenue source (the federal income tax). He felt that in the long run, the states would become the winners in shedding the Medicaid financial burden. In the light of Gramm-Rudman, he may have been right.

It was clear that a number of the governors were unalterably opposed to the Medicaid/welfare trade; however, there was also a consensus that we should give the President some support. Governor James Thompson (R., Ill.), for example, felt that "Ronald Reagan is the governors' only hope to a New Federalism." He correctly pointed out that any proposal was going to face stiff opposition from Congress, and that it would clearly fail without the President as an ally.

In crafting an alternative proposal for consideration by all the governors, the executive committee essentially adopted my proposal with some modifications. We applauded the President for setting out "a bold and specific proposal to realign the federal system to achieve more effective and accountable government at all levels." We indicated that we shared the President's sense of urgency in placing federalism reform at the top of our agenda and that we agreed with many of the principles and guidelines contained in the President's proposal. Nevertheless, there were some elements, specifically AFDC and Food Stamps, which were not consistent with existing NGA policy, and the governors were unwilling to concede that basic, long-held point of view.

We also served notice that the federalism proposals were linked to the budget debate, clarifying our position that "support for state and local governments should not be cut in the 1983 budget to the extent that state governments are weakened and left without the capacity to meet the new service delivery requirements of the president's plan for 1984 and beyond."[1]

The governors pledged that they were ready to enter into immediate discussions with the administration concerning areas of agreement and to leave unresolved subjects open for future discussion. Our goal was to keep the federalism issue alive before the American people and to work with both the President and the Congress at every opportunity to restore balance to our system.

The National Conference of State Legislators (NCSL), reportedly after heavy lobbying from the White House, adopted a resolution in support of the President's initiative, but with qualifications and concerns about the scope of the program and some of the specifics. In fact, the proposed $10 billion in cuts in federal aid to state and local governments contained in the President's fiscal year 1983 budget were of concern to both Republicans and Democrats. NCSL President Ross Doyen, the Republican president of the Kansas Senate, indicated that the new cuts Reagan proposed would have "an adverse effect on our ability to cope with citizen needs."[2]

The governors met with President Reagan on February 22, 1982. While the President was disappointed that we had not agreed to the AFDC takeover, both sides agreed there was enough common ground to attempt to negotiate the differences. On the final day of the NGA winter meeting, Governor Snelling announced the selection of five governors who would join with him on a negotiating team that would meet with the administration. The governors included Democrats Bruce Babbitt of Arizona, George Busbee of Georgia and myself; and Republicans Richard Snelling of Vermont, James Thompson of Illinois and Lamar Alexander of Tennessee.

"I am pleased to name this bipartisan negotiating team," Snelling said. "The governors have a great deal of experience in the issues at hand and are in an excellent position to articulate the concerns of my colleagues. . . . We share with the administration the strong desire to move forward constructively on federalism."[3]

The administration was represented in the negotiations by Edwin Meese, III, counselor to the President, James Baker, White House Chief of Staff, Richard Williamson, assistant to the President for intergovernmental affairs, David Stockman, director of the Office of Management and Budget, Richard Schweiker, Secretary of Health and Human Services, and Ed Harper, director of the White House Office of Policy Development. The first meeting of the governors and the administration was scheduled for March 6, 1982.

In the meantime, we took our case to Congress. Several governors testified on February 24 before the Joint Economic Committee's "Hearing on New Federalism." I stressed the poor fiscal conditions of the states and our inability to take additional cuts in the context of New Federalism.

I also took the governors' case to the Senate on March 12, before the Committee on the Budget. I articulated the governors' position on the federal budget, indicating that the state and local share of the federal budget had shrunk from about $105 billion in 1980 to $78 billion in 1982. The $5 billion in additional cuts proposed by the administration for fiscal 1983 would require substantial reductions in benefits to individuals who are totally or partially dependent upon government assistance. "Those cuts far exceed potential savings from reductions in fraud, waste and abuse."

While I endorsed the President's federalism initiative, I said, "We cannot divorce it from the proposed budget cuts" in fiscal year 1983. I indicated the governors' support for congressional efforts to curb the size of the federal deficit — feeling that major targets had to be defense and non-income-related entitlements. But I argued that governors would not subscribe to a "shift and shaft" theory where the federal government passed down responsibilities and expected states to find the money to pick them up. That simply was not true federalism.

The Federalism Negotiations

The first negotiating session between the governors and the administration took place at the White House on Saturday, March 7. Snelling presented the governor's position and Williamson and Stockman spoke for the President. It was clear that Williamson wanted to reach an agreement and was supported by Secretary Schweiker. Stockman, however, performed in his familiar clinical fashion. Baker was inscrutable.

While a detailed position paper had been provided to the governors by their staffs to discuss specific issues related to the governors' counter proposal, a basic impasse was reached with the administration officials over the AFDC/Food Stamp issue. Mr. Williamson indicated that the administration's definition of a swap contained all three components: Medicaid, AFDC and Food Stamps.

One of our main objections was the incompleteness of the administration's plans for the federal takeover of Medicaid. We questioned eligibility rules, scope of benefits and reimbursement procedures, which varied greatly among the states. While we did not represent to the press our discouragement, it was clear that governors were disappointed that they had not succeeded in making any substantive progress at the first meeting.

A second negotiating session was held March 17. Prior to that meeting, one of the chief negotiators, Rich Williamson, reportedly stated that the President was considering withdrawing one element of his proposal that the state and local groups liked most, Reagan's plan for the federal government to assume responsibility for the Medicaid program, because the states were unwilling to assume AFDC and Food Stamps. According to Williamson, the President had given something, and now it was the governors' turn.[4]

What the White House proposed on March 17 was a restructuring of the swap along the lines proposed, at one time, by Governor Busbee but rejected by the governors. It provided that the federal government would assume responsibility for AFDC and Medicaid for a certain group of eligible people and the states would be responsible for another group. Under an illustrative proposal, Medicaid, Food Stamps and cash assistance were suggested as state responsibilities for the AFDC population, with suggested federal responsibility being the SSI, or elderly population. The governors countered with a suggested federal assumption of specific functional elements of the Medicaid program financed by the states, if a full federal assumption of Medicaid as originally proposed by the administration was no longer possible.

What most troubled me about the character of those negotiations was that they were driven solely by dollar tradeoffs without any kind of underlying philosophical basis for sorting out the program elements.

The administration had originally hoped to have draft legislation ready by the end of March, but at that time, their Medicaid assumption criteria were still in flux. The *New York Times* reported, on April 7, 1982, that an OMB official indicated that while the idea of a swap was not dead, the administration had no plans to press for the necessary legislation.

A similarly pessimistic report was prepared by Governor Snelling to all governors on April 28, 1982, indicating that "No agreement on the swap is possible without a full accord on Medicaid. To date there is no such accord; in fact, we have not yet received *any* details of the administration's Medicaid proposal." A final meeting of the negotiating team was held June 23. We had made progress on minor details but the major stumbling block was still there: Which level of government appropriately holds responsibility for maintaining a minimum level of economic security? In a July 8 speech to a "New Federalism" Conference in Portland, Oregon, I noted that all fifty governors were united in believing that "the national responsibility extends beyond providing national defense, servicing the national debt and administering the Social Security system."

Despite the administration's lip service to the establishment of a "safety net" for the poor, its effort to shift AFDC to the states was totally inconsistent and suggested to me that they had no clear concept, nor any genuine philosophy, concerning the nature of the federal system.

The final 1982 federalism initiative by President Reagan, announced in a speech in Baltimore on July 13 before the National Association of Counties, provided no basis for compromise with the governors. The President proposed dividing the Medicaid responsibility between the federal government and the states, with the primary Medicaid responsibility for low-income persons assumed by Washington, and long-term care remaining with the states. To help pay for this, the states would receive a block grant of $8.5 billion. Reagan also proposed transferring about thirty programs, including AFDC, with an annual cost of $38.7 billion, to the states.

The *New York Times* editorialized on July 15 that "Washington got into the welfare business in the Depression because the states couldn't or wouldn't provide adequately for the jobless. Poverty is even more a national program now. Recession touches every region. Even affluent Texas is telling the poor of the states not to come looking for work . . . So far, new federalism sounds mostly like a nice name for old poverty."

The governors considered and rejected the final administration package at their annual meeting on August 8-10 in Afton, Oklahoma. However, they agreed to a federalism action plan that called for continued discussions with the President regarding his federalism initiative and the development of a separate NGA federalism reform proposal. In his report to the governors, outgoing Chairman Snelling said, "It no longer seems prudent to pin our hopes for a new federalism on the outcome of any negotiations with the White House which proceed from the assumption that the public policy convictions of the President and the governors regarding the substance and design of a proper federal-state relationship can or must be reconciled."

Snelling basically believed there was broader agreement among the governors concerning appropriate specifics than among the key advisors to the President. He shared my belief that those advisors lacked a central, philosophical basis for their federalism proposals. "Our negotiations with the White House seem to have floundered on the question of whether, in the end, the federal government would maintain any responsibility for assuring minimum levels of essential services or for dealing positively with the problems which the disparity of fiscal capacity among the states pose for state and local officials," Snelling concluded.

In my August 10 remarks, upon assuming the NGA chair, I said, "The governors of the American states have been concerned about restoring balance to the federal system for many years. If we are to obtain the balance we seek, each of the partners must recognize that our federal system consists of both sovereign states and a sovereign nation. . . . Federalism cannot be departmentalized into a single bill or package of legislative initiatives divorced from other issues. Rather, it must provide discussions of virtually every domestic issue that comes before Congress."

"The nation's governors are anxious to become responsible and responsive partners in the federal system. I intend to devote my efforts, as chairman of the National Governors' Association, to helping the states assume the role intended for them by the founding fathers. They can do no less if the term, 'these United States,' is to have any meaning at all."

In remarks later that month to the Citizen's Forum/National Municipal League, I said that fundamental to the belief of the governors is that the federal government is responsible for maintaining a minimum level of economic security. The states were not in a position to control poverty or unemployment, since federal tax, monetary, regulatory, fiscal and foreign policy decisions are the major determinants of the economic climate in individual states, and all of those decisions are under control of the federal government. Thus, the seventeen percent unemployment in Michigan and the immigration of Cuban refugees into Florida were national, not state, problems.

We had spent nearly five months of intense but ultimately unsuccessful negotiations with the White House to resolve our differences. Although the Reagan Administration is the strongest advocate of a revised federal system to occupy the White House in many decades, we had to face the fact that the administration's view of federalism was, in many ways, not the states' view.

I was invited to meet with the President at the White House on September 30 and to express, along with other state and local officials, the governors' concerns over issues of federalism and the federal budget. The President said he would welcome a comprehensive counter proposal to his federalism package, but later events disproved that offer.

In a follow-up letter to the President on October 7, I stated that the fiscal year 1984 budget must bring the federal system toward a clear and more rational division of responsibility among federal, state and local governments. Any move to reduce federal support for such areas as education, law enforcement and transportation must be balanced by expanding the federal role in income security programs, which are a national responsibility.

On November 10, the NGA executive committee made a final attempt to revive the governors' proposal of an exchange of Medicaid for selected categorical programs. Since the administration had not presented details on their Medicaid initiative, we outlined a specific proposal which would provide for the federal government taking over all or part of Medicaid in exchange for state acceptance of a comparable level of categorical programs. It was designed in three major components so that federal assumption could take place on a phased basis if necessary.

In a letter to the President on November 19, 1982, we noted that our proposal was built upon the initiative that the President announced in January of 1982. It would end direct federal responsibility for a number of categorical programs. It would more clearly focus accountability for certain areas on the states and build on the current role of the federal government in financing Medicare.

Our attempt was to adopt a simpler swap and one easier to explain in the event that we could attract congressional consideration. In conclusion, we said, "Clearly, a successful federalism initiative must have the strong support of your administration, the Congress, the governors, state legislators and local officials. Accordingly, we pledge our continued cooperation in working with you and others on the present proposal and on other options to accomplish federalism reform."

The reaction to our initiative was a resounding silence. Nineteen eighty-two, which began with such high hopes for cooperation and fundamental change in the intergovernmental system, ended with the nation in the greatest recession since the Great Depression—a budget deficit of $111 billion in fiscal year 1982, a projected deficit of near $200 billion for fiscal year 1983 and the promise of further cuts from the President that would damage the fiscal health of state and local governments.

The President's 1983 Federalism Initiative

On January 25, 1983, President Reagan announced, in his State of the Union address, that he would shortly submit a comprehensive federalism proposal that will "continue our efforts to restore states and local governments their roles as dynamic laboratories of change in a creative society."

The President's legislative proposals consisted of four block grants which consolidated thirty-four programs. The proposed total for fiscal 1984 funding was approximately $21 billion. It provided level funding for each of five fiscal years from 1984 through 1988 but proposed some initial reductions. The four separate blocks, each in a separate bill, were the following:

1. A local block grant combining general revenue sharing with the entitlement portion of the community and development block grant, involving approximately $7 billion annually;

2. A transportation block grant consolidating six highway programs covering urban and secondary road systems, some bridges and safety activities, involving some $2 billion annually;

3. A rural housing block grant to states consolidating four programs for low-income rural housing construction and repair, involving $850 million annually, a sixty-five percent cut from the previous fiscal year; and

4. A state block grant, financed by federal excise tax revenues and alcohol, tobacco and utilities, combining twenty-two health, social services, education and community development programs involving approximately $11 billion annually. A fourteen percent cut from fiscal year 1983 levels was proposed for these twenty-two programs.

There seemed to be no coherent rationale for the state block grant. In testimony on March 2 before the Joint Economic Committee's hearing on New Federalism, Governor Snelling noted that the "megablock grant proposed for the states puts in everything but the kitchen sink — as a matter of fact, the kitchen sink, too — into the proposal, putting together child care programs and sewage disposal programs together with a fourteen percent cut . . . " Snelling concluded that the governors continued to believe that "some day we ought to try a new federalism . . . block grants are not by themselves federalism, block grants which deny the advantage of flexibility are certainly not federalism, and budget cuts can never be characterized as federalism."

President Reagan's 1983 federalism package was never considered seriously by Congress. The lawmakers were consumed by the growing problems of the federal budget deficit. The governors were actually supportive of the transportation block grant and the local government block grant and were willing to discuss a rational state block grant, but there was no inclination in the Congress to seriously address the federalism issue; the federal budget deficit had assumed center stage.

It's easy to see why the governors got involved in the federal budget debate at their 1983 winter meeting, even with their unease over the issue. Most economists were arguing that the projected federal deficits would provide a continual drag on the economy and threaten another recession. For the states, every one percent drop in the gross national product reduced revenues to the states by $1.8 billion dollars, or about two percent of expenditures. Every one percent increase in unemployment raised state expenditures by nearly $1 billion. Thus, even a slight recession had major budgetary implications at the state level.

The states also saw Congress whittling away state and local programs funded at the federal level in an attempt to address the deficit. The word from Congress was that the governors had come into Washington, D.C., as they had traditionally done, simply to testify for more federal funds for their projects. New Federalism had fallen on hard times.

Reflections on the Federalism Negotiations

The President clearly captured the tide of popular sentiment when he proposed a limit on the expanding role of the federal government through his federalism initiatives. He was aware of the general attitude of most Americans about their national government. It had simply become too big, too indifferent, too wasteful, too remote, and too powerful. The time was right for another look at the states. Ronald Reagan certainly did not create that national feeling but he sensed its historical impact and took full advantage of it. Neither did the President create the environment which would support such a revolution. He simply capitalized on it. His series of initiatives, the tax act, the block grants, the swap and his constant pressure on the domestic budget turned back the pendulum of power and responsibility flowing to the federal government. He sought nothing less than a domestic revolution. But from 1982 to 1985, following the tax cut and the new block grants, his revolution was blunted by Congress' unwillingness to provide necessary legislative support. It is indeed ironic that the ultimate change was not proposed by the President, but by a spontaneous uprising in the Congress which led to the initial passage of Gramm-Rudman.

Congress provided the President with the capstone to his domestic revolution, but it is Reagan who will nevertheless receive the credit for reversing a twenty-five-year era of federal domestic activism.

Had the governors been more prescient, or perhaps a bit more courageous, we might have been willing to be flexible on the 1982 Reagan proposal and thereafter fought together to push it through the Congress. True, we were hung up on legitimate, philosophical concerns and not-so-legitimate concerns over the dollar figures. If we had recognized the coming revolution, I suspect we would have cut our best deal while we still had something with which to bargain. One of the great failures of public officials is to remain too long fixed on an admittedly sound general principle, when the problem requires a pragmatic solution in the public's best interest.

Governor Busbee had warned the governors that we needed to "trade the horse while it is still alive." But we couldn't accomplish the trade. Gramm-Rudman may make any future trade unlikely, if not impossible, and now the horse is surely dying.

CHAPTER 5

The Future of Federalism

DESPITE the failure of the negotiations between the governors and President Reagan over his new New Federalism initiatives, it is clear that a major restructuring of roles will take place. This may have happened without the passage of Gramm-Rudman, but most assuredly will happen now with its enactment. The pressures to balance the fiscal budget, and the dramatic cuts in domestic programs which we can expect, will force the governors to redefine their role in the federal system. Properly addressed, that role can be translated into a new opportunity for the states.

As a participant in the national debate over New Federalism, and previously as well, I have reflected on the appropriate distribution of powers between the federal government and the states. Those views are provided here along with examples of state leadership that provide real promise for the states ultimately regaining their proper place in the federal system.

A Realistic Approach to Federalism

In general terms, I think that policies affecting the entire society on a more or less equal basis are appropriately assigned to the federal government. National defense, for example, is easily assigned to the national government. I believe broad social policies, such as anti-discrimination laws, federal environmental goals and income distribution policies, are also most appropriately assigned to the national level.

In contrast, policies that affect only one lower unit of government and no others are clearly local responsibilities. People in individual communities should decide whether the benefits are equal to the cost of public programs.

Probably the most difficult area for sorting out are policies that primarily benefit one area but may impose external benefits or costs on neighboring states or jurisdictions. If those policies are left to the states, they may pay less than what is necessary for the good of a whole society, or they may actually impose costs on a neighboring jurisdiction. For example, although good interstate roads and a good education system are of primary importance to municipalities and/or states, they also provide benefits for the entire society. Air or water pollution, on the other hand, flowing downwind or downstream from one state to another, causes external costs that may require outside intervention.

Federal intervention (through regulations or funding) is often described as developmental, redistributive or regulatory. Developmental efforts occur in such areas as transportation, water development and economic development, where a cooperative effort between a state or local government and the federal government is appropriate. Federal matching programs in these areas in the past may well have stimulated such cooperation. However, in the post Gramm-Rudman era, states may be the jurisdiction that is forging a partnership with local government and the private sector, without their federal partners.

A second major area of federal intervention is in redistributing benefits to assist those in need. The logic of federal government responsibility in this field is that low expenditures by one locality may drive the needy to an adjacent jurisdiction that gives richer benefits. Further, migration of the poor — for example, of refugees from Cuba — may impact one state disproportionately. And the fiscal capacities of the fifty states are not equal. That is the major reason why the governors continually argued that the basic income maintenance programs were a federal responsibility.

There is no ideal answer in this category. A solution is to take a pragmatic and cooperative approach to federalism issues. We have to recognize that we cannot roll back the calendar to 1960. We have already built substantial expectations among constituent groups — the aged, the handicapped, the poor — that have benefited from federal redistributive policies. Through 1985, most of these groups had been only marginally affected by Reagan in his budget-cutting initiatives. Even the President says he accepts the "safety net" concept, although that net is surely shrinking.

We also must recognize that the world is more complex today than it was in 1960, and the private market system is not perfect. Therefore continued federal regulatory efforts in many areas are likely. Environmental problems that went unnoticed ten years ago are now more obvious. Their consequences, whether we are dealing with Love Canal or disposal of high-level nuclear waste, are better known. Television also heightens the expectation of various deprived groups in our society, creating a greater demand for equality and fair treatment. The federal role in protecting people against discrimination or dangerous drugs is obvious and necessary.

In a 1980 study, the Advisory Commission on Intergovernmental Relations suggested a three-part litmus test to unscramble governmental functions.[1] That litmus test includes:

1. A history of *local* versus *national* involvement,

2. The relative amount of federal financing, and

3. The effect of turning the responsibility over to the states, which could result in destructive competition among programs between states.

This pragmatic test does not raise the philosophical or economic questions which I discussed earlier, but in applying the test, we reach similar results. For example, while federal financial assistance to state educational programs does provide some benefit to the nation as a whole by producing a more educated society, the history of education and funding responsibilities has been primarily at the local level. Thus, in any sorting out of program functions, the funding of education should return to states and local school boards. In contrast, programs such as those designed to assist states affected by refugees were initiated by the federal government and designed for a population group over which the states have no control. Thus, it makes sense for those functions to remain with the federal government.

While environmental programs historically are a state responsibility, it is clear that there is a new consensus on the need to have national goals and standards. Turning this program over to the states without national controls could lead to destructive competition which could create external costs in neighboring jurisdictions. Thus, the kind of cooperative program that exists today, where the states can assume primacy (administrative responsibility) over federal programs if their state laws conform to national standards, provides a basis for state-federal cooperation in the environmental area.

The governors have consistently argued for a comprehensive national policy for the sick and the poor. Thus, the Reagan swap ("I'll take the sick — you take the poor") makes no sense to the governors. A potential area of compromise is the development of a federally-funded national "basic" program of income maintenance and medical services administered by the states with the option to the states to provide additional income support and health benefits above the national floor.

If we are to make progress with the current administration, the governors need to advocate some compromise along this line that is acceptable to President Reagan and which maintains a national commitment to the needy. The difficulty in reaching a consensus is that there appears to be no driving philosophy behind President Reagan's federalism initiatives — no central rationale, other than to shrink the scope and cost of the federal government.

The states need to assert their own will. In general, governors do not believe that representative democracy works best when their representatives are far from home. On the other hand, just as with Congress, governors tend to support or reject positions on the narrow basis of how they affect their states. We will never come to an appropriate sorting out of responsibilities if the governors continue to exhibit a "computer printout" mentality with respect to any swap proposal. Short-term gains or losses must be viewed in the context of long-term solutions.

We are never going to come up with a proposal that makes everyone whole and continues the status quo. The status quo is rapidly evaporating. It makes no sense to get bogged down in the development of a trust fund which guarantees that no state will lose any dollars. I think what we really need to do is come to an agreement on the philosophical underpinnings of a core federal income security program and let that philosophy, not the budget numbers, lead to the sorting out of a solution.

State-Local Distribution of Responsibilities

In attempting to reassert state responsibility for programs, governors also need to focus on appropriate state and local intergovernmental relations. We need to have the same kind of sensitivity to local concerns that we ask from our federal partners. In Utah, during the last year of my administration, we began to work with local officials to review jointly-administered programs in an effort to discover which level of government would most efficiently and most appropriately take over those administrative duties. We also examined the impact of state mandates on local government. For example, largely at local government's urgings, Utah assumed the financial responsibility for the circuit court system, a change which will go a long way toward eliminating the problems resulting from joint administration by the states, cities and counties. We also succeeded in changing the distribution formula for the state sales tax, providing a broader, more reliable revenue base for local governments.

State Leadership Opportunities

The Chinese characters which signify "crisis" contain a double message: "danger" and "opportunity." Unquestionably we are faced with a fiscal crisis of major proportions for state and local governments, creating an imminent danger. But we also have an unparalleled opportunity for state and local leaders to seize the initiative they lost in the 1960s and to regain their traditional roles in the federal system.

Federal devolution of domestic programs will provide the states with the opportunity to assume a leadership role in many areas of domestic policy. New fiscal realities in the late 1980s will require the states to reassume total responsibility for education, economic development, housing and community development, transportation, and some health and welfare programs. The federal presence, including regulations and judicial oversight, will remain to provide protection against arbitrary actions of state and local government.

It's comforting to point out that recent state programs, in Utah and throughout the nation, have been innovative and responsive to modern social problems. Several state experiments have drawn national attention, and reports by the Council of State Governments and the National

Governors' Association have documented state successes. I have selected three areas of examples: education, economic and community development, and human resource management.

Education

The states took up the gauntlet thrown down by *A Nation at Risk* even before the report was issued by the National Commission on Excellence in Education. The state share of the cost of public education has been increasing and, in fiscal year 1983, stood at over fifty percent. In contrast, the federal share was 7.3 percent and declining. School finance reform has led to an increase in per capita expenditures and equalization of expenditures. And governors and legislators have increased their focus on education, in part because of its relationship to economic development programs in the states.

A 1984 survey by the Council of State Governments indicated that state reforms were underway in all states, with more than half responding favorably to thirty-six of fifty recommendations of the Education Commission.[2] Recent initiatives reported by states as enacted or proposed include: increased high school graduation requirements (forty-seven states); new student evaluations and testing (forty-four); raised teacher certifications and standards (forty-nine); performance based incentives (thirty-seven); increased instructional time (thirty-four); academic enrichment programs (forty-two); and improved school discipline (twenty-seven).[3]

Economic and Community Development[4]

As the federal government has moved out of the economic development area, the states have increased their presence. I think the most encouraging aspect of state involvement is the move away from the traditional "smokestack" chasing of industries, a zero-sum game for the nation.

State efforts are becoming more comprehensive, strategic and constructive. Forty states, for example, have initiated programs designed to promote development of technology. Michigan's strategic plan, "Path to Prosperity," proposes revitalization of the state's industrial base by creating "factories of the future" through technological development for existing industries and by financing new products.

States are placing a priority on education, infrastructure and the general business climate in attracting and developing new industries. A NGA survey found that twenty-six states developed new public-private partnership organizations between 1983-85. They administer loans and grants, oversee development policy for some states and help attract private capital.

A new emphasis is on state promotion of foreign investment and trade opportunities. Thirty states have established foreign offices to promote international trade. States are also developing policies and programs to support small business and to stimulate indigenous industry. Emphasizing innovation and entrepreneurship, these programs include research and development, venture capital and management assistance.

In the battle to create adequate public infrastructure, states have created housing authorities to subsidize low- and middle-income housing and have created a number of mechanisms (bond funds, community impact accounts) to assist local governments. In Utah, for example, we have developed several low-interest loan accounts to assist localities in water resource management, including the development of new sources and of wastewater treatment. State credit will become an increasing source of funding for local governments.

Human Resource Management

It was the states, not the federal government, who took initiatives on health care cost-containment and work programs as alternatives to welfare. Medicaid cost-containment efforts include alternatives to nursing homes for long-term care patients and restricting a patient's choice of providers by using either a case management or health maintenance organization approach. The efforts have paid off. Medicaid costs rose more than fifteen percent annually from 1975 to 1981, but rose only 6.7 percent in 1982, 9.6 percent in 1983 and 7.1 percent in 1984. States have at least begun to slow the annual growth rate in this program.

Utah, Arizona, California and Massachusetts have all developed innovative alternative work programs for welfare recipients. Arizona, for example, began a Work Incentive Program in 1982 to help people who receive welfare assistance to develop the skills they need to make it on their own. Their self-sufficiency effort has four major components: job motivation and positive work habits; marketable skills training; job development and placement; and supportive services.

No one has suggested that state programs in human services are panaceas to solve the nation's welfare and health care problems. What it proves is that a variety of programs and approaches are being tried by the states. Information on those programs — successes and failures — are shared. The states are meeting social issues in a responsive and professional manner.

Tough Choices Ahead for States

Changes in the intergovernmental system clearly take time. Woodrow Wilson suggested that they occur only over generations. Nevertheless, we are at a crossroads in intergovernmental finance; the ascendancy of the Reagan philosophy of returning programs to state and local

governments to help resolve the federal budget crisis points to continued devolution of program responsibilities to state and local governments. Governors, state legislators and local officials, in confronting
the risk side of Gramm-Rudman and the federal efforts to balance the
budget, will have difficult problems to solve in the next few years. The
states must articulate what their appropriate role is in a sorting out
process of the federal system; they must also be equally concerned with
and sensitive to the local role in a state-local intergovernmental setting.
I am not optimistic that we can do this in a totally rational manner
given the increasing fiscal problems, but we must try.

We cannot let the ideas of New Federalism die in the throes of the
federal budget crisis. Governors must continually place this agenda
high on their list of priorities. Several important tasks are before them.

First, they must forcefully fight for continued, adequate federal funding for those programs which provide an essential level of food, shelter
and financial assistance to those unable to provide for themselves. Cuts
in AFDC, Medicaid and Food Stamps hit hardest those resource-poor
states who are least likely to replace federal revenues. This would create
an unacceptable, dual standard of care for our nation's poor. At the
very least, we should negotiate an adequately funded floor of benefits.

Second, governors must seek a shift of tax resources from the federal level to the states as part of any package of reduced federal responsibilities. Federal excise taxes (e.g., cigarettes and alcohol) are a good
place to begin, even given their uneven distributional impacts among
the states. With the Federal Highway Act up for reauthorization in
1987, states should support a new program that is primarily funded by
each state, with perhaps a modest federal trust handling interstate population and fiscal disparities.

Third, governors should understand that federal withdrawal from
programs that are investment-oriented (education, housing, community development) may adversely affect both local and national productivity. A careful prioritization of human and capital investment
programs is essential for funding those that provide the maximum possible benefits given limited state resources.

Finally, state leaders must prove to their populations that they have
the ability and judgment to make responsible choices, so that they can
raise appropriate revenue to fund essential programs. We simply cannot allow a federal default brought about by the federal deficit to become
a state default.

Along the way there will be opportunities for governors and other
state leaders to influence the federal process in the states' interests. Each
of those opportunities will require the best the states have to offer.

Aggressive leadership will ultimately measure the success. I am confident the states are up to the challenge.

PART II

Balancing State Interests Against National Security

CHAPTER 6

Confronting MX Deployment

THE United States' race for supremacy over the Soviet Union in intercontinental ballistic missile technology and strength has always been an awesome, almost incomprehensible issue for me, and during the late 1970s, preliminary discussions about our newest weapon, Missile Experimental—more commonly known as MX—had me even more bewildered. I was looking forward to my first detailed briefing on the topic. I wanted to know as much as possible about this new missile, since there was talk that the Air Force wanted to base it in Utah.

The briefing was scheduled for March 28, 1979 in my office, and although I did not realize it at the time, the meeting signaled what was to become the most time consuming, challenging and divisive federal-state debate I would participate in during my entire eight years as governor. Opposition to the MX basing scheme consumed more than half of my time for two years. My dealings with the Air Force often frustrated and angered me, but in the end, with a significant nudge from the Mormon Church, we won. In retrospect, it was a perfect example of what can be done to resolve a major federal-state conflict if you are willing to roll up your sleeves and go after it.

Model intercontinental ballistics missiles, the Soviets' in black, ours in white, provided a dramatic focus for the briefing, which was one of the most exhaustive and detailed I experienced as governor. Lieutenant General Thomas Stafford, the U.S. Air Force's deputy chief for research and development, brought them to me as a gift, but they also served as a sobering prop for the message he and his aides delivered that day. The Air Force was becoming increasingly worried about what it considered to be the growing age and vulnerability of our ICBM force, and the models dramatized the perceived imbalance between our missile arsenal and the Soviets'. It was not a "top secret" briefing, but some of the information was regarded as confidential, and the press was not present.

By the time the briefing was over, I felt that I had been given chapter and verse on the Air Force's views regarding national security. The brass was well polished, and they did a smooth, professional job on us. The Air Force chalked up plenty of credibility points that day, points that would dwindle considerably over the following two years. But, in terms of strategic considerations, what the generals had to say made sense.

In summary, the briefing pointed out that the aim of our strategic nuclear weapon systems is to deter aggression. To achieve that goal, we have implemented a TRIAD of strategic forces designed to survive a first strike by the Soviet Union and still have the capacity to inflict heavy losses on the aggressor. The TRIAD consists of the following components:

— Land-based ICBMs,

— Submarine-launched ballistic missiles (SLBMs), and

— "Air-breathing" systems, such as manned aircraft, capable of delivering nuclear weapons and unmanned cruise missiles.[1]

The strongest of the three legs is the SLBMs. Their mobility and deep water capacity make them capable of surviving most attacks. The manned aircraft leg consists of B-52s armed with conventional bombs and cruise missiles. This system is old, and there is concern as to how long it can remain effective. President Carter had made the decision to forego funding the B-1 bomber, the latest available technology, and instead pursue the "stealth" bomber, designed to thwart radar detection. The stealth bomber is not seen as a likely addition to our arsenal until the late 1990s.

Our ICBM force then consisted of approximately fifty Titan missiles and one thousand Minuteman II and III missiles. Continued upgrades in technology have improved the reliability, operating costs, accuracy and yield of the Minuteman, and the Titans have now been retired. The Minuteman III is equipped with multiple, independently-targeted re-entry vehicles (MIRVs) which allow the firing of three warheads from a single missile. Continuing advanced technological programs for the Minuteman include the development of maneuverable reentry vehicles (MARVs), designed to increase the probability of penetrating an enemy's defenses.

The entire ICBM force is housed in hardened silos — vertical launching structures buried in the ground with self-contained electronics and support equipment necessary to launch a missile. The silos are spaced so that a nuclear blast close to one would leave the others operational. They are dispersed in several areas throughout the United States so that an attack on a single area would not wipe out the entire arsenal.

While the U.S. ICBM force appears sufficient, the Air Force made a persuasive case that a new generation of missiles was needed. The fixed positions of our ICBMs are known by the Soviets, making them increasingly vulnerable to their new high-payload missiles. The Soviet missiles are deployed in super-hard silos which, in case of war, would make it necessary for the U.S. to use higher yield missiles, fired with pinpoint accuracy. At that time, we did not have such weapons, and the

Air Force felt that we needed them in order to pose a real threat to the Soviet missile arsenal.

The "fourth generation" Soviet missiles, SS-17, -18 and -19, with a MIRV capability of ten or more warheads each meant that fewer of their missiles could destroy more of ours, leaving a significant Soviet nuclear force intact after a retaliatory strike by the United States. In addition, the Soviets were implementing mobile-based missiles, which would be more difficult for us to target.

In analyzing options to the perceived threat and vulnerability of U.S. ICBMs, the Air Force found it had some limitations. SALT II (Strategic Arms Limitation Treaty) proposed to place constraints on the total number of ballistic missile launchers; therefore, we could not continue to build more Minuteman IIIs. Defensive measures were limited by the Anti-ballistic Missile Treaty; therefore, the survivability of the Minuteman could not be assured.

Increased heavy reliance on Trident submarines would leave U.S. strategic weapons only one leg of TRIAD, since both the Minuteman and the B-52 were viewed as potentially vulnerable. This would allow Soviet war planners to concentrate on anti-submarine warfare, with the possibility of a technological breakthrough that would make our submarine fleet vulnerable to location and attack. The essence of TRIAD is that no two legs are vulnerable to the same Soviet countermeasures. This rationale would "guarantee" survival of two-thirds of our nuclear forces given any single breakthrough in Soviet technology.

The MX Solution

The Air Force's solution to the perceived vulnerability of U.S. strategic nuclear weapons was MX. It involved two concepts: First, the development of a larger missile than the Minuteman, with increased accuracy and payload; it would have ten warheads, giving greater retaliatory effectiveness with fewer missiles. Second, the basing mode of the missile would incorporate a deceptive multiple aimpoint (MAP) concept; the missile would be mobile rather than fixed in silos, and suitable precautions would be taken to prevent the knowledge of its exact location.

I had already indicated initial support for MX on November 30, 1978 in response to an Environmental Impact Statement on MX. In a rather patriotic statement to Carlos Stern, Air Force deputy for environment and safety, I noted that the missile would have enormously positive impacts on Utah. The two primary ones were in the production of the missile (two local contractors, Hercules and Thiokol, were scheduled to receive contracts in excess of $100 million for the project) and in the possible deployment of the missile in the state. I noted that the proposed missile site in southern Nevada and Utah would "have very little impact socially, economically or environmentally within the state." Later, however, I would change my mind.

Following the March 28 briefing, I sent telegrams of support for MX to President Jimmy Carter and Defense Secretary Harold Brown as "a vital and necessary part of our national defense capability."[2] I reiterated my view that there would be "no adverse environmental impacts" associated with MX or its possible launching sites. On June 8, following the President's decision to proceed with the missile's development, I issued a news release supporting the President's decision and indicating that the "$20 to $30 billion project could provide substantial economic benefits to the state of Utah, particularly in the southern part of the state" which was being considered as a possible deployment site.

In retrospect, my early and unqualified support for MX was naive and did not represent the detailed analysis characteristic of my administration. My support was based on three factors: a genuine belief that the Air Force had made a good case for the vulnerability of our existing ICBMs and need for a better missile, the job potential from its development and deployment, and the perception that I politically needed to support the Carter administration on a key defense policy issue.

On July 5, 1979, General Guy Hecker, who had been appointed special assistant in the Defense Department for MX matters, sent me a note of thanks for my continued support. He said, "There is no doubt that your early support of MX was one of the keys to a favorable decision by the President. . . . " While later events would prove that my support was far from crucial, General Hecker's comments are now embarrassing to me.

The Basing Decision

On June 27, 1979, I was in a two-hour briefing with General Hecker and Colonel McGuire to examine alternative basing modes for MX; the President's June decision to deploy MX had left the basing mode for further discussion. The meeting was a turning point in my unqualified support for the missile.

The basing mode favored by the Air Force was horizontal shelters. The missiles would be placed in sealed concrete and steel tubes, and a mechanism would erect them for launching. They would be moved from one shelter to another, using a huge transporter. Each missile would be in a network of twenty-three shelters spaced seven thousand feet apart and interconnected by a roadway system so it could be moved periodically to prevent detection.

When viewed in isolation, parts of the concept seemed sensible, but as I considered a total of two hundred missiles and forty-six hundred shelters, expandable to double that number, I was looking at a colossal system extending over one-third of Utah and two-thirds of Nevada. From that briefing, I decided I would have to become much more familiar with MX and its basing mode.

On September 7, 1979, President Carter announced his support for a horizontal, mobile, multiple protective structure basing of MX. While Arizona and New Mexico were listed as other potential deployment areas, it was clear, from a later briefing on September 26 by General Hecker and Seymour Zyberg, deputy undersecretary for research and engineering at the Department of Defense (DOD), that the Great Basin desert area of Utah and Nevada was considered the most desirable deployment area. The missiles and shelters would be located in the "remote areas of the West where economic, environmental, and population impacts will be minimized."[3]

The Air Force planned to deploy each of the two hundred missiles on a transporter-erector launcher (TEL). Each TEL would have a deployment area consisting of twenty-three horizontal shelters interconnected by a loop road. Security measures would allow for verification to comply with SALT II by opening the shelters for inspection by satellites to confirm that only one missile existed in the twenty-three-shelter area. After verification, the TEL would be moved to another shelter faster than an ICBM could travel from the Soviet Union to the deployment area. Theoretically, the Soviets never could know which of the twenty-three shelters housed the missile.

Against the projected Soviet threat of an ICBM attack under the constraints of the SALT II treaty, two hundred missiles and forty-six hundred shelters were viewed as "adequate." Dr. William J. Perry, DOD undersecretary for research and engineering, indicated in a press statement that larger Soviet ICBM forces were possible to envisage. In the absence of SALT II or a new SALT III, the Soviets could build up their ICBM forces. However, the press release said "we can maintain our deterrence by deploying more shelters . . . we can build shelters at a rate of two thousand per year. We could have, for example, a ten thousand shelter system completely deployed by 1989, if we concluded by 1984 that this was necessary."[4]

The enormous growth potential and complexity of MX deployment were now becoming more clear. I immediately felt that the citizens of Utah did not have a good grasp of the implications of the system, and on October 10, 1979, I wrote each member of our congressional delegation seeking public hearings in Utah on MX. While still supporting the missile and its deployment in Utah, I noted that the state "will experience unprecedented socioeconomic impacts, a drain on our scarce water resources and prohibitions on our use of public lands. The citizens of Utah deserve full participation in the MX debate." While our two U.S. senators were not yet interested in the issue, Congressman Gunn McKay responded by setting up hearings in Cedar City on November 5th.

At the same time, I requested that State Planning Coordinator Kent Briggs form an MX Task Force consisting of members of state agencies and local governments most likely to be affected, and asked him to draw up a planning budget for assessing necessary mitigation measures if MX were deployed in Utah. It seemed essential to broaden the scope of knowledge about MX beyond the governor's office. I also began to think about funding for the task force and a full-time project manager. I did not see how we would handle the enormity of the analysis necessary with the few people in my office. Kent suggested Ken Olson, a former state planning coordinator with good contacts in Washington, D.C. and throughout the state. I later appointed Ken to the position.

On October 22, I met with generals Lew Allen, Guy Hecker and John Murphy, with key planning staff and members of the Nevada planning office to discuss our need for funds to assess impact mitigation, and they agreed to support a supplemental appropriation for that purpose. On November 1, Kent chaired the first meeting of the MX Task Force. For many state officials, it was their first opportunity to learn the details of the program.

Since my briefing on March 28, I had received nothing but positive statements about MX from my closest advisors. However, when I met with State Representative Frances Farley and ex-CIA official Herbert Scoville on October 18, both expressed open opposition to MX. That meeting intensified some of my own concerns about whether I had made a premature judgment. I also had a breakfast meeting with my good friend, Senator Frank Church (D., Id.), chairman of the Senate Foreign Relations Committee. He raised some strong concerns about the military need for MX. The issue came to a head during a November 3 staff meeting in preparation for my Cedar City testimony.

Maggie Wilde, my press secretary, and Mike Graham, my executive assistant, had serious reservations about my further support for MX based on concerns about the magnitude of the impacts in southern Utah. Kent also thought it was time to back away from our enthusiastic support, although he remained optimistic that proper planning could take care of the impacts, and he urged continued, albeit more reserved, support. Members of his planning staff were concerned that the cumulative impacts of MX and energy development would be impossible to handle. The discussion was heated. My own intuition was that it was time to make a break from my previous commitment, even if it caused embarrassment. I told Kent to prepare a speech listing all the concerns that had been expressed, utilizing material developed by the planning office.

My statement on November 5 before Congressman Gunn McKay's Subcommittee on Military Construction of the House Committee on Appropriations came as a shock to him and to the military representatives who had lined up to testify in support of MX. I first noted that unlike other projects that come to Utah, "there is an ominous, almost unreal, dimension of MX, in part due to its magnitude and in part due to its purpose."

I explained that Governor Robert List of Nevada and I had established a Bi-state Management Committee to cope with the problems associated with the project, and that we had created an MX Task Force, funded from the Four Corners Regional Commission. While I complimented the Air Force on their briefings, I indicated that I was extremely displeased to hear that geologists working for the Air Force had been drilling core samples for about two years in Utah near the Nevada border. I said that I didn't want "consultants and contractors . . . scampering around the state of Utah poking, digging, scraping or rummaging unless I know what is going on and why."

While indicating that I personally still supported the MX weapons system as a means of maintaining a survivable ICBM counterforce, I was concerned with the issues affecting the quality of life of all Utahns.

In my testimony I tried to dramatize the colossal nature of the project that was three times the size of the Alaskan Pipeline and the projected socioeconomic impacts of an accumulation of major projects that were underway or planned. The MX would be in full swing at the same time as peak construction for the Intermountain Power Project (the largest coal-fired plan in the U.S.), the Central Utah Water Project and projected synthetic fuel developments.

As a state our construction industry had barely passed $1 billion in annual construction. We were looking at several multibillion-dollar projects. The MX could easily consume "all building and construction material, equipment and manpower," threatening home and office construction and raising a costly competition for labor.

It was not simply whether we could build the MX in the Great Basin, but at what cost:

> It is not enough to simply ask whether or not the human, physical and technological resources can be mustered to build this project. I have no doubt that they can. But at what cost and to whom, and with what long-term result? This is the over-arching question that subsumes all others and the one that must be answered to my satisfaction. We need to be absolutely clear on these points: We do not consider the construction of an MX missile base in the Great Basin of Utah and Nevada a foregone conclusion; we do not consider the scoping and environmental impact procedures empty exercises to satisfy the requirements of

the National Environmental Policy Act; and we do not intend to allow the economic and social well-being of our people to be abated, eroded or engulfed by this project.

I continued by detailing a number of social and physical impacts that I saw occurring in the specific region where deployment was projected, including a doubling of the population in the four rural counties of Juab, Millard, Beaver and Iron in six years. That would have created social problems of enormous magnitudes. I recited the likely strain on municipal infrastructures and the inadequacies of public service personnel and educational facilities. We had seen the enormous strain on facilities and social problems created by rapid growth in our neighboring state of Wyoming. "What impact assistance will these communities receive?" I asked.

I indicated my concern for the potential disruption to public lands, both federal and state, and for the network of roads that would require security measures limiting access to large portions of the state. I asked what provisions were considered for eventual technological obsolescence. Unlike the Minuteman project where little is visible, the MX would be as permanent as the Pyramids. I also wanted assurance that the Air Force would follow state procedures in reserving water for the project.

I concluded by asserting my belief that the stress on physical resources would not be as acute as the competition for and the strain on our human resources, our social fabric and our long-range capital requirements. I said: "If these concerns . . . can be resolved, then MX should be deployed in the Great Basin. In the decision-making process, the people of Utah must be assured that their concerns will be pressed early, openly, honestly and aggressively."

I had crossed the Rubicon with my Cedar City statement. Henceforth, my relationship with the Air Force and DOD would be at arm's length and somewhat adversarial. To say the generals were surprised by my testimony was an understatement. They were shocked. I had given them no indication that I had backed away from my one hundred percent commitment to the MX.

I next moved to shore up our capability to monitor and analyze MX issues. I named Ken Olson as project manager for the MX Task Force and notified state and congressional leaders of my actions and of the new position. Ken was to play a vital role in the development of our strategy with respect to MX.

I had discussions with Undersecretary of the Air Force Antonia Handler Chayes, concerning the process for the Environmental Impact Statement (EIS). She assured me that the Air Force would follow Utah law on water appropriation and would cooperate closely with the state MX

Task Force on the EIS. Secretary of Defense Harold Brown reiterated, in a November 19 letter, the need for coordination to "assure that there is adequate planning and timely assistance in resolving serious impacts that may be related to a new defense system of this magnitude."

On November 29, 1979, the Air Force announced it would prepare an EIS for "use in decision making regarding the selection of a basing area or areas" for the MX system. A draft EIS was scheduled for completion by June 1980 with a final decision in late 1980 or early 1981. The Air Force scheduled a series of "scoping meetings" to determine "the nature, extent, and scope of the issues and concerns that should be addressed in the environmental impact statement related to the proposed action."[5]

Growing Concerns over the EIS Process

November 1979 was the major turning point for me in terms of my attitude toward MX and the Air Force. My son, Scott M. Matheson, Jr., was attending Yale Law School, and I had been invited back to talk to his class and faculty about the environmental issues associated with MX. While my speech contained the same issues I had raised in my Cedar City testimony, it also contained some rather harsh remarks about the Air Force process.[6] I had just learned, from reading a November 18 article in the *New York Times,* that the Air Force was planning on "fast track" legislation that would allow them to withdraw the entire land area of potential MX basing in Utah and Nevada—about 7,000 square miles—and return the portion they didn't need to the public domain—at their own leisure. It also proposed to exempt MX from the Environmental Impact Statement review required by the National Environmental Policy Act of 1969.

I was angry. First, because I viewed this move as an attempt to circumvent a legitimate environmental impact statement which would require them to isolate specific locations and analyze impacts and mitigation strategies. Second, I had not been informed of this action in advance; I had to read about it in the paper. Earlier, it had seemed that the Air Force was dealing with me in a positive and professional manner. Suddenly, they were planning an end run to circumvent the orderly process which they had agreed was essential.

I don't know who initiated the end run, but do not believe it was President Carter. He was too committed to environmental protection and the EIS process. I suspected Antonia Chayes.

After the Yale speech, I went to Washington, D.C. to meet with Undersecretary Chayes. She was a lawyer assigned as the civilian policy officer regarding MX. We had a confrontation over the fast track legislation, and although she indicated that it was not in final form, I was neither assured nor mollified by her answers. It confirmed my suspicion that she may have originated the fast track concept. I later had some opportunities to testify against the fast track approach, and after the public was fully aware of what the Air Force was proposing, the Air Force made a hasty retreat from its position. The legislation was never introduced.

One of the major procedural issues that developed in early 1980 was the scoping process for the EIS. Responsibility for preparing the statement was assigned to Major General Forest B. McCartney at Norton Air Force Base in California and a new set of Air Force personnel. At the beginning of the EIS process, there was a major effort on the part of the Air Force to do what is called a "narrowing" of the scope. They had enlisted the support of the Council on Environmental Quality (CEQ) to cooperate with them in meeting the very tight timetable commitments they had received from the President. Recognizing they were on a difficult time schedule, the Air Force, through Undersecretary Chayes, asked the CEQ to support and provide assistance in doing the minimum requirements of the statute so they could end up meeting the time frame.

CEQ discouraged the Air Force in January 1980 from pursuing the fast track legislation and recommended that some EIS process was better than nothing. CEQ's comments mirrored my own concerns that the narrowing of the EIS process would bring about only one selection and that would be the Great Basin desert of Utah and Nevada, and the basing mode would be limited to an analysis of the one proposed, the racetrack, or horizontal, mode. Split basing would be gone, other alternatives would not be examined, and we would end up being the winner, or loser, by default because it would be the racetrack or nothing. And "nothing," it was obvious at the time, was not in the Air Force's lexicon.

We wrote a tough letter to General McCartney on August 20 asking what the scoping process was and outlining what we thought it ought to be. We enlisted Gus Speth, chairman of CEQ, to respond to our concerns. In responding, he attached correspondence which the general counsel of CEQ had sent to the Air Force outlining the difficult prospects they were facing if they attempted to narrow the scoping. The letter pointed out the pitfalls, problems and difficulties associated with it, particularly if other alternatives were not considered.[7] The scoping issue thereby became an important factor in how we preserved our role in monitoring the EIS.

We had strategically decided that we would carefully make an elaborate paper record of every single step in the environmental impact process and document it from the state's perspective to keep all of our options open for attacking the ultimate EIS product. Ken Olson spent a great deal of time with our counsel, who was an expert in environmental law, to guide us carefully along a circuitous paper trail that would eventually become a complete record, harmonious with all of the requirements and sufficiently convincing if we ever had to go to court.

Public Hearings in Utah

On February 7, 1980, I announced four town meetings to discuss the impact of MX deployment. I wanted to explore the attitudes of those who would be most affected by the development, both positively and negatively. I personally attended each of the meetings: in Provo, for Utah and Juab Counties; in Delta, for Millard County; in Milford, for Beaver County; and in Cedar City, for Iron and Washington Counties. Because of the public interest, I later held meetings in three other major Utah cities in March: Salt Lake City, Ogden, and Logan.

We provided a forum for anyone who wanted to get on the soapbox. Most of the supporters of MX and the proposed basing mode appeared at the Ogden hearing; many of these witnesses worked at Hill Air Force Base — mostly civilians who had had experience with the Minuteman Missile. They were strong supporters of national defense. Some professionally articulated their points of view and provided excellent technical information. In the Milford hearing, there was strong support for the MX basing; their economic situation was desperate. The mayor and the city council, chamber of commerce, even the school superintendent, came forward in strong support. There were also articulate spokesmen for the opposition, and they had equally persuasive presentations. This point of view came strongly from Delta, a city much closer to the proposed basing site. Delta had already had the single whammy of coping with the development of the 3,000-megawatt Intermountain Power Plant (IPP). They were concerned that IPP was going to overrun them.

The hearings brought out all sizes, shapes, and varieties of points of view — and tremendous press coverage, and I feel they raised the level of concern and interest. It gave me a good opportunity to be reflective and to listen to people. During the hearing process, I was moving toward opposition of MX in the proposed basing mode, although I was not publicly outlining where I was coming from on the basing issue. Governor List and I were arguing for split basing during that time, and during testimony that we were giving nationally we were arguing for the consideration of alternatives.

MX Testimony

I testified twice before Congress in early 1980, on January 24, before Congressman John Seiberling's Subcommittee on Public Lands of the House Committee on Interior and Insular Affairs and on March 26, before Congressman Gunn McKay's Subcommittee on Military Construction Appropriations. My principal concern before Seiberling was to kill the idea of a fast track legislative approach. Since Seiberling was a strong public land use advocate, he was receptive to my testimony. He was not in favor of a large withdrawal of public lands and, with his support, we were able to effectively kill that legislative alternative. I wanted to maintain the integrity of the EIS process and expressed my concerns with the proposed narrowing of its scope.

Finally, as the consequences of the full magnitude of MX deployment became known, I indicated I had "serious doubts about whether or not MX should be deployed in *any single* geographical area such as the Great Basin." List and I jointly urged the consideration of "breaking up deployment of the system to smaller and more manageable subunits which might be within the capacity of a larger number of states and localities to accommodate."

Before Chairman McKay's committee, my primary concern was the socioeconomic impacts of the proposed development—first, whether the states and localities could handle it, and second, what mitigation funds might be available for communities suffering the greatest impact.

Although I continued to support MX in theory, I indicated that "with regard to the proposed basing mode and deployment area, I have serious, unresolved concerns, questions and reservations. The President's proposal combines a basing mode decision—the horizontal shelter race-track—and a deployment area decision—the Great Basin desert—in a double whammy that raises profound anxieties, fears and doubts among the citizens of Utah, including myself."

After citing a list of physical and social concerns, I said that I believed that "in order for the President's proposal, or any alternative, to be implemented, the people of Utah, Nevada and the entire nation must be persuaded that all possible alternatives for the deployment of MX have been thoroughly examined. The relative costs and benefits of each alternative must be known and understood by an informed citizenry, and there must be a reasonable consensus among the technical, political, military and non-scientific members of the national community that the alternative finally selected is the best, is workable, is reasonable and is supportable."

Two interesting things occurred in the McKay hearings. One of the reporters who had covered what I had done early in the process said: "See that gentlemen sitting over there—that is a reporter from Pravda. I can't understand how we can have open hearings and allow Russian reporters present when we're talking about serious matters of military security." I thought that was interesting. I reread my testimony later and couldn't find anything that would expose any military secrets. It does emphasize one of the valuable democratic principles that we follow in this country. Except where we can prove and establish some legitimacy for secrecy, we're an open society and even those who are competing against us, economically or politically, are still entitled to be involved in the process. Frankly, I ended up being proud of our system that day.

The second thing that happened was a spirited conversation with Representative Joseph Addabbo (D., N.Y.), who was on the committee. List and I established the fact that as governors we were just as concerned about national security as members of Congress, but we were also there from a totally different perspective. We were there to protect our constituents, and we were entitled to be a part of the resolution of the issue; we didn't deserve to get run over in the name of national security or patriotism.

Congressman Addabbo claimed we lacked concern for the solution to a national problem. I remember him looking at me and saying, "This has got to go somewhere in the United States, Governor Matheson!" We got a tongue lashing from him — almost an implication that we were somehow unpatriotic in insisting that our concerns be a part of the solution to the overall problem. I wish I had responded to him. It was late in the day; the hearing was nearly over and it was not a good time to respond to him, but I regret that I didn't, because he really deserved a return volley, and I didn't fire one.

I should have explained to him that the people in Utah are fully cognizant of their responsibilities to national causes; that we are fully supportive of national defense and want to be helpful in solving problems. But that I also had the responsibility of maintaining the integrity of Utah's ability to survive as a viable economic, political and social entity. National security involves economic success as well, and to destroy the ability of a state to maintain its economic integrity in the name of national security absolutely defeats the principle.

The Local Planning Effort

Part of my early strategy was to involve local officials who would be most affected by MX deployment in our statewide planning effort. We encouraged those local officials to form a Four County MX Policy Board to provide a vehicle for involving their constituents in all our deliberations. The local officials hired a full-time staff director, Ralph Starr, and Ken Olson made sure that he and board chairman, Chad Johnson, commissioner for Beaver County, were full partners in our activities.

Congressman McKay had been responsible for getting a $1 million supplemental appropriation for fiscal year 1980 through Congress in late 1979. It was to supplement our original grant of $400,000 from the Four Corners Regional Commission (a Title V Commission composed of Colorado, Arizona, New Mexico, Utah and Nevada). The legislation included language that required us to spend the funds for studies associated with the MX basing proposal. We set up offices in Utah and Nevada and began to incur expenses, but it took us several months to receive the funds.

The Air Force handed the administration of the grant over to the Department of Commerce and by the time they were prepared to turn the money over to us, they wanted us to sign a detailed and complicated executive agreement. When we looked it over, we decided its language and restrictions were an affront to the intent of Congress. We weren't able to resolve this problem with the Air Force or with Commerce. Undersecretary Chayes proved unhelpful again.

We ended up going to the White House on this issue by involving Jack Watson, President Carter's special assistant for intergovernmental relations. I remember we were going to have a meeting with Secretary Chayes and all of the players, but Ken Olson and I went over to the White House to have a pre-meeting with Watson to see whether they were behind Secretary Chayes on this matter. We wanted to explain that we had appreciated all the help from the White House and that it was now time for the White House to support us without putting extra burdens on our funding.

I sensed it was time to draw the line, and I had the feeling that if I had gone along with the agreement, we would have been enveloped in their control; we would never have an independent opportunity to do what we needed to do for our own planning. I was prepared to lose the money and I explained to Jack, and later on to Secretary Chayes and others, that if we didn't get the money on terms acceptable to us, we didn't want it. But we assured them we would make the issue public. We finally got the money without signing the agreement. After the meeting, Secretary Chayes told me, "I don't know why you went to the White House; we could have worked it out over here." I'm sure she was unhappy, but she had not helped before and seemed unlikely to support us now.

The difficulties with the planning fund (really an insignificant figure in the total federal budget or even the MX budget) was a perfect example of what happens when you deal with the federal bureaucracy below the policy-making level. When you ask somebody to implement something, they don't care about policy; they care about process. This is one of my great objections to the federal system. I'm sure it happens in the state and local funding processes as well, but that doesn't make it any more acceptable.

Public employees, whether governors, cabinet secretaries, or office clerks, are public servants. They are supposed to implement policy in a manner that supports the public purpose, not hamstring the process so that it merely serves to bolster their own bureaucratic egos. We have to create a culture in government of *wanting* to serve and to meet the policy goal. We can't let the goal become secondary to the mechanics of its implementation.

The Meeting with President Carter

Because List and I had had problems with the planning funds and we were both concerned about the narrowing of the EIS scoping process, we requested a meeting with the President. We got that opportunity on February 27, 1980. Defense Secretary Harold Brown, Dr. William Perry and Jack Watson were also present.

We discussed a series of our concerns. By this time, we were dealing with both military and civilian representatives of the Air Force and with the Army's Corps of Engineers, who would have responsibility for building the base. We were also dealing with people in the Department of Defense, primarily Undersecretary Chayes and General Hecker, MX project liaison. We were dealing with General Forrest McCartney, of Norton Air Force Base, on the EIS. As a result, we were beginning to get a little confused about who was really the spokesman for the federal government in the ongoing saga of MX deployment in Utah and Nevada. List and I got together and decided we wanted to have someone we could work with who would be responsive and responsible, someone who would be helpful and keep us up to date on what was happening.

Our first strategy was to get rid of Antonia Chayes. I think both List and I had had about all we wanted from her. We wanted to deal with someone in whom we had confidence. President Carter selected Dr. William Perry, undersecretary of defense for research, which pleased us both. He was responsible and, I think, maintained his integrity throughout the process. We wanted also to maintain our contact with the White House, and the President assigned Jack Watson the responsibility of dealing with us.

We next talked about the narrowing of the EIS scoping process. We explained to the President how concerned we were about the dramatic nature of the narrowing, and we advised him that the administration was not going to be able to sustain an EIS under the National Environmental Policy Act (NEPA), because they'd narrowed it to where it wouldn't meet the minimum legal standards. The President was concerned about that and agreed he would review the question of alternative deployment sites and split basing but he did not want to delay the beginning of construction proposed for July 1986.

There is no question in my mind that the President was committed to the schedule he was on and to the racetrack basing system. The President was also well prepared. He had spent a great deal of time looking at alternatives for the basing of MX and had looked at the air system, a number of proposed sea systems and a whole range of land-based systems. We didn't go into the alternatives in much depth. I was pretty anxious to have the sea basing alternatives maintained as a part of the scoping because that resolved so many of the problems, particularly those of mitigation. The President had his mind made up, however, and he went with the racetrack system for good reasons sufficient to him. One of the important ones was the verification provisions under SALT II (signed in 1979 but not yet ratified by the Senate). He had to support a system consistent and compatible with SALT II. I was not critical of that. Consistency between SALT II and MX was a very important factor. We were all concerned about alternative sites and split basing, and we told him if we didn't get a scoping that included those alternatives, we were going to oppose him. He understood that clearly.

We talked about impact aid, raising the earlier question with respect to the source of mitigation funds for deployment. We argued for a line item approach, where we would negotiate mitigation directly with the Air Force. The Air Force would put the funds in a line item in their budget, and Congress would look at it as a line item. This approach had been used before in developing a Trident submarine base.[8] The Air Force wanted to use a regional approach to impact assistance, and we could see massive control developing outside Utah and Nevada. We would also end up competing for mitigation funds with all federal defense programs. We didn't want to compete for mitigation funds with forty-eight other states where federal national security programs were underway. My understanding from the meeting was that the President had no objection to the single line item and actually supported that approach. In fact, the legislation finally adopted by Congress in late 1980 agreed with the concept as we proposed it. Carter didn't oppose the legislation, even though by then I was on record against his MX proposal.

The meeting with Carter was valuable. It was the first time I had had the opportunity to observe the President at close range. He began the meeting on time and ended on schedule, thirty minutes later. He was cordial and businesslike. No one present doubted his grasp of the issues and his commitment to the basing proposal. He conducted the discussion; in fact, Secretary Brown, Perry and Watson said virtually nothing.

In matters of procedure, the President was supportive and cooperative. His selection of Perry and Watson, as liason, his willingness to examine NEPA alternatives and to support the line item approach for impact aid were clear victories for List and me. On the substantive issue of MX basing we already knew the President had made up his mind.

The real value of the meeting for me, however, was the feeling, as we left the White House, that Carter had not made a persuasive case on the basing proposal and that those of us opposed to the racetrack had the better of the argument.

CHAPTER 7

Deciding Against the MX

BY the spring of 1980, I was beginning to form a negative opinion of MX in the horizontal racetrack basing mode, but I continued to assimilate an enormous amount of material from experts on both sides of the issue. Ken Olson sent me written material on a daily basis, and I met with Sidney Drell, who was advocating submarine basing for MX, William Van Cleave who argued for a retrofitting of the Minuteman silos, and others.

We organized a one and one-half hour live PBS television public debate on MX — a co-production of KUED-TV in Salt Lake and "Bill Moyer's Journal" of WNET, New York City. "The MX Debate" was held at Symphony Hall in Salt Lake City on April 24, 1980 and attracted a national audience. The three panel discussions and topics were: *Why Do We Need the MX?* (with David L. Aaron, deputy assistant to the President for National Security Affairs, Dr. John F. Lehman, defense analyst and former deputy director of the Arms Control and Disarmament Agency, and Herbert Scoville, Jr., author of *The Monstrous MX*); *How Should the MX be Deployed and Based?* (with Dr. William Perry, representing President Carter, William R. Van Cleave, professor of International Relations, USC, and Dr. Sidney Drell, deputy director of Stanford Linear Accelerator Center and a member of the President's Science Advisory Committee); and *What Would be the Economic, Social and Environmental Impacts of the MX?* (with Antonia Handler Chayes, undersecretary of the Air Force responsible for assessing impacts in the deployment area, and Dr. Frederick Wagner, associate dean of the Utah State University College of Natural Resources). There was also a five-member citizen panel from the proposed impact area.

Much of the debate was predictable, although it was a good airing of the issues before a national audience. A couple of incidents stood out.

Just before the live broadcast was to begin, a highway patrol trooper came to where my wife Norma and I and Bob List and his wife were sitting and told me there was an emergency and I was needed backstage. It turned out that the "emergency" was a glare the cameras were getting from my balding head as they panned the audience. Not wishing to disrupt the production, I agreed to a little powder.

Undersecretary Chayes was strident throughout her panel discussion, basically duplicating her customary modus operandi. Undoubtedly, she felt a hostile audience, but she didn't do the President any great service in her presentation. Finally, one of the residents of southern Utah, noted for his colorful ways, made the statement during the question and answer period that he had heard about the sea mode and the land mode, but if it were up to him, MX would go into the commode. He cracked up the audience.

About the time of the debate, I had another interesting conversation with Senator Frank Church, who had just announced for reelection. I was still in the process of finalizing my views, but he had made his mind up on MX. After we had discussed the strategic TRIAD and the problems associated with land-based missiles, it was his view that the land-based leg of the TRIAD in the 1980s was a lot different than land-basing the Minuteman in earlier years; attitudes had changed. It had become a political problem. Local opposition could not be overcome, and the solution was to move away from the land-based method for missiles. That's when he gave me his poem:

Take the MX out to sea,
Where the real estate is free,
Far away from you and me.

I had decided not to announce my formal position on MX until after the PBS debate. I had gone through the learning curve, a tremendous attitude adjustment and the process of digesting an enormous amount of information and debate on how this public policy question ought to be resolved. In terms of the process itself, my attitude had long since been jaded by the way the Air Force and the federal government had proceeded in their efforts to make Utah a deployment state.

Finally, I felt that Utah could never absorb and manage the MX system and still maintain the integrity of its own future. MX would so dramatically change the state that I didn't feel it was a proper or reasonable trade-off.

The June 16, 1980 Statement

On June 16, I issued a statement and held a press conference strongly opposing the racetrack basing mode. I tried to explain my rationale and to offer some alternatives for deployment of MX. I cited a number of process problems and indicated that the state had "been ill-served by the general unwillingness of the Air Force to promptly and candidly share all of the information in their possession about the MX missile system and its impacts."

However, my chief concerns and reasons for my opposition centered around my growing belief that MX, deployed in the multiple shelter land mode suggested by the Air Force and the President, was not a survivable long-range solution to the perceived obsolescence of the Minuteman in fixed silos. Given my doubt over the timely value of MX, the potential problems associated with deployment in the Great Basin of Utah and Nevada loomed as sufficient reason to oppose MX as proposed.

I was still of the opinion that "the increasing age and relatively smaller size and warhead capacity of the Minuteman system requires the continued development and deployment of a new, far more capable missile." But I stressed: "The vulnerability of our land-based missiles does not translate directly into *immediate* fear of nuclear war . . . I am persuaded that failure to respond to the vulnerability of these land-based missiles will free the Soviet Union to concentrate on means of attacking the deep water submarine-launched and bomber or air-breathing components of the strategic TRIAD."

I concluded that the administration's proposed "multiple aim point" or "shell game" approach works in theory "only if the United States is prepared to enter into a race with the Soviets in which we try to build protective shelters faster than they can build missiles and warheads." I was not prepared to believe that we could do that; the price, in terms of land use and financial resources, seemed too high, and the timing of system implementation did not meet the strategic needs as articulated by DOD. Even if we could meet the optimistic timetable suggested by the President, it would be 1990 before the system was totally deployed, and there appeared to be no constraints on the ability of the Soviets to match our protective shelters with additional warheads. The Soviets would end up with a lot more weapons after such a race, while we would end up with more concrete and steel "garages."

I also questioned the shell game concept itself. It relied totally on deception by attempting to hide the missiles among many shelters. Technological advances might easily make deception more difficult or impossible in our open society. The result would be tighter security in a widening area of deployment, an anti-ballistic missile system, or both.

I urged the administration and Congress to consider alternatives. Recognizing my own limited scientific background, I had spent considerable time talking to experts, reading technical reports and examining alternatives. I suggested a proposal advanced by Professor William Van Cleave, Director of Defense and Strategic Studies at USC, to build additional Minuteman silos and convert existing silos to a type that could contain mobile cannisterized weapons which could be moved among these multiple aim points and later be converted for use by the larger MX.[1] While this did not solve the inherent problems with the shell game, it did provide a more timely alternative. It was apparently less costly, and it was far less disruptive of the deployment areas, both environmentally and socioeconomically, since it built upon existing operational facilities and personnel.

I made it clear that I was not proposing an "ABU"—anywhere but Utah—alternative. I stressed that this option would also permit the deployment of some Minuteman III or MX missiles within the state of Utah in vertical silos built on land already under military control in the western desert of Utah and serviced from Hill Air Force Base. The citizens of Utah, I stated, "are willing to do their fair share by accepting some reasonable proportion of an expanded Minuteman-MX vertical system under this option."

If we were to continue to follow the TRIAD strategy, I thought we would inevitably have to reconsider utilization of anti-ballistic missile systems for the land-based system. Although contrary to the ABM treaty, it seemed a less destabilizing option than continuing to expand missiles and silos. However, I thought a serious alternative was an air, deep-sea and shallow-sea TRIAD.

The shallow, underwater mobile submarine, or SUM, was a proposal attributed to Dr. Sidney Drell and Dr. Richard Garwin.[2] While equal in cost to the proposed land-based system, it had the advantages of not disturbing the land or the communities adjacent to where the system would be deployed. I was convinced that a large number of small submarines posed an entirely different war-planning problem for the Soviets than attacking deep-water submarines.

In a theme I was to develop in later speeches, I noted that Utah already played a strong role in our nation's defenses and that national security is measured in many ways, not just in the number of nuclear missiles. The West and Utah are important areas for the achievement of national energy independence and the production of strategic materials. We had been targeted for coal development, large power plants, the development of synthetic fuels from tar sands and oil shale and the development of such strategic materials as beryllium, aluminum and molybdenum.

"Utah has a finite capacity to bear the burdens and demands of large scale development," I said. "We have only a finite amount of water, and we cannot manufacture more. Our labor force and mechanisms for developing capital have limits to their capacities. Our cities and towns have limits to growth."

"As citizens of Utah," I concluded, "we are concerned for the way of life we have come to cherish, and we are committed to preserving it. As citizens of the United States, we are concerned for the security of our nation, and we are prepared to do our part to defend it. When issues as complex and demanding as national defense are involved, these two commitments are inseparable. For on issues such as MX, we must give effective voice to our immediate concerns while, at the same time, educating ourselves to the wider aspects of policies whose consequences extend across states and across generations."

Reaction to My June Statement

I don't think anyone was all that surprised when I came out with my opposition to the horizontal land-based mode. It opened up a dialogue on MX in the state of Utah in a definitive way because the governor had drawn a pretty tough line after having gone through the metamorphosis described earlier. The press coverage was good, and my statement became the subject of letters to the editor, which are at least a superficial way of determining public interest. I was both praised and abused. The public's attitude, as reflected in local polling, was beginning to respond to the issue, and my position opposing the racetrack basing continued to gain support.

I had informed the Utah congressional delegation in advance of the position that I was taking, but they were noncommittal. They never really got involved in the MX debate until mid-1981. 1980 was an election year. I was up for reelection. President Carter was running against Ronald Reagan. Three of our four-member congressional delegation were up for reelection.

I thought that when I went into my campaign, MX would be the primary issue of the debate. I had presupposed my opponent, Robert Wright, would make that an issue and go out and take up the cudgel on behalf of the MX and on behalf of the basing mode. That would have made a classic gubernatorial campaign but the MX issue turned out to be a minor part of the process. And Mr. Wright's campaign contained little substance at all.

During the campaign, Ronald Reagan indicated that he had serious misgivings about the racetrack approach to basing the MX but didn't have a specific alternative to propose. I don't think it was a material factor in the 1980 campaign. The people of the state of Utah were so down on Jimmy Carter and so up on Ronald Reagan that the outcome of the campaign in Utah was preordained, with or without the MX issue. Our polling showed that when I publicly supported Carter I lost votes. In Utah, Ronald Reagan got the highest percentage of the vote in any state that year—a little over seventy-three percent. Despite my open support for Carter, I won reelection, with fifty-five percent of the vote—significantly smaller than my eighty percent approval rating.

The Debate is Joined

I had briefed Brigadier General James P. McCarthy, the Air Force's new special assistant for MX matters and deputy chief of staff for research and development, the morning of my June 16 public statement in opposition to MX deployment in the racetrack mode. McCarthy had replaced

General Hecker. Naturally, the Air Force was disappointed with my open opposition, even though I had been moving in that direction for some time. During the summer, General McCarthy and I exchanged letters, which for the first time contained a thoughtful response to MX alternative issues.

Initially the Air Force supported the vertical shelter (silo) multiple aim point concept, similar to the Van Cleave proposal. However, the Secretary of Defense and the National Security Council raised the question of whether concealment alone was a long-run solution to the land-based missile problem. The horizontal shelter, racetrack concept was developed to give the missiles a second means of survivability, i.e., mobility to move quickly from one shelter to another in the event of discovery.

McCarthy contended that "The decision to shift from vertical to horizontal shelters for the MX basing system was not dictated primarily by arms control verification considerations; rather, survivability was the driving factor."[3] I questioned this assessment. The time that DOD and the National Security Council were raising their questions was the same time that the President's negotiators were finalizing SALT II. SALT II required a verification system for the number of ICBM delivery systems. If such verification was by satellite, missiles in a vertical shelter would have to be "uncovered" for a period of time to allow counting. McCarthy contended, probably correctly, that the missiles could not be moved in time to prevent a preemptive Soviet strike. This assumed the unwillingness of the United States to launch "on warning" in the event of the appearance of such a strike. The horizontal basing provided a "dash" capability that allowed the missiles to be moved quickly to a new shelter after verification.

Regarding the Minuteman option, McCarthy stated that it was technically feasible to modify the missiles and deploy them in a multiple vertical shelter system, but he disputed the Van Cleave assessment, stating that their analysis had indicated it would be more costly and that they could not do the engineering, land purchases and EIS as fast as the preferred MX option. Western public lands appeared easier to deal with than private lands and a state road system. He stated that because of road loading limitations, "the maximum growth potential would be to a new technology missile with . . . about fifty percent the capacity of MX."[4]

McCarthy had rejected the SUM alternative on the basis of maintaining the TRIAD. His conclusion was that "to deploy one-third of our strategic deterrent forces in large, deep-water submarines and another third in small, shallow-water submarines would subject two-thirds of our forces to the same Soviet countermeasure." This, he said, was contrary to the TRIAD concept which attempted to guarantee against losing two-thirds of our strategic forces to a single breakthrough in Soviet technology. They believed there was no technological difference in anti-submarine warfare between shallow- and deep-water submarines. SUM, as an addition to our Trident submarines, "would be no more effective than painting our submarines different colors," said McCarthy.[5] Other defense analysts disagreed on the technology issues associated with SUM versus Trident. I believe that at the core of the SUM opposition was an unwillingness to consider abandoning the land-based ICBM which had been the traditional heart of our nuclear strike force during the 1960s. Nor was I persuaded that continuing to build additional shelters to outrace the Soviets made any sense.

"To put this issue as bluntly as possible," I stated in a letter to McCarthy, "the Air Force apparently believes that the Soviets might think it sensible to launch about 2,100 warheads at fairly hard vertical silos, but it would not be irrational enough to launch 4,600 warheads at less durable horizontal shelters. We are being pressed to believe that the likelihood for a 2,100 warhead attack is a compelling reason for building a very high-cost system against which a 4,600 warhead attack would, apparently, be about equally efficient. It seems to me, we are asking the Soviets to expend the net cost of about 2,500 additional warheads and the missiles to carry them (which I assume might cost them up to $8-10 billion dollars) against our investment in an MX-MPS System which will cost us at least $33 billion dollars."[6]

The bottom line on the Air Force's argument still, to me, seemed tied to the SALT requirements and expectations of a warhead limitation, the policy of not firing ICBMs on warning and thus requiring a "survivable" deterrent and the reluctance to give up the traditional land, sea and air TRIAD. In total, these assumptions required a Rube Goldberg scheme like the MX racetrack. I was simply unwilling to concede the validity of the assumptions.

Preparing for the EIS Response

During all of 1980, MX Project Coordinator Ken Olson was organizing the local and state response to the EIS. We had viewed our ability to effectively respond as the key in taking the MX fight to Congress or, if necessary, to the courts. I was involved, from the beginning, in the creation of the local MX Policy Board (chaired by Chad Johnson) and two separate teams put together from state agencies and the state's three major universities (University of Utah, Utah State University and Brigham Young University) to analyze all of the information flowing from the Air Force and the EIS. In all, there were nearly two hundred people working on thirty task forces reviewing the project.

When the MX draft EIS was issued on December 22, 1980,[7] I was sufficiently prepared to immediately issue a preliminary statement. I was very concerned over the short ninety-day response time, especially since all of the technical documents were not going to be available until late January. The draft EIS asserted that the basing mode had been resolved in favor of land-based, horizontal shelters and had made no analysis of alternatives. It did contain a limited analysis of the split-basing mode, with Texas and New Mexico as a proposed second area.

I also had serious concerns about proposed "tiering" which asserted that the EIS would be area-specific but not site-specific, making mitigation strategies somewhat general. No consideration was given to the cumulative effects of energy development activities and MX on the communities. The Air Force had also used a "quick and dirty" methodology on the construction labor force which they admitted had to be revised. In all, it was a rather disappointing effort after the expenditure of some $17 million by the Air Force, but it provided us with a lot of ammunition for our attacks.

Our first attack was against the tiering approach. In a December 24, 1980 letter to Gus Speth, chairman of the Council on Environmental Quality, I argued that the lack of a construction management plan and specific sites made it "impossible to determine the construction-related impacts on specific communities in Utah and Nevada." I questioned whether CEQ had previously endorsed the tiering approach and whether it believed such an approach was acceptable under federal law and regulations.

Speth responded on January 16, 1981 indicating that no advice had been given, that council staff was studying the draft EIS and would shortly prepare an answer to the Air Force. "At the same time the Council replies to the Air Force on this matter, a copy of the Council's response will be provided to you." Because of subsequent events, the council never did respond.

I also asked for an extension of time to comment on the draft and solicited other governors and officials to pressure the Air Force for more time.[8] It was all part of our strategy in opposition to deployment. I felt the momentum was building on our side, and further delay in issuing the final EIS would accrue to our benefit. I also objected to the arbitrary way the Air Force was proceeding. There were hundreds of technical papers in addition to the basic set of documents, and we had two hundred people involved in the review. The project itself was bigger than the Alaskan pipeline. It all argued in favor of more time for the comment period. The Air Force announced, on the 19th of January, that they would extend the comment period to May 1, 1981.[9]

Meeting with the Reagan Team

Ronald Reagan was the new president. As a Democrat, I was disappointed in Carter's loss, but as an opponent of MX deployment in Utah, I was encouraged by Reagan's campaign comments and initial reports concerning the views of the new Secretary of Defense, Caspar Weinberger. List met with Reagan at his California ranch even before inauguration. I was not invited, but List told me he got no commitments from the President-elect.

List and I were of the view that we had better do our homework quickly. We sensed that Reagan might be going a different direction but that was not clear, so we decided it would be a good idea to see Weinberger soon. We met with him on February 10, 1981, in his Pentagon office. Though we had sent him briefing materials on the issue, it was a total waste of time. We had wanted to find a spokesman in the Department of Defense we would work with. We wanted to get any information we could about the direction they were going. We wanted to know whether he would support the mitigation approach if we failed. All of those things were on the agenda, and Weinberger didn't seem to know a thing about the MX issue. He was either unprepared or had decided not to give us any response.

We sent a follow-up letter on February 24 urging him to read our materials and asking for a designated representative to work with. List had wanted Frank Carlucchi, Weinberger's deputy, because of his past experience with the domestic agencies we might have to deal with for impact aid. But Weinberger designated Dr. Dick Delauer, who was Bill Perry's replacement as undersecretary of defense for research and engineering.[10] As with Perry, we enjoyed a good professional relationship with Delauer.

The Opposition Gathers Momentum

During early 1981, I met with a number of members of Congress, including representatives Ron Dellums (D., Ca.), Bo Ginn (D., Ga.) and John Seiberling (D., Oh.), and anyone else who expressed an interest in hearing our side of the story. I had accepted an invitation to deliver a speech on March 4 at Santa Barbara City College for their "Challenges of a Nuclear World" lecture series. It was a memorable speech, both because it represented my toughest public statement on the MX and because of the surprising weather.

The Santa Barbara trip was another example of broadening our base of opposition to the MX basing mode. We had reached the point where we had completed our homework and the next step was to expand the influence of the point of view we were espousing outside the state. The weather was horrible. They canceled all the commercial flights into

Santa Barbara. We had trouble getting there. We took the state plane through an absolutely *cats and dogs* rain storm. It was so bad that when we landed at the airport, you couldn't see a hundred feet. We had no coats. When we got to the terminal from the airplane, I was soaked. One favor had been done. Sam Battistone (an owner of the Utah Jazz) lived there, and he sent his car to take us to Santa Barbara College for the speech. I remember I was very uncomfortable giving the speech, but not because of the subject matter; I was still dripping. Although the auditorium had a roof, the sides were all open to the elements. It continued to rain hard during the speech, so although I had a microphone, I could barely be heard. Despite the storm, the auditorium was still two-thirds full because the subject matter was so important to this particular group. The speech was solid, probably the toughest I ever delivered on the subject.

I called the MX deployment scheme of the Carter administration "a serious challenge to 'Alice and Wonderland' . . . In what is surely the grandest, officially-sanctioned scheme of deception, the missiles would be moved from time to time in an attempt to insure position location uncertainty, or "PLU", thus requiring the enemy to target many structures in order to destroy one missile. Imagine if you will, forty-six hundred shelters scattered across some nineteen valleys in the Great Basin deserts of Nevada and Utah, connected by nearly eight thousand miles of roadway upon which the missiles would be moved. The deployment area would cover some twenty thousand square miles — about the size of the state of Michigan."

I said that I was convinced that MX, in the racetrack basing mode, would be "just as vulnerable in 1990 as the Minuteman." I added that in the absence of a negotiated limit on the number of Soviet warheads similar to that contained in SALT II (not ratified by the Senate and rejected by Reagan), MX simply cannot survive. Without SALT II, MX in the proposed basing mode made no sense. It could lead to a race between the Soviets building missiles and warheads and the U.S. building shelters which would only become a destabilizing force, rather than an effective deterrent. "*If* the MX missile is a sufficiently frightening weapon to make its destruction a Soviet priority, and the MX basing mode offers no real protection, such an attack would be more likely. The consequences are, of course, incalculable."

We had a question and answer period, and the audience clearly supported our position in Utah. They didn't have any interest in supporting MX at all. We flew back that same night and got home about three A.M.

In mid-March, the President appointed a group headed by physics professor Charles Townes, of the University of California, to conduct a review of the MX basing options and report back by July 1 to Weinberger who would make his final recommendation to the President. The Townes Commission examined a number of options and heard testimony from Governor List and myself. I was able to submit the state's complete comments on the draft EIS.[11]

We had arrived at a point of fruition in the process that was critical in terms of the future relationship between the state of Utah and the Air Force. I thought we had whipped them thoroughly. Their draft EIS was a tremendous embarrassment. They spent $17 million and pulled together a proposal that was certainly unworthy, in my opinion, of the United States Air Force. An example of gross negligence was the attention given to the problems associated with boom towns in the MX deployment area. The draft EIS devoted thirty-one pages of discussion to the pronghorn antelope, seventeen pages to rare plants, twelve to sage grouse, but only five and one-half pages to the impacts on human beings.

In contrast, our product was carefully organized. Even though individual technical and staff people did their assigned evaluations without knowing what their colleagues were finding, Ken Olson and I were amazed at the consistency and coherence of the finished product. As far as I was concerned, our comments on the draft EIS were more professionally done than the draft itself.

In a summary letter of April 23, 1981 to Defense Undersecretary Vernon Orr accompanying the detailed analysis, I stated: "The subject DEIS does not permit either a responsible decision maker or a concerned citizen to make informed judgments about the crucial issues pertaining to MX deployment. . . . Since this DEIS clearly fails to consider the full range of impacts associated with a reasonable set of viable alternative methods of basing the MX missile, the state of Utah believes this omission fatally flaws the current DEIS. . . . Even assuming prior decision on the MPS linear basing mode, my evaluation of the DEIS suggests that split basing (Alternative 7) has been inadequately considered." I also detailed seventeen serious "generic" defects in the draft which ran throughout the document.

I felt that the combination of the inadequacy of the EIS, the President's appointment of the Townes Commission, and the growing negative attitude of the public and policy makers toward the racetrack basing had shifted the prospects of victory to the MX opposition.

Then, on May 4, 1981, the Church of Jesus Christ of Latter Day Saints (Mormons) came out officially against the proposal.[12] In my opinion, it sounded the death knell over the project.

The LDS Church Statement

Early in the process, at the time when Ken Olson came on board, we talked about the LDS Church, and I made a decision that the Church should have the opportunity, if they chose to take it, of being updated monthly on the MX issue. We had an initial meeting with their Public Affairs Committee members, including President Gordon B. Hinckley, first counselor to President Spencer W. Kimball. I don't remember if I met with them personally on the matter or talked to them on the phone about it, but they were very pleased. We worked through Public Affairs Director Richard Lindsay. Our objective was to have Ken meet with them about once a month, or once every two months, to keep them up to date on everything we were doing, without asking anything from them. It was simply a briefing proposal for their benefit, if they chose to use it. They were very receptive to the idea.

I had never asked the Church to take a position on MX and they had never told me they were going to take a position on it, although the official statement of the Church was brought to my attention before they publicly announced it. I received a phone call from a member of the LDS Church's Council of the Twelve Apostles indicating that they were going to oppose the basing, viewing MX as a significant moral issue. They felt strongly about it and wanted me to know about their decision before it was officially published so that I could be prepared to respond.

From my perspective, all of the influence and all the things we did paled by comparison to the position of the Church. The fun thing about it was that even though I was not privy to why they did it nor when they were going to do it, it happened to coincide with my own views and was a major factor in influencing public attitudes in Utah.

The LDS announcement was a precipitating cause in bringing the Utah congressional delegation on board, albeit with a bit of grumbling. Apparently, they had been kept out of the discussion as much as I; they learned about the LDS position when I learned about it. Senator Jake Garn was extremely unhappy that the Church had not consulted him. He viewed himself as the defense expert in the state, but there wasn't anything he could do.

The LDS Church's statement stressed the danger of the worldwide buildup of arms and the potential unlimited extension of the racetrack system in the absence of the ratification of SALT II. Such a system, they said, "may even invite attack under a first-strike strategy on the part of an aggressor. If such occurred, the result would be near annihilation of most of what we have striven to build since our pioneer forefathers first came to these western valleys. Furthermore, we are told that in the event of a first-strike attack, deadly fallout would be carried by prevailing winds across much of the nation, maiming and destroying wherever its pervasive cloud touched."

After discussing the tremendous social impact of such a development, the First Presidency of the Church concluded with this widely quoted statement:

> Our fathers came to this western area to establish a base from which to carry the gospel of peace to the peoples of the earth. It is ironic, and a denial of the very essence of that gospel, that in this same general area there should be constructed a mammoth weapons system potentially capable of destroying much of civilization.
>
> With the most serious concern over the pressing moral question of possible nuclear conflict, we plead with our national leaders to marshal the genius of the nation to find viable alternatives which will secure at an earlier date and with fewer hazards the protection from enemy aggression which is our common concern.

The Mormon Church's statement drew worldwide attention, not all of it favorable.[13] But all of the Utah congressional delegation is Mormon, and seventy percent of Utah's population and thirty percent of Nevada's population are Mormon. Senator Garn soon began to develop alternative basing schemes. The Townes Commission was still deliberating, but in my mind the victory was won.

President Reagan Kills the Racetrack

Ronald Reagan is a strong supporter of national defense, the MX missile and the military structure of the United States. I'm sure the military felt they had an ally in pursuing their racetrack proposal. My view in terms of the outcome was quite confident, despite some last-minute lobbying by the Air Force to knock down the various alternatives proposed. By this time, the draft EIS was over, our comments were in, we were now looking at the package. I was sufficiently confident, after reviewing our legal and our other procedural remedies, that we had a strong hand to play.

The President didn't try to keep me in touch with his thinking on MX. On October 1, 1981, however, I received a phone call from the White House informing me that Reagan was going to oppose racetrack basing in Utah and Nevada. I was pleased because it was now official and all of the things we had presupposed and concluded came together. But it was not an emotional or exhilarating pleasure, it was a conclusion — the last nail in the lid. It was predictable and satisfying, but somewhat anti-climactic. We had already enjoyed the emotional exhilaration of the expected result.

While I got hooked into the MX issue without appropriate review, I felt it was incumbent and an inherent part of the job of the governor to do exactly what I did — to get into such an issue as thoroughly as possible, to take positions on it consistent with interests of the state, respecting the national objective and yet being aggressive in terms of the state perspective.

In retrospect, my view about President Carter on MX is positive. I think he was trying to do a first-class job for the people of the United States. I believe that he tried to carry policies out in the public interest and that he worked hard, studied hard and thought about the issues carefully. He basically is a fair man and did not want to abuse anybody politically, economically or any other way. Even though he would disagree on basic issues, he was not the type who would react emotionally and take advantage of you if you disagreed with him. That was not his make-up. He was totally professional in terms of how he dealt with public issues, and even though we disagreed on the basic substantive issue of MX basing, we could disagree on that and still agree on the best approach to the mitigation side.

Even though President Reagan has scored a partial victory with MX funding, I feel there is significant deterioration of support for the weapon. I still feel the MX basing mode, even given the remodeled, super-hardened Minuteman silos in which they will be deployed, is vulnerable. Someone still must come up with a reasonable rationale for our spending billions of dollars for a vulnerable system.

At this writing, the President has managed to get congressional approval to spend $1.5 billion for twenty-one more MXs.[14] Many thought that obtaining the funding would be a breeze, since the White House had so deftly tied the issue to our chances for success in the new Geneva arms control talks. But it took a monumental selling job to do it, and many have already stated flatly that they will not support funding for the additional forty-eight missiles the President has said we must have.

MX's future remains highly problematic. In terms of its deterrent value, many proponents in the early debates said we simply had to have MX ready to go by 1989. That timetable is no longer discussed, even among those who adamantly claim we are behind in the missile race. The primary argument for MX during the last couple of years has been that we need it as proof that we are tough and dangerous. That image is supposed to bring everyone to the bargaining table, ready to reduce missile stockpiles. Yet the MX was not a significant issue at the Geneva Summit in 1985.

I frequently wonder if the original arguments about our vulnerability were true, or whether we were being set up. All the deadlines we were looking at are long gone, and nobody seems to care. The lack of support for MX has not produced more concern about our alleged vulnerability.

The whole MX issue has now taken a back seat to President Reagan's Strategic Defense Initiative (SDI) or "Star Wars" as it is popularly known. The President is suggesting we substitute lasers from space for land-based ICBMs. Thus, our defense TRIAD would be changed to SEA, AIR and SPACE. Whether this approach is technically possible is an open question. Perhaps former Senator Church was right. In today's political environment, additional land-based ICBMs may simply not be feasible.

The MX issue was one of the most critical events in my service as governor. Our approach to the issue established a very important pattern for states to follow in dealing with federal-state issues, even though national interest issues are involved. It certainly proved that states do not have to quietly swallow everything the federal government throws at them. That was an encouraging lesson for Utah, and it set the right pattern in dealing with other issues.

CHAPTER 8

The Tragedy of Atomic Testing

IN the spring of 1953, nearly forty-three hundred sheep from herds grazing in the high desert country ninety miles southeast of Cedar City, Utah died mysteriously.[1] There were eleven different herds in the area, with a total of some eighteen thousand sheep; and though all of them did not die, most became ill, losing significant amounts of weight and spontaneously aborting lambs. It was a devastating loss for the sheepmen who owned the herds.

At first, the sheepmen were completely dumbfounded by the incident. The animals had small, blister-like lesions on their skin. That, coupled with the weight losses and abortions, puzzled the ranchers; it was unlike anything they had ever seen. Some of them had reported seeing clouds of dust passing over their lands following an above-ground atomic bomb test conducted in the Nevada desert just west of where their sheep grazed. But at first, no one linked the dust clouds with the sheep deaths. However, after they had time to think about the incident, they began asking questions. Primary among their queries was the issue of radioactive fallout: Had their animals been killed and injured by the deadly byproducts of the atom bomb tests?

The Atomic Energy Commission (AEC) looked into the matter and, in a report issued in January 1954, concluded that their "extensive research" showed the sheep had not died from exposure to radioactive fallout from the Nevada Test Site. Malnutrition was a possible culprit, the AEC claimed.[2]

That was not an easy answer for the sheep ranchers to swallow. They knew they were not starving their sheep. In February 1955, five of the Iron County sheepmen, in a suit filed against the U.S. government, asked for $176,964 in damages they claimed they sustained as a result of the atomic testing. The complaint alleged that the herds were within sixty to eighty miles of the probable detonation point of the blast, and that "government agents negligently performed, conducted, discharged and executed such nuclear tests and experiments, causing damages to the plaintiffs."[3]

My wife and I were living in Cedar City at the time of the sheep deaths, and we were somewhat concerned about the spectre of radioactive fallout. We had no inkling that it would later become a major public health and freedom of information issue for me as governor.

It was in 1951 that the U.S. government began the series of aboveground atomic tests at the Nevada Test Site, northwest of Las Vegas.

Previously, the testing had been conducted at Eniwetok, an atoll in the Pacific Ocean, in order to minimize radiological hazards. However, the isolated island presented security and logistical problems, and in 1950, the AEC began to seek a continental test site.[4] United States security and the protection of democracy were major concerns in 1950. The Soviet Union had the atomic bomb, war had broken out between North and South Korea, and Senator Joseph McCarthy had begun his personal war against Communists in the U.S. I was in Salt Lake City in my second year of law school at the University of Utah, and I can remember the bitter campaign between incumbent U.S. Senator Elbert Thomas and Republican Wallace Bennett. Bennett and the Republican Party wanted badly to unseat Thomas. They accused him of being "soft" on communism and of associating with known Communists. It was a scathing and unprofessional attack, a sad commentary on politics, the type of campaign I've always deplored. Bennett won in a close race, and the Republicans have held that Senate seat ever since.

The 1950 election, postwar nationalism and the developing conflicts in Korea created a very patriotic mood in Utah. I remember that President Harry Truman's popularity was at a low ebb until he made the decision to send U.S. troops to Korea. That decision almost made him a national hero. Utahns were ready to wholeheartedly back just about anything the federal government wanted to do in the name of national security.

On December 18, 1950, President Truman made another momentous decision. He granted permission for the AEC to begin aboveground testing at the Nevada Test Site. Like most Utahns at the time, the decision and the beginning of the tests had little impact on me. In 1951, I had made two important decisions: to transfer to Stanford University for my final year of law school and to marry Norma Warenski, daughter of Dr. L. C. Warenski, a prominent Salt Lake City obstetrician.

We moved back to Utah in 1952, and I passed the Utah Bar examination. My father was also an attorney. He was born and reared in Parowan, a small southern Utah town in Iron County. After graduating from the University of Chicago Law School, he returned to Utah and formed a law partnership in Cedar City with a longtime friend, Durham Morris.

My father felt that I should get some on-the-job training with Durham, and after some consultation, we all agreed that a rural legal practice would provide the right experience. Norma and I moved to southern Utah, initially to Parowan and, later, to Cedar City, and I learned how to be a country lawyer. It made a big difference in the professional style I developed and how I later dealt with legal problems and people.

I was appointed Parowan City Attorney and got to go to city council meetings once a month. I received twenty-five dollars a month, but no expenses to do whatever legal work had to be done in Parowan, which was eighteen miles north of Cedar City. I think I almost paid the city to be their attorney, but I wouldn't have missed the opportunity to do it, especially in my "Mother City." It was a great experience.

The legal issues I dealt with were typical for a rural setting, a far cry from the battles I would later encounter in connection with radioactive fallout. For example, an eight-months pregnant woman was chased by a ram one day. This ram pursued the woman up the back steps of her home, and she barely escaped his attack. She was unharmed physically but was very disturbed—almost hysterical. I found an ordinance that prevented anyone from keeping a vicious ram within the confines of Parowan City, so I filed a complaint against the animal's owner. Before we tried the case, he knuckled under my relentless prosecution and disposed of the ram. The complaining witness, my aunt, was vindicated.

The fact that she was a member of my family was not remarkable; many of the area's population are related to me. I had no way of knowing it at the time, but the fallout issue would later have a direct effect on many of my relatives, and I would find myself defending them again, as their governor rather than their attorney.

Iron County, and all of southern Utah for that matter, is traditionally rural. The people are dependent on agriculture, ranching, some mining and tourism. The state didn't have a travel council to encourage tourism at the time, and Cedar Breaks National Monument, an awesome geological wonder in the tops of the mountains of Parowan, was a well-kept secret. Cedar City has a college, and that produced some jobs, including a part-time one for me; I couldn't earn a living from my law practice alone.

People in southern Utah were mainly concerned with making a living, and I don't recall anyone being too upset about the brilliant flashes and thunder-like blasts that were part of the 1953 atomic testing. The Upshot-Knothole series, conducted from March to June 1953, included the "Dirty Harry" explosion that carried an enormous amount of debris downwind, over southern Utah. People *were* concerned about the sheep deaths that occurred in May 1953, but when the AEC said there was nothing to worry about, we all just shrugged our shoulders. No one really accepted the malnutrition rationale, but we were used to accepting whatever the government said, especially during that very nationalistic period.

The people in southern Utah, then and now, grow up with great respect for our system of government. Generally, they are patriotic and supportive of whatever leadership says is in the public interest, both locally and nationally. Utah is, in a sense, a patriarchal state, and many of its citizens are used to obeying authority without question.

That was the environment in which southern Utah willingly accepted the testing in the beginning of the early 1950s, without any real concern about possible adverse health impacts on any of its citizens. Early concerns were raised in minor ways and, of course, they increased as years passed, particularly as people began to question the unusually high death rate due primarily to cancer.

From the beginning, the AEC stressed the need to carefully "manage" information about the atomic tests. In their recommendation of the Nevada site to President Truman on December 13, 1950, the AEC stated: "It is recognized that the problem of radiological safety is most critical in site selection. Not only must high safety factors be established in fact, but the acceptance of these factors by the general public must be insured by judicious handling of the public information program."[5] The all-out public relations campaign by the AEC to assure everyone that "there was no danger" effectively quieted most fears.

I've tried to recall my reactions to the Nevada atomic testing during the 1950s and the growing concern of some scientists about the amount of radioactive fallout and its potential impact on Utah residents, the "downwinders." Negative articles began to appear in the news media, and there was even some editorial concern, but it was always balanced by arguments concerning the need for testing because it was in the national interest. And, of course, the AEC was still claiming there was absolutely no danger from fallout. The sheep losses created a major stir; and by the time of the 1958 moratorium on testing, Utahns were glad to see the tests concluded, but there still was little concern over long-term health consequences. I lost track of the issue until after I became governor.

Uncovering the Information of the Impacts of the Atomic Tests

Anxiety that the atomic tests of the 1950s were responsible for increased cancer among the exposed populations living in Utah, Nevada and Arizona began to mount in the late 1970s, although it was never an issue in my 1976 campaign for governor. In 1977, Salt Lake City news media and the nationally-distributed *Parade Magazine* chronicled the grim story of a Salt Lake City cancer patient who had participated in the military exercises in Nevada.[6] The account evoked an outpouring of telephone calls to the National Center for Disease Control in Atlanta, Georgia from former army personnel involved in the tests.

While my office received some inquiries, it was really the Utah press that kept the story alive. Mike Youngren, who was my press secretary in 1977, had moved to KUTV, a local television station, and was very interested in the work of two of the station's reporters, Lucky Severson and Carl Idsvoog. They were doing a piece for "Extra" (a weekly news magazine show) entitled "Clouds of Doubt," which examined the story of southern Utah residents who had been downwind of the atomic testing.[7] Margaret "Maggie" Wilde, my press secretary from 1978-1981, had seen some of the footage and thought it very damaging to the government's credibility. On an October weekend in 1978, we all sat down in my office and watched several hours of taped interviews.

The tapes had a tremendous impact on me. National figures, such as Linus Pauling, were interviewed and had strong views about how small amounts of low-level radiation could threaten human health. There was substantial professional and scientific information on the cumulative impacts of low-level radiation, and most of it was ominous.

They also interviewed a number of people from southern Utah who claimed they had lost large numbers of family members to cancer. Many were relating those losses directly to the fallout from the above-ground testing. Particularly, they were talking about leukemia, and how radiation incipiently invades youngsters, manifesting itself after a number of years. Much to my amazement, I knew about a third of the people who were being interviewed. The realization that these people were my former neighbors, many of them my cousins, hit hard.

When I watched that part of the interview, I was immediately struck with the realization that a lot of people down there were asking questions and not getting any answers. They suspected they were being abused, and nobody seemed to be listening to their pleas for help. I decided, at once, that I would see what I could do to wring some answers from the federal government.

Several members of my family from southern Utah have died from cancer. I'm sure some would argue that the cause, or at least one of the causes, was exposure to low-level radiation. I have no definitive evidence on which to base that claim, but when the overall mass of evidence about the relationship between the radiation fallout and the area in which the fallout occurred is examined, and those events are related to the incidence of cancer death, it is difficult to find a reasonable explanation that does not point to low-level radiation fallout. There are difficult technical and legal questions that require scientific explanations, but the important point was that a lot of people were dying from cancer.

We became extremely concerned about the way the government had handled the entire issue. I felt there was a public duty to get the facts and to determine if state government could offer treatment, diagnosis and/or research. The second issue at that time was what to do about those who had already contracted cancer and died. I was equally interested in that. However, as governor, it seemed to me that my first responsibility was to get all of the information together and then see if there was a possible public resolution.

The first thing I did was to go to southern Utah. I spent many hours talking with people who had gone through the experience, and I listened to what they had to say. We visited St. George in early November 1978 and arranged to have a number of people come in from the surrounding communities, including Parowan.

We simply sat down and talked about it. They told their story. The common theme was loss of loved ones. They blamed the 1950s atomic testing, and they were very frustrated about it since they had been assured by the U.S. government that everything was perfectly all right — there was no danger. It was a public relations effort on the part of the federal government in those days to make the whole project look good, and everyone in southern Utah bought their story. In that limited sense, their project was a total success. Now, in retrospect, with the tragedies a matter of record, I know those people had a very emotional, negative feeling toward the federal government for the way they were abused. That was the recurring theme of almost everyone I interviewed on that trip.

I decided to assign the issue as a top priority to my personal staff. I thought we first should go into our files and find out what information we had. We found a lot more information than we thought existed. In fact, there were some significant reports in the archives that had come into our Division of Public Health in the 1960s that had never been published. And no one had taken the trouble to call the information to the attention of the governor or any other policy maker.

Our investigation showed that the managers of the Division of Health felt the radiation issue was of no real concern. All of the information we uncovered had been handled in a merely perfunctory manner. Someone stamped it in, and it isn't clear whether it was reviewed carefully or not. It all went into archives, apparently with no decision-making process associated with it. Therefore, instead of getting one of the agencies like the Division of Health to take responsibility for the new investigation, I felt I would be better off relying on somebody in my own office.

Maggie Wilde took on this assignment with great zeal. As a journalist, she was angry about what we had learned. Someone was supposed to provide information, and they had withheld it; some of the information provided was not true, and those who provided it knew that. That offends journalists; it also offended the governor. One of the facets of Maggie's assignment was to gather information. There was a storehouse of knowledge on this subject that had never been carefully evaluated by state policy people. As a matter of fact, you can hardly send out kudos in the way the state of Utah handled any aspect of the low-level radiation issue during the 1950s and 1960s. It was pretty much a default.

In late November 1978, just before Thanksgiving, Maggie and I went to Washington to try to get some help from the federal government. We had sent information in advance to Jack Watson, President Carter's assistant for intergovernmental relations, to Joseph Califano, the Secretary of Health, Education and Welfare, and to the Department of Defense. I had talked to Jack on the phone in advance to make the appointment with the President and, since this was the first time I had ever personally requested assistance from the Carter Administration, I was hoping for a positive response.

The meeting with Watson was a real frustration. Despite my phone call, he had not read the briefing material and offered no assistance. I thought, "Here is the President's assistant for intergovernmental relations, and he can't provide any help in my search for the facts." It was disappointing and disturbing. I was about to leave empty-handed when he mentioned that the President had given Califano the responsibility of studying the problem of servicemen who were exposed to fallout from the Nevada tests and suggested I talk to him.

After meeting with Watson, I met briefly with Assistant Secretary of Defense Charles Duncan, to brief him on our efforts, but he also was unable to offer any concrete assistance and seemed little concerned with the issue.

After my two fruitless meetings, I went back to the hotel and asked Maggie to try to get an appointment with Secretary Califano. I was frustrated and angry and determined not to continue tilting at windmills. There had to be someone in Washington interested in this problem. After a number of phone calls, Maggie talked to an assistant secretary, Sue Foster, who had received our briefing materials.

Califano had just returned from Europe and was scheduled to leave for the Thanksgiving holidays the next day, and Foster doubted we could get in to see him. Maggie pressed, indicating that I would be available any time that evening or early in the morning to accommodate the secretary. An appointment was arranged for eight o'clock the next morning, November 22. We sent some additional briefing papers to Foster.

I admit I wasn't very optimistic about the prospects of a successful meeting, but Califano quickly changed my mind. He was knowledgeable on the subject and had been thoroughly briefed on everything I wanted to talk about. He was very well versed on his assignment about the military personnel. He had his general counsel there to give me an update on what they were doing about that issue. When we were finished, I said I needed help in getting the administration involved. We needed them to open their files. He offered to speak to the President. I said that would be absolutely great. He said he was going to the White House later on that day and promised to ask the President if he would do something. Califano kept his word.

I had no prior knowledge about Mr. Califano, but the one time I asked him for help, he followed through, and I respect him for that. In any event, he did talk to the President, who referred the matter back to Mr. Watson. Watson was with the President when he came to Salt Lake City five days later, on November 27.

The President was appearing at the Mormon Tabernacle for the National Conference on Families. I went out to the airport to meet Air Force One and when I got there, I found another very important individual waiting to meet Carter. It was the President of the Mormon Church, Spencer W. Kimball. We greeted the President jointly, and we returned to town in the same automobile.

I had met Carter earlier, but I had never discussed the issue of low-level radiation fallout with him. Jack Watson advised me at the airport that the President was going to do something about it while he was in Salt Lake City and would issue a brief statement indicating he was committed to offer some help. Watson told me he had personally typed the statement on Air Force One and, in fact, the first time he was able to discuss the matter with the President was after the plane was airborne.

Carter's statement read:

> Governor Matheson has expressed his concern over the possible health implications for people in Utah who were exposed to radioactive particles as a result of Defense Department testing of atomic bombs in the 1950s.
>
> The Governor has asked me to review the findings of earlier federal studies in Utah on the effects of exposure to radioactive particles on health, and to determine whether or not a more comprehensive study is indicated.
>
> I am today directing the Secretary of the Department of Health, Education and Welfare to take the following actions:
>
> — Reevaluate the findings of earlier studies conducted in the state to determine whether or not the rate of illness or death from leukemia is disproportionately large in Utah, particularly in the southwestern counties;
>
> — Reopen a study conducted in the late 1960s on the incidence of thyroid disease; and
>
> — Consult with state officials and consider the possibility of developing a larger, more complete study if indicated.

—I have asked Secretary Califano to work closely with the state of Utah as he proceeds, and I have asked the Secretary of Defense to cooperate fully in this endeavor.

Responding to the Carter memorandum, Secretary Califano established a joint Federal-State Radiation Effects Management Committee, with members from Health, Education and Welfare (HEW), the Utah Division of Health, the University of Utah Medical School and the Center for Disease Control. Maggie Wilde and Michael Zimmerman, a Salt Lake attorney assisting us in this effort, were also added to the committee. This select group would oversee the reevaluation of past studies, as well as the formulation and implementation of any new studies.

The public's concern spread with the publication of a 1979 study in the *New England Journal of Medicine* by University of Utah medical researcher Dr. Joseph L. Lyon; it indicated significantly increased incidences of childhood leukemia among the exposed population.[8] Dr. Lyon's findings documented a twofold increase in leukemia among children born during the open air test period in the high fallout counties of southern and eastern Utah.

Other information became available, including a previously unpublished report by Dr. Edward S. Weiss of the University of Utah (1965) which suggested similar findings.[9] The unexpected discovery of the Weiss report by State Archivist Harold Jacobsen prompted my request in January 1979 that Secretary Califano undertake a document search of "all relevant information concerning past studies that may have been suggested or actually undertaken, as well as other fallout data collected over the years." Citing President Carter's commitment, I made similar requests to the Departments of Labor, Defense, Energy and the Environmental Protection Agency, as well as various divisions of Utah state government.

On February 27, 1979, Secretary Califano reported the findings of an HEW study that suggested a higher than normal incidence of leukemia among individuals present at the "Smoky" nuclear bomb test in August 1957. Such findings, he said, "underline the need for additional research to determine whether the risks associated with low-level radiation are higher than scientists have predicted in the past."[10] At the same time, he announced that the University of Utah "under an HEW contract . . . will study the possible long-term health effects from radioactive fallout in areas downwind from the Nevada weapons test site."

A $250,000 contract was signed by the University of Utah Medical Center with the Center for Disease Control for a one-year study to identify parameters of a possible full-scale epidemiological survey. On the strength of President Carter's commitment, Dr. Chase Peterson,

Vice President of Health Services (and later president of the university), expanded his staff in the anticipation of additional funding from the National Institute of Health (NIH). Chase and I entered into a pact: I agreed not to decide how to do the research, prejudge the outcome or determine the amount of money that would be required to do the research correctly, and he agreed to leave all of the political problems associated with the issue to the governor's office. We never violated that rule.

"You see, governor, we couldn't release all our radiation data. You know how uptight the public can get over this sort of thing."

One particularly distressing piece of information the state archivist had uncovered was an historical account of the 1953 sheep deaths, kept by Dr. Monroe A. Holmes, a veterinarian in what was then the Department of Health. The record was astonishing. It portrayed a federal bureaucracy that was using every tool at its disposal, including intimidation, to keep the facts from the public. It was no wonder that the sheepmen did not prevail in their 1955 lawsuit against the federal government; they simply didn't have the facts, facts essential to their case. The uncovering of this record, shortly before congressional hearings on the issue in Salt Lake City, undoubtedly colored my testimony.

The following are excerpts from my April 19, 1979 statement to the joint hearings of the House Committee on Interstate and Foreign Commerce (Subcommittee on Oversight and Investigations) and Senate Labor and Human Resources Subcommittee on Health and Scientific Research, chaired by Senator Edward Kennedy and Congressman Robert Eckhardt:

> The evidence shows a willful refusal to investigate evidence of threats to human health and a suppression of relevant information on health dangers. The primary responsibility for this appears to rest with the AEC, although others

aided and abetted that agency. The reasons for this incredibly irresponsible course of conduct appear to have been all too human, and all too petty.

The 1953-1957 Southern Utah Sheep Investigation Documents I have furnished this Committee . . . read like a case study in government misfeasance and callous disregard for health and property.

Samples of a few of the sheep thyroids and other organs indicated that the sheep had been exposed to very high levels of radiation. Preliminary analysis, based on what appears to have been erroneous assumptions about the time of exposure that minimized the doses received, showed the thyroids to have had concentrations of from 250 to around 1,000 times the maximum then established as a permissible human level. Although the sheep symptoms were clearly of a type that radiation can produce and had never been encountered before in the area, the AEC refused to acknowledge the possibility that radiation could have played a role.

This scientific myopia appears more sinister when other events are considered. Not long after the investigation got underway, a senior AEC representative met with a number of scientists investigating the problem and pressed them to endorse a conclusion that the radiation was not a causative factor in the sheep incident. The AEC representative told the scientists—most of whom were AEC employees or Public Health Service people—that unless the commissioners were presented with a satisfactory resolution of the sheep problem, they would not "open the purse strings" for further continental weapons testing. The "no cause" conclusion that the AEC representative suggested was forwarded to the commission. And, as we know, the testing continued.

The final aspect of the story relates to the AEC-funded follow-up study. The AEC invited a proposal from Utah State University to study the possible causes of the sheep deaths and illnesses. In inviting the proposal, the AEC made it clear that it only would fund a study that looked into ranching practices and malnutrition as possible causes of the sheep losses. It would not permit further study of radiation as a possible causative or contributing agent. The study was funded under the AEC's conditions. Not surprisingly, damage that occurred to the herds in 1953 could never be duplicated. A 1964 study that has just been provided me by the Department of Agriculture indicates that symptoms *exactly* like those that killed many of the sheep are the by-product of radiation exposure at levels far higher than the AEC thought it was possible for the Utah sheep to have received. That paper might have been written ten years earlier had the USU study not been limited by the AEC.

Through all of this dismal chronicle, one thing stands out: There is no mention of the obvious implications the sheep injuries and deaths might have had for the safety of humans in the area downwind of the test site.

I told the committee we had to answer two critical questions: What were the health risks for those who lived in the area, for themselves, their children and grandchildren, and how do we mitigate those risks? Also, what can we learn about these events for the future? In addition, I was interested in assessing responsibility against those who made the critical decisions regarding precautions taken during testing and their later cover-up of relevant information.

While we certainly know more today than we did in the 1950s, I could not help but draw a comparison to the Three Mile Island nuclear reactor incident in Pennsylvania. Governor Richard Thornburgh (R., Pa.) recommended evacuation of pregnant women and children who were within a five-mile radius of the reactor when the radiation doses were two to twenty-five millirems per hour. Residents in Utah and Nevada received doses of one thousand millirems after a single explosion in 1953 but were told nothing.

The documents discovered prior to my testimony demonstrated severe failures by the federal government to deal responsibly and candidly with the human health consequences of the fallout, a serious underestimation of its geographical scope and failure to keep a central repository of information on the health implications. I indicated that it was imperative to institute an independent conclusive study on the cause/effect relationship of the fallout to health.

I also urged Congress to fund an independent library or central depository where all data concerning the fallout and its health implications could be preserved for researchers and the public. I noted that this had been done for the Japanese and the Marshall Islanders and for those affected by the Three Mile Island incident.

Following this highly-publicized testimony was a three-year effort by me to get adequate funding for the research that the experts thought was necessary; a continuing effort by attorneys representing alleged victims of the testing to get redress in the federal courts; and an attempt by some members of Congress to find a legislative solution for those persons downwind of the testing, who felt they had been harmed. My primary effort was getting the funding for the scientific studies.

Even before my testimony, the University of Utah Medical Center was proceeding with its contract with the Center for Disease Control, and on May 8-9, 1979 hosted a conference to develop its proposal for a long-term study. Among the federal representatives were Drs. Guy Newell and Victor Zeve, representing the National Institute of Health. The proposal included provisions for:

1. The establishment in Utah of an archive of all available documents pertaining to the Nevada atomic bomb tests.

2. The reconstruction from these documents, as best possible, of the levels of radiation emitted into the atmosphere and received by the residents of Utah, Nevada and Arizona (the dose assessments).

3. A full-scale epidemiological survey of the health effects of this fallout on these residents.[11]

Dr. Zeve telephoned Michael Zimmerman on May 11 to say that neither he nor Dr. Newell had any questions about the soundness of the

Utah proposal. He expressed confidence in the ability of the University personnel to conduct the projected study but indicated some concern about the divergent approaches of the separate Utah and Nevada proposals.

That same day, Dr. Guy Newell called Zimmerman, saying he was preparing a rough fiscal year 1980 budget for Congress and would like an estimate of the amount necessary to fund the Utah and Nevada studies. He indicated the estimate should include both the Utah and Nevada research, as well as the document depository. Furthermore, he said he expected little or no difficulty in getting the research proposal funded. He pointed out, however, that HEW preferred to fund a single research package that would cover the other affected states as well.

Together with the University of Utah researchers, Zimmerman worked out a rough budget projection which would cover radiation dose assessment (dosimetry), epidemiology and the document repository. He conveyed an estimate of $1.5 million for each of five years to Dr. Newell, who reemphasized the importance of Nevada and Utah coordinating their research plans so that HEW could fund one scientifically consistent and credible proposal.

Two days later, Drs. Newell and Zeve called Zimmerman again. They informed him they had spoken to Sue Foster at HEW who wanted to know how Utah would like its contract handled. He was told that although the contract would have to go through normal National Institute of Health (NIH) grant channels, it would be written so that the University of Utah and the Nevada medical schools would be the sole eligible applicants. Again, Zimmerman was assured the studies would be funded.

In July 1979, Newell and Zeve returned to Salt Lake City and declared they had been asked by Washington authorities to develop a program to study the problem of radioactive fallout. Newell indicated that approximately $9 million had been set aside in the budget to support studies by investigators on the issue. In order to coordinate the interests of Utah, Nevada and Arizona, he requested that a tristate administrative commission be established to review proposals from the area. He reiterated, in a telephone conversation with Zimmerman on July 6, the importance of coordination among the states and indicated that HEW would be willing to fund such an administrative commission.

Robert Edmundson and Dr. Aaron Smith of Nevada, Dr. James Sarn of Arizona, Dr. Chase Peterson of the University of Utah, Mike Zimmerman and Maggie Wilde met in Reno and spent considerable time later by telephone and correspondence designing a proposal to establish a tristate commission to coordinate and oversee the various health study proposals.

This grant effort was beginning to concern me. The process began to appear more important than the product. I expressed my concerns to Mike and Maggie. However, since both my office and the University of Utah Medical Center were assured that the tristate proposal would be funded — that NIH would commit the money — we still seemed on track. It was always emphasized to us that HEW felt compelled to fund health studies in the affected states and that in order to assure the scientific credibility of the studies, coordination among the states through the tristate commission was essential.

We submitted the proposal to the White House and to HEW in September 1979 and it proceeded through the system at an agonizingly slow pace. It was subjected to extensive peer review by the Committee on Federal Research into the Biological Effects of Ionizing Radiation and was rejected on November 23, 1979.[12] The committee, in direct contradiction of earlier communications by Drs. Newell and Zeve, concluded that in the absence of a specific health research proposal, it would be inappropriate for NIH to fund an administrative mechanism for such a study. The review committee recognized the "chicken and egg" dilemma posed by this unusual situation, but rejected the tristate commission.

Rejection of the tristate commission proposal was a serious setback to the momentum that had been building to fulfill President Carter's November 1978 commitment. I was furious. It was also the first indication of what was later to become a history of changing representations, flagging interest at the middle and lower levels of bureaucracy (if not intentional delay tactics), changing ground rules and self-destructing procedures. Furthermore, it gave credence to confidential reports we were receiving from some federal officials that key bureaucrats had no interest in seeing these studies funded and these issues exposed.

During the next several months, however, a three-state proposal to study possible health effects from the above-ground weapons tests was prepared at the request of Dr. Donald Frederickson of NIH and personally delivered by Dr. Peterson on April 16, 1980.

A rigorous scientific evaluation of the study proposal ensued in June 1980 by an ad hoc technical merit review subcommittee of the Interagency Radiation Research Committee. In September 1980, the group unanimously refused funding of the studies, primarily because it believed the proposal did not address well-framed scientific questions.[13] Additionally, NIH lawyers maintained they could not grant the contract before going through competitive bidding procedures. Again, a new hurdle was introduced by mid-level management.

After refusing to fund the proposals, the subcommittee identified study topics within the proposal which they believed should be pursued through the Department of Defense, Department of Energy, Environmental Protection Agency, the National Institutes of Health of the Department of Health and Human Services (HHS) and the Veterans Administration. In a press conference held in Washington, D.C. on September 22, HHS Secretary Patricia Harris announced that these five federal agencies "will negotiate with scientists in Utah, Nevada and Arizona to conduct $4 million worth of research on the possible health effects of radioactive fallout from the testing of nuclear weapons."[14] Study areas included incidence of leukemia and thyroid gland malfunction, reconstructive dosimetry using thermoluminescent technology (a new tool which examined radiation in the quartz contained in fired bricks) and tissue sections, and reconstructive dosimetry of uranium miners in Utah.

True to Secretary Harris' announcement on September 22, "negotiations" did ensue between the five federal agencies and researchers in Utah, Nevada and Arizona. But those negotiations bore precious little fruit.

In telephone conversations on October 16, 1980 with Dr. Chase Peterson, Dr. Charles Lowe of NIH emphasized the delicate nature of the funding process. He repeated that it was illegal to issue a contract for work which had already been turned down as a grant. Negotiations continued along those lines until January 13, 1981, when the press reported that NIH intended to waive the competitive bidding procedure and quoted Dr. Frederickson as saying he wanted to move ahead rapidly with the studies.[15] Dr. Lowe was also reported to have said that on a commonsense basis, the University of Utah was the sole available bidder with direct access to the state cancer registry and the LDS (Mormon) Church genealogical records. The files were deemed vital to a study of cancer deaths in southern Utah since atomic tests began in Nevada in 1951.

The news account indicated that final approval of action to waive the competitive bidding procedure would require the signature of HHS Secretary Patricia Harris or someone in her office, a process "expected to take about a week." That same week, Dr. Peterson received a phone call from NIH confirming the competitive bidding requirement was being waived and that funding would be forthcoming within two weeks.

Weeks passed, and no funds came. I arranged a trip to Washington to visit with the new HHS Secretary Richard Schweiker on February 10, 1981, who incidentally had been present at the joint congressional hearings in Salt Lake City two years earlier. This was the third cabinet secretary that I had personally dealt with on this issue. Secretary Schweiker assured me that the University of Utah would receive funding within sixty days.

Two months later, however, the rules were to change again. In a meeting on April 6 with Drs. Donald Frederickson, Charles Lowe and Joseph Perpick, all of NIH, Dr. Chase Peterson of the University of Utah learned that the NIH procurement procedures required competitive bidding after all. Accordingly, NIH had distributed a "Sources Sought Circular" on March 23, soliciting the names of individuals and organizations interested in bidding on the health effects study. The awards would be made by the National Cancer Institute (NCI) within NIH.

In early 1982, the University of Utah's proposal was selected over other competitors by a scientific review board. In February, the National Advisory Board to NCI reviewed the proposal and approved it. But after having selected it on its scientific merits, they recommended that NCI fund only one-third of it and requested that the Departments of Energy and Defense each contribute one-third toward the total cost of $6.4 million.

Following this disclosure, I again appealed to Secretary Schweiker, who had assured me one year earlier that funds would be forthcoming within sixty days, to use every means at his disposal to impress upon NCI director, Dr. Vincent DeVita, the importance of funding their scientifically-approved study immediately from available funds within NCI. Following a February 11, 1982 letter and a personal visit to Secretary Schweiker on February 22, I was assured, again, that funds would be forthcoming. In that meeting, Schweiker promised to try to influence the departments of Defense and Energy.

When the promises produced no action, I again appealed to Schweiker to press DOE and DOD for funds. I also testified at the U.S. Senate Labor and Human Resources Committee hearings in April. In those hearings, I indicated I was even more cynical and less optimistic about the outcome of the hearings than I had been three years ago when I first testified on fallout. The contract was finally awarded to the University of Utah in May 1982.

Four Years Later, Limited Success

I consider my final success on this issue a limited one. We did get some funds for studies, but the reassessment of the radiation dosage from the atomic testing is led and funded by the Department of Energy. Unlike the health effects study, the Department of Defense and Department of Energy did not undertake competitive bidding, and Dr. Ed Wrenn of the University of Utah received funding for reconstructive dosimetry using thermoluminescent technology and tissue samples as part of an overall reevaluation of the radiation at the time of the atomic tests.

I believe DOE is doing a competent job, and Utah is represented on their advisory committee by one citizen and one scientist. But I feel a completely independent study would have been preferable. DOE also took the initiative in establishing a repository for documents in Las Vegas. Here, again, I believe an independent agency, such as the University of Utah, would have been preferable to avoid any appearance of bias. DOE had the funds and basically moved in to fill the vacuum while we were getting the run-around by federal HEW and NIH officials.

The epidemiological study, headed by Dr. Joseph Lyon at the University of Utah, was not as comprehensive as it should have been. It was funded only after constant political pressure by me. Why we were not told about the existence of NIH's procurement requirements and the restraints inherent in them before the private statements of Dr. Guy Newell (summer 1979) or the public statements of Drs. Lowe and Frederickson (October 1980 and January 1981) is difficult to explain.

The evidence of bureaucratic foot-dragging, if not actual sabotage of the grant proposal, is substantial. Was this the result of attempts to protect the careers of those individuals who might have underestimated the radiation impacts years earlier? Or was it simply a case of the professionals feeling that there was no scientific reason to spend more money on a "dead issue" when there were more interesting research agendas to pursue? I'll probably never know, but I suspect it was a combination of these two concerns that led mid-management to sidetrack those who made department policy.

There may never be conclusive scientific proof that the increased incidence of cancer in southern Utah was related to the atomic bomb testing in the 1950s. But I hope the additional information generated by the studies will at least alert the people most at risk to annually check for thyroid cancer symptoms and other illnesses that may manifest themselves after a long period of dormancy.

I am still angry about the way this issue was handled by the federal government. It points to a continuing need for governors to be vigilant concerning both short-term and long-term impacts of federal decisions on their residents. If the citizens in a state are to be sacrificed for the "national interest," then, at the very least, those citizens need to be fully informed and protected as much as possible.

CHAPTER 9

The Politics of Nerve Gas

USUALLY, important federal-state public issues develop in a predictable, forthright way and can be addressed in the normal decision-making process. Occasionally, however, an issue will sneak up and blindside you before you have the opportunity for proper evaluation. This happened to me in dealing with the Weteyes, several hundred nerve gas bombs stored at the federal Rocky Mountain Arsenal near Stapleton Airport in Denver.

The Department of Defense (DOD) had decided to transfer the Weteyes to Utah, but in the process of making that decision, failed to tell the governor of their plans, or, for that matter, anyone else in the state of Utah. DOD's proposal to relocate the bombs in Utah, without notice, was a perfect example of a failure of the federal-state partnership and illustrated the callous disregard federal agencies have for the states, particularly those involved with national security matters. This situation, once I became involved, was mostly a game of frustrating catch-up to marshall the necessary information to make an appropriate decision in the overall public interest.

I first knew of the proposed transfer from a third party outside the loop of the federal agencies, Congresswoman Pat Schroeder (D., Colo.). Schroeder was involved early in the issue and was very aggressive about it. She wanted to get rid of the nerve gas because of her safety concerns over the possibility of a Stapleton-bound airplane crashing at or near the storage area.

The Department of Defense was required by federal statutes to file an Environmental Impact Statement (EIS) on the proposed move. In most cases, when a governor disagrees with a federal policy objective affecting his state, there are limited tools at his disposal to fight it. He can try to rally public opinion, and he can take his case to the administration or to the Congress. But he seldom has an opportunity to take his case to the federal courthouse with a solid procedural weapon and really lock horns. We found that weapon in the Environmental Impact Statement process analyzing the Weteye proposal.

My views on the proposed move were colored by health and safety factors associated with moving and storing nerve agents GB, VX and mustard gas. I didn't get deeply involved in the philosophical argument over whether nerve gas should be used, (although it is an abhorrent thing to me), or whether we needed nerve gas in our defense arsenal at all. Those questions were raised, however, during the debate over why we shouldn't simply detoxify the Weteyes at the arsenal.

The problem should have been resolved in 1973 when the Army promised the Colorado congressional delegation that the Weteye bombs and all toxic material at the Rocky Mountain Arsenal would be destroyed there. Apparently, however, this commitment was made with some understanding that Congress would first fund the development of a modernized, "binary" type chemical weapon. The binary concept is to separate the nerve gas components, which are inserted into the weapon. They mix enroute to the target; the ingredients are therefore inert until after the missile is fired. Because Congress had not approved the binary approach, the Department of Defense had suspended detoxification of the Weteye bomb.

The MK-116 (Weteye) is a 530-pound bomb designed and built at the Rocky Mountain Arsenal for the Navy during 1964-65. The bomb is ninety-two inches long and fourteen inches in diameter; the nerve agent (GB) accounts for 352 pounds of the weight. The bomb is made of extruded, one-eighth inch, seamless aluminum. The fins are folded in storage and pop out when the weapon is deployed. The bomb is "fused" when loaded aboard a plane and explodes on impact. The bombs are contained and stored in hermetically-sealed containers resembling coffins. Originally there were 901 bombs, but one developed a leak and was destroyed.[1]

After notice we had to scramble for information. We went into the periodicals and obtained articles about the nature of nerve gas itself, what its chemical makeup was and the history of how it was developed. It happened to be part of the research done in Nazi Germany in World War II. GB nerve agent affects the central nervous system by destroying an enzyme, causing muscle contractions which lead to heart failure. The deeper we got into it, the more intrigued I became. It turned out that over a period of years, the Tooele Army Depot in Utah had received a high tonnage of GB, VX and mustard gas. We were, and we remain, the grand champion storage site in the entire country for this product.

I remember getting the startling information from the Army that eighty percent of all our chemical weapons were stored at Tooele. Up to that time we had absolutely no idea of that volume, because of the pattern of impunity followed historically by the military. Once a mission has been assigned the military, they proceed with a plan of execution. They tell those affected nothing unless they have to.

Prior to the National Environmental Protection Act (NEPA) in 1969 there was no public notice requirement to warn the affected state. The military simply loaded their chemicals onto railroad cars and trucks, transported them over the public roads and railroad rights-of-way of our state, delivered them to Tooele and stored them in "igloos." We were never told about it and went on, blithely going about our business for years without appreciating the nature of the chemicals. Then we learned how lethal nerve gas is. A drop on your skin, I was told, if not attended to properly, is fatal. We had enough of it already stored at Tooele to destroy mankind.

The more we learned the more disturbed I became. Our briefings continued to be perfunctory; therefore, we were forced to keep digging for information. We got very little for our efforts; but the more I got stonewalled, the more committed I became to finding out what was going on. The potential risk was so great that the health and safety aspects of bringing in additional quantities of the product were ominous. After all, I had worked for a railroad company for fourteen years and was certainly aware that accidents could happen.

The deeper we probed, the better our chances of stopping the transfer became. DOD had filed the EIS in late 1977,[2] and a number of state agencies found problems with the safety aspects of the transfer. In early 1979, in addition to the already known problems, leakage was discovered in other Weteye bombs. Leaking occurred around the weld plugs where the product had been loaded in liquid form and sealed. All leaking happened to occur in exactly the same place. The evidence showed that, ultimately, all of the Weteyes were going to leak. The issue became a matter of whether the leaks were significant and whether those leaks would cause health and safety problems. That became the issue in the lawsuit we filed with federal court at Salt Lake City to force a supplemental EIS.[3]

At the same time we entered the courthouse, we stepped up our campaign in other areas. We continued to press the administration for a reassessment of the need to retain the Weteyes[4] and we began to develop public interest in the potential problems associated with the move.

In the heat of the public debate one of the employees at the Rocky Mountain Arsenal was taken to the hospital with symptoms of nerve gas exposure, but it turned out that the gas was probably not the cause of the problems.[5] Nevertheless, that incident dramatically triggered public concern on the issue. The leaks were difficult to explain. The Army concluded that they were small, inside another container and that the bombs were entirely safe. By then, however, no one was willing to buy that explanation.

We developed solid support for our side of the issue. The press and the public rallied behind the cause. Our congressional delegation, however, was not willing to support my position and took the view that the military could do a safe job of handling the nerve gas.

During the debate, I became convinced that the entire Weteye system was completely obsolete. The agents had all been manufactured in the 1960s and the deterrent argument for the Weteyes for the 1980s and beyond seemed meaningless. We were also planning to store them in a hard-to-reach location. Most notably, there never was a delivery system for the Weteyes; those who were advocating that we needed to have the materials in storage for retaliatory purposes never could answer the question of how they would ever get the bombs to a target for purposes of retaliation.

The final unanswered question was, how much do we need? The quantities of nerve agent stored at Tooele are absolutely mind-boggling. Our storehouse has the capacity to do a lot of mischief in the world. We never addressed that issue head-on, never really got to the philosophical question of how much of that stuff we really need. When we tried to get the military to respond to that question, the answer was simple. The Joint Chiefs had determined it was needed for defense—a familiar, if somewhat unsatisfactory, response.

The Weteye issue exemplifies, therefore, public officials defaulting their public policy responsibilities. The President and the National Security Council should have been the ones to make the decision as to whether or not we really needed the Weteye bombs in our defense arsenal. But this decision was turned over to military technicians. Faceless people made that decision. Clearly, when you turn a matter like that over to the military, it will predictably maintain the weapon no matter how obsolete.

In the course of the battle, I did meet some very competent people in the Department of Defense, particularly William Perry, undersecretary for research and development, who had been so helpful with the MX issue, and who understood and was most helpful in explaining the chemical makeup, capacity and lethality of the nerve gas agents. Deputy Secretary Charles Duncan, Jr., though he ended up as an adversary, did so professionally.

We dropped our lawsuit once we decided we could resolve the differences outside the courtroom. Even so, the suit had an impact. We went in with a good case, and I think the willingness of the Department of Defense to do a supplemental EIS was based primarily on the merits of our arguments in the case. It was nice to have some leverage for a change.

After the supplemental EIS was completed, we had access to even more information.[6] It was now clearly established that all of the welds were ultimately going to leak, but no one could predict just when. That placed the proposed transfer into a nose dive. We were starting to get important people and organizations to support our case, the *Washington*

Post among them.[7] Our homework and stubbornness had paid off, and DOD backed away from the proposed move.

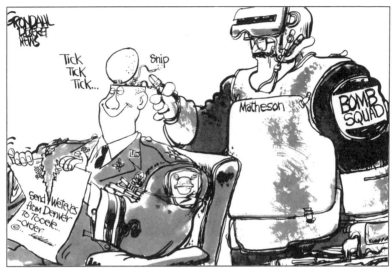

DOD's formal announcement on February 26, 1980 occurred when I was in Washington for the National Governors' Association mid-winter meeting. William Perry announced that he was going to make a public statement of what the Carter Administration would be doing with the Weteyes. We assembled in a hearing room in the Capitol Building. Colorado Governor Dick Lamm, Representative Pat Schroeder (D., Colo.) and Senator Gary Hart (D., Colo.), and lots of press were there. Bill Perry announced that the decision had been made to continue to store the Weteye bombs at the arsenal. He indicated there were some health and safety problems with the move and said the administration was backing off. Hart immediately came over and said, "Congratulations, Scott, you're the winner." But he was very unhappy about the decision. I advised him that, in my view, the Weteyes shouldn't be inflicted on either Utah or Colorado; I had hoped they would be detoxified at the Rocky Mountain Arsenal.

Pat Schroeder was comfortable with the decision and said that the next step was to go for detoxification. Dick Lamm, however, was very displeased about the decision. He apparently interpreted the announcement as a kind of political victory for me based on an informal deal I had made with either the White House or the Pentagon strictly for political purposes. He felt that I had turned my back on Colorado.

I tried to have a conversation about it with Lamm that night at the Kennedy Center, but he wouldn't even discuss it with me. He thought

I had politicized the issue deliberately for my own 1980 reelection, and he was very emotional about it. In truth I had never talked to the President about the issue. Lamm and I didn't speak for more than a year, but we are now good friends again.

I had no information that President Carter ever got personally involved in the Weteye issue, unless Jack Watson, assistant to the President for intergovernmental affairs, visited with him sometime on an informal basis. Our contacts had basically been with Bill Perry, and I had been to the Pentagon a number of times to discuss it. The victory, of course, was gratifying. We had started out as David against Goliath and had earned the win the hard way.

One interesting fallout of the Weteye issue was my political relationship with the people of Tooele County. Tooele County is traditionally Democratic and, over the years, Democrats have counted on strong support from Carbon, Tooele and Weber counties. As a result of my opposition on the Weteye, I thoroughly stirred up the traditional political alliances there. This had a very adverse impact on maintaining traditional Democratic support, and, as a consequence, I did not do well in Tooele County in the 1980 campaign. The residents felt that since they had grown up with chemical weapons and nerve agents in their backyard and had never had an accident, they didn't need outsiders from Salt Lake to come in and tell them how to do things.

One particularly emotional rumor was a supposed statement from an unidentified person at the Pentagon who allegedly said that my personal attitude on the Weteye matter would have an adverse affect on the growth of the Tooele Army Depot.[8] When that came to my attention, I knew it was now important to get the facts promptly. I flew to Washington and met with Charles Duncan at the Pentagon. He gave me an unconditional commitment that my position on the Weteye issue would have absolutely nothing to do with the Pentagon's decision about the growth or lack of growth at the Tooele Army Depot. I followed up with a public statement to that effect, but heavy political damage had already been done in Tooele County.

People naturally worry about issues that might affect their jobs. That certainly is human nature, particularly where we have major federal installations and major federal employment. Employees certainly don't want anyone coming in and jeopardizing their jobs. So when people started talking about losing jobs, it fanned the flames of antagonism. I think Tooele County went Republican later on at least partly, and perhaps substantially, because of my views on the Weteye issue.

Hart Snatches Victory From Defeat

Senator Hart was a very unhappy man on the day that Bill Perry announced the decision on the Weteyes. But he did not throw in the towel. After a careful analysis Hart determined that he could attach an amendment to the military appropriations bill which would require that the Weteyes either be detoxified or moved from the Rocky Mountain Arsenal within twelve months.[9] He was successful in restoring the amendment to the bill in conference committee and the President signed it.

Hart knew all along that the arsenal near Denver couldn't set up for detoxification that soon (their detox facility was mothballed), and that they had no budget for detoxification. It simply could not have been done in twelve months. He also knew that without detoxification, the only feasible place to store the bombs was Tooele. The language was innocent enough, but it was deliberately and carefully designed. He didn't say, "We're going to take these over to Utah," he simply said, "Either these Weteyes have got to be detoxified within twelve months, or they must be moved." When that time passed, he had, in effect, won a victory because he also legally exempted the move from the environmental statutes of the United States. DOD didn't have to do an EIS. Consequently, Hart turned a major victory for the state of Utah into a major victory for the state of Colorado.

Hart did not consult with me or even inform me of his actions in advance. At the time, I was extremely unhappy that he was depriving Utah, and me, of victory; but on reflection, I can understand his motivation. Gary Hart is a pragmatic senator. He was running for reelection in 1980, and he was having a tough race. He had to have a couple of victories in Congress.

At that time, I had Deputy Attorney General Don Coleman examine the language of the amendment. I asked him if we had any reasonable expectation of successfully pursuing litigation. In his July 21, 1981 opinion, he concluded we had very little, if any, legal argument left. Senator Hart had successfully cut away both our political base and our legal base. I ended up backing away from further litigation.

It turned out, after examining our options, that we had none. We had played out the hand and I had no more resources to use. I could have gone down swinging but that is not an appropriate thing for a governor to do. I ended up withdrawing my opposition to the move and addressing the safety precautions which, ironically, were the reasons I got into the Weteye issue in the first place.

I was dealing with another general by then, General Niles Fulwyler, who had been assigned the Weteye matter. He told me he would play it straight, and that he would give us all the facts, all of the time, and that whatever baloney we had put up with from the military over the years was about to end. It did.

Fulwyler advised me, in a letter on July 23, 1981, just before the move in August, that they had significantly improved their overall safety and security because of the concerns I had raised. The military was so anxious to meet every health and safety precaution that the design of the move was much more sophisticated than originally planned. We did force the military to do a totally professional job on the move, and General Fulwyler was pleased that they did it that way. The public interest was served. The health and safety of the people of both Utah and Colorado were protected by the careful design of the move. It was done without a hitch.

In retrospect, I probably would have done at least one thing differently. At the time I filed the lawsuit, we had developed the data to argue successfully against any move. If I had known that I was going to expose my win to reversal, I would have pressed the suit with more vigor. That's the one thing I had going for me that was under my own personal control, to the extent that you can control one side of any lawsuit. The suit was in Salt Lake City, not in Washington. I had a lawyer who knew the issue well. And we had a good case. Another valuable political lesson was learned: Never relax with victory until it is assured.

I never pursued the Weteye issue through the Pentagon and the White House by trying to persuade anyone politically. I was perfectly willing to abide by the facts. I had no idea what Bill Perry was going to say the day he announced the decision. I was totally open and professional about it and I got burned for that, but I understand the process. I probably was not as tough an infighter in terms of the issue as I should have been. I do know that in later years as governor I would have been a more worthy adversary to Senator Hart as he pursued his amendment.

Conclusion: Balancing State and Federal Interests

From the often frustrating and always difficult experiences of MX, low-level radiation and Weteye transfers, I learned that states sometimes must be very aggressive in their dealings with the federal government. Tradition has long held that governors and other state administrators are expected to keep their noses out of federal business, unless they are invited to participate. I came to abhor that attitude, and I feel that we made some dents in it.

When I first became governor, I was naive about the attitude of the federal government toward the states. However, as I chalked up more experiences with federal-state relationships, I became more "streetwise." Among other things, I realized that most federal-state issues are interrelated, and that together they have profound implications for a state. As I thought through some of those relationships, I began to realize just how monolithic the federal system can be and what a challenge it is to inject Utah's voice into the issues. By the time the Nuclear Waste Repository Act was adopted by Congress in 1982 and had reared its ugly head in Utah, I was a scarred veteran of intergovernmental relations, and I was quick to make an issue of the proposal to place a repository near one of Utah's national parks.

National security is a national issue. It is important to everyone, and states must be fully cooperative and helpful in the process of ensuring it. But states must also consider *all* the relevant factors before endorsing any proposal the federal government might make in the interest of protecting its citizens. Blind obedience serves neither the national nor the state interest. The value of full state participation in national security decision making had become very apparent in dealing with the MX issue.

Traditionally it has not been the custom for governors to go forward and grapple with the federal government on national security issues affecting their states. Our history has been largely one of acceptance and compliance. Utah has been a perfect example of that approach for decades. In my view the role of governors is inherently different than the role of advocates for federal interests. While we are citizens of the federal system and have a solemn obligation to help solve national security problems, we also must speak for the people of the states. Our duty is not only to accommodate federal interests but to protect state interests as well.

I still believe that the federal government would rather roll over states on these crucial issues. That realization still makes me angry, but the experience has not made me cynical. Federal officials are doing what they consider to be their jobs. There is no reason to expect them to have any real concerns about the state of Utah and its future. They're assigned to solve federal problems; their focus is properly directed to their own objectives, not to whether their objectives are interfering with or challenging state value-systems and resources. I do not fault them for that, but I do object to the attitude many of them still have that states should consider their own interests secondary to national ones.

That approach can ultimately thwart both state and national interests. Healthy state economic, political and social systems are important to the national good. They are the key ingredients of a healthy federal system, and unless states are aggressive in establishing and protecting these interests, they can be swallowed up in the federal machine. I was not about to allow that to happen.

My view is that we must recognize both federal and state interests and work together to serve them. Trade-offs are often necessary, but compromise is more palatable when it is forged cooperatively by everyone involved. That takes full and early disclosure, and the active involvement of the states in federal decisions.

Historically, Utah has been left out of far too many of these decision-making processes. MX, low-level radiation and nerve gas bomb storage were all defense-related issues, but we have had similar experiences in dealing with the management of water and public lands.

PART III

New Directions in Natural Resource Policy

CHAPTER 10

Public Lands: Rebellion or Cooperation

ON July 4, 1980, about 250 residents of Grand County, Utah celebrated the anniversary of the American Revolution with a protest gesture of their own—the bulldozing of a road into a proposed Bureau of Land Management wilderness area. County commissioners termed the "road improvement" a symbolic protest against what they felt was an attempt by the federal government to deprive them of their right to use the land and to earn a living.

The demonstrators gathered at Moab City Park early in the morning, formed a caravan of more than one hundred four-wheel drive vehicles and made the trek to the proposed wilderness boundary. The region has sandstone knobs and fins, sandy hills covered with sagebrush, juniper and yucca and a few rough dirt roads. Many of the protestors wore insignia boasting, "I am a Sagebrush Rebel."[1]

The protest punctuated a decade of growth in environmental and management controls which had frustrated many westerners. The root cause of the dissatisfaction was the enormous amount of public land owned and controlled by the United States, and the administration of those lands by the federal government.

While the Grand County protest came midway in my eight years as governor, public lands issues dominated the entire period. Since more than two-thirds of the land area of Utah is owned by the federal government and managed by the Bureau of Land Management, Forest Service, National Park Service, Department of Defense or the Bureau of Indian Affairs, I sometimes joked that I was really only the governor of one-third of the state. While this was undoubtedly an exaggeration, the intergovernmental problems of dealing with the five separate federal agencies and in working closely with local officials, who felt impotent against the federal establishment, occupied a great part of my time.

Because of the Sagebrush Rebellion, we were able to launch several initiatives in Utah concerning public lands that will have long-range impacts on the management and development of the state, including cooperative agreements with federal agencies, wilderness legislation and the development of a proposal to block scattered state land sections into consolidated areas for more efficient management. These initiatives were controversial and precedent-setting for western public lands states. Our battles to protect state interests were waged in the halls of Congress, the Departments of the Interior and Agriculture and the

United States Supreme Court. At the heart of the debate was whether Utah and other western states would control their destinies or have their development and growth charted by forces emanating from the Potomac.

What It Means to Be a Public Lands State[2]

It would undoubtedly surprise many people in the United States that two-thirds of our total land area falls within the public domain. I use the term "public domain" to describe land held by the federal government. About one-half of that land is in Alaska, and the remaining one-half is almost entirely located in the eleven contiguous western states extending from Colorado to California.

The percentage of each state under federal control varies greatly. For example, in Connecticut, less than one percent of the total land is under direct control of the federal government, but in Nevada, the total is nearly eighty-seven percent. Even in the western states, the total varies greatly, from the Nevada high to a low of thirty-six percent in Colorado. In Utah, approximately sixty-seven percent of the land is under the jurisdiction of federal land managers.

Easterners, having limited public land acreage in their states, tend to envision western public land states, such as Utah, as vast, wide-open wastelands, except for national parks. In the case of parks, most easterners have strong emotional ties and look on public lands as important personal and national resources. Locals, however, tend to consider public lands as their own property, and think that easterners should keep their noses out. Federal governmental agencies have a slightly different attitude. They see western public lands as easy places to locate almost every controversial or unpopular federal project because their sparse populations and limited political clout in Washington make those sites fairly indefensible.

The era between 1785 and 1896 was one of public lands disposition, because the United States was primarily concerned with building a new nation. It saw the key to this development as the promotion of economic and physical development. Achieving this goal required an aggressive colonization effort in the vast, unpopulated areas of the new nation in order to encourage settlement.

The federal government also provided land grants to the western states as they joined the union. Utah received four sections (640 acres each) in every township for schools and other specific land grants totaling 7.5 million acres. The state's Enabling Act requires the proceeds from the lease or sale of "school sections" to go into trust for the benefit of the state's public school system.

Beginning in the 1890s, however, Congress began to recognize the importance of conservation for the long-term economic health of the nation. In 1891, it passed the General Revision Act which provided executive authority for the withdrawal of certain public lands containing valuable forest resources. By 1901, the nation had established nearly forty-one forest reserves, which are now part of the national forest system.

The passage of the landmark Antiquities Act on June 8, 1905 allowed the President to set aside certain areas of significant natural, cultural and historical value. In addition, the General Withdrawal (Pickett) Act of 1910 gave the President authority to withdraw lands containing "nonmetalliferous resources." Other specific acts and actions which withdrew areas of the public lands included the Reclamation Act of 1902, the Petroleum Placer Act of 1897, withdrawals for Indian reservations and for various military reservations, including naval oil reserves.

During the 1930s and 1940s, withdrawal of public lands for specific purposes increased dramatically. The federal government began to take an active role in the conservation, maintenance and improvement of public lands. In 1934, the passage of the Taylor Grazing Act brought new grasslands and grazing areas into the fold of actively-managed public lands and provided the essential area that was later to be managed by the Bureau of Land Management. The Fish and Game Sanctuary Act of 1934 provided a new role for the federal government in protecting the nation's wildlife resources. In the late 1930s and 1940s, World War II resulted in large withdrawals of land for Army, Navy and Air Force bases.

In 1964, a major piece of legislation established wilderness as an aesthetic value to be protected for its own sake. The Wilderness Act required the U.S. Forest Service, the National Park Service and the Bureau of Land Management to select and recommend to Congress those lands which were pristine enough that they should be preserved as part of a National Wilderness Preservation System.

In 1969, the National Environmental Policy Act (NEPA), one of the most significant environmental policy and land use measures, was adopted by Congress. The act, signed by President Nixon in 1970, declared as national policy the encouragement of "productive and enjoyable harmony between man and his environment" and the promotion of "efforts which will prevent or eliminate damage to the environment and biosphere and stimulate the health and welfare of man."[3]

In a single, sweeping declaration of national policy, Congress sought to improve and coordinate federal plans, functions, programs and resources for the benefit of present and future generations of Americans. The key requirement of NEPA was the filing of an Environmental Impact Statement (EIS) by a federal agency on any major federal actions significantly affecting the quality of the human environment. This EIS is the same document whose scope so much concerned me during my fight against MX deployment in Utah. It has become the cornerstone of federal efforts to manage the lands of the public domain.

In the West, because of the interrelationships of public, state and private lands, virtually any major activity has required the filing of an EIS. Such a statement requires a discussion of the need for the proposals, an analysis of alternatives, a discussion of environmental impacts of the proposals, suggested alternatives and potential mitigation strategies, and a proposed course of action. The EIS process was designed to be open, allowing for affected federal, state and local agencies and individuals to participate in the discussion and debate on federal policies and actions.

Between 1969 and 1976, a series of additional environmental laws were adopted to protect endangered species, wild and scenic rivers and other environmental concerns.

Such environmental legislation culminated in the passage of the Federal Land Policy and Management Act of 1976 (FLPMA). This act completed the full evolution of federal land policy from an approach of rapid disposition for economic development to one of retention for conservation and environmental protection. It declared that the policy of the United States was to retain public lands for present and future use. FLPMA is often referred to as the "BLM Organic Act," because in addition to establishing a federal policy for its public lands, it provided an administrative charter for the Bureau of Land Management (BLM).

The second major function of FLPMA was the reassertion by Congress of its authority over public land withdrawals and management. Previous legislation had allowed the executive branch to withdraw public lands for various purposes such as national parks, wild and scenic rivers, etc. The new legislation for the BLM set up specific rules and regulations for withdrawal, including approval by Congress for withdrawals over certain acreage limits. It also set up a method of land exchanges and a leasing structure requiring fair market value for grazing lands. Finally, it mandated a wilderness review with recommendations to go to the President and to Congress.

While FLPMA represented a major grant of authority and responsibility to BLM, it provided that authority within a framework of coordination with state and local governments and specifically provided that BLM land-use plans had to be consistent with state and local plans to the greatest extent possible, except where the Secretary of the Interior viewed such consistency as contrary to a national purpose. Thus, embodied in FLPMA was the opportunity for major state and local consultations with BLM managers.

Utah State Lands Litigation

During the ninety years of Utah statehood, many land exchanges with the federal government have taken place. In nearly every case, they were relatively small and have had little effect on overall land ownership patterns. During the same period, however, Congress reserved additional areas in Utah for national defense, national parks, national monuments, national recreation areas, Indian reservations and other federal uses without regard to the state sections which might be impacted. It was fairly common for many Utah sections to be preempted for federal or private purposes by the time the state got around to a survey.

In an effort to make sure the states were treated equitably, Congress established procedures known as the Indemnity Selection Process, or in-lieu land selections, which meant that if a state is denied one of the designated school sections through a withdrawal it was entitled to select other available land from the unappropriated public domain (managed by BLM) to compensate for the land loss.[4] The law provides that a state may select other lands of equal acreage with one condition: If the land lost was non-mineral in character, the state could only select a section that was non-mineral in character; but, if the land lost was mineral in character, then the state could select mineral-character land.

By the mid-1960s, Utah was eligible for extensive in-lieu selections. From September 1965 to November 1971, Utah identified a package of 157,256 acres of school sections we requested as in-lieu selections. Interior did not process our selections; the Secretary of the Interior claimed that under the 1934 Taylor Grazing Act he had the duty to classify lands, not only on their mineral and non-mineral character, but to measure the equivalent value of the preempted land sections versus the land sections we had requested. Utah claimed that it was entitled to an acre-for-acre selection based on constitutional precedent nearly two hundred years old.

The matter came to a head in Utah during the mid-1970s energy crisis, which followed the Middle Eastern oil embargo. Utah has the second largest land area of oil shale, and its processing was thought to be one answer to the energy crisis. Part of Utah's unprocessed in-lieu selections included large tracts of the oil shale land. Over Utah's objection the federal government offered for bid ten thousand acres in two small tracts of the oil shale land we had selected, and it received a large bonus payment for that property. Governor Rampton indicated he would sue the Secretary of the Interior if he attempted to lease the oil shale tracts we had selected, but Interior went ahead and processed it anyway. It was agreed, in the best interest of Utah and the United States, to proceed with a lawsuit. It was filed on March 4, 1974, requesting the court to direct the Secretary to act upon and approve our in-lieu selection.

The court ruled in Utah's favor on January 8, 1976, but the United States appealed to the Tenth Circuit in Denver. In April 1978, a three-judge court ruled unanimously in Utah's favor. By this time, I had become governor and tried to get Interior Secretary Cecil Andrus to agree with the Court of Appeals' decision. However, the Solicitor General of the United States and the Justice Department felt very strongly that the case needed to go on to the Supreme Court and review was granted. This time, in a five-to-four decision issued in May 1980, the United States Supreme Court reversed the Tenth Circuit Court of Appeals, and Utah lost the case.[5]

The four judges who dissented were highly critical of the finding, indicating that it was a significant change in policy and that it departed from the sanctity of agreements between the states and the federal government that existed for nearly two hundred years. In my opinion this was one of the most parochial, federally-oriented decisions in the Supreme Court's history. Utah was, in a real sense, denied its inheritance.

At that point I had to reexamine our entire land policy. I concluded that we needed to strike a better partnership with the federal government in the management of public lands within the state. And we also had to find a better way to manage our scattered state sections, a problem related directly to our failure to block up sections of land in the in-lieu selection process.

Management Problems of Scattered State Sections

In 1984, over eighty-five percent of the total land holdings of the state of Utah existed in five thousand isolated six-hundred-forty-acre (one square mile) sections surrounded by public lands. They are therefore virtually immune from any logical state management strategy, and a significant number of the sections (nearly half a million acres) exist as inholdings within national forests, park lands, military lands and Indian reservations. While, in Utah, earnings from state lands are used for public education, the use of the inholdings is severely limited, and they generate little or no return to the school trust fund for which they were originally granted.

The mingling of state and federal lands frequently also leads to serious conflicts between the state and federal governments over the use of specific lands.

The Alton coalfield, located in Kane County, northeast of Kanab, Utah and south of Bryce Canyon National Park, illustrates those conflicts. A significant portion of the low-sulfur reserves in the field can be surface mined, which makes Alton development more economically attractive than deep-coal reserves in the same area. The Bureau of Land Management manages the federal coal properties, including some existing leases. The state of Utah also owns and leases a number of scattered state sections in the area.

In November 1976, citizens and environmental groups petitioned the Secretary of the Interior to declare portions of the Alton field unsuitable for surface mining under provisions of the Surface Mining Control and Reclamation Act. The petition alleged difficulties in reclamation, impacts on water resources and adverse impacts on Bryce Canyon National Park, which overlooks the northeastern portion of the field.

In December 1980, after completion of an EIS, the Secretary of the Interior responded to the petition, agreeing that development of the easternmost portion of the field could adversely affect the park and declaring unsuitable for surface mining those lands visible from the park.[6] This decision is the subject of litigation that may take years to wind through the courts. In the meantime, more than twelve thousand acres of state coal land are preempted from development by the federal decision because the sections are simply too small to support a mining operation without the adjacent federal coal. The impact on the state inholdings frustrates our Enabling Act requirement that state land be managed in trust for the schools.

The state shares the concerns which led to the filing of the unsuitability petition. At the same time, the state, as land manager and trustee for the land grant, is obligated to manage those lands for the economic benefit of the trust. The logical solution is to address problems such as Alton through site-specific exchanges which eliminate the particular management conflict. For example, if state coal lands could be blocked up in an area that is suitable for mining, state and federal management objectives could be realized simultaneously.

The state of Utah frequently has proposed small exchanges to address potential management conflicts or to facilitate management of specific resources. Unfortunately, experiences with existing exchange procedures have been singularly unsuccessful. As of 1984, more than twenty-two exchange applications covering more than 200,000 acres and dating back to June 1967 were pending, with little hope of favorable action.

Sagebrush Rebellion

The 1960s and 1970s probably saw more extensive resource management reform and certainly more environmental controversy than any other period of American history. The tradition of natural resource conservation established by President Theodore Roosevelt was expanded by presidents of both political parties during that period. For example, NEPA was adopted under Richard Nixon; FLPMA under President Ford; and Jimmy Carter's administration gave us an expanded Clean Air Act and the Super Fund to clean up toxic waste.

These were decades of far-reaching legislative activity. But of equal significance was the philosophical upheaval that dominated the period. The classic dilemma of preservation versus development focused the American mind on our national heritage. That focus, and the ambiguities of the inherent conflict, are built into the Federal Lands Policy Management Act. Among the legislative mandates for the BLM are sustained yield on the public lands, prudential development, public recreational use and preservation. These inherent conflicts heighten the special interest group competition for use of the public lands.

"SIR, THERE'S A GENTLEMAN WAITING TO SEE YOU WHO CLAIMS TO KNOW A THING OR TWO ABOUT REBELLIONS AGAINST FEDERAL INTERFERENCE."

The so-called Sagebrush Rebellion that erupted in the public lands states in the late 1970s was a reaction by users of public lands, as well as state and local governments, to inflexibility and insularity on the part of federal land managers, particularly in the Bureau of Land Management. It was a reaction to the growing volume of environmental legislation that, in total, seemed to overwhelm public land states and make it impossible for even prudent development to take place.

There were bills introduced in almost every western state legislature that asserted jurisdiction over all the public lands in the states, invoking the constitutional doctrine of "equal footing." The Rebellion was stoked by a perception that the system was out of balance and that the pendulum had swung too far in the direction of preservation and away from the tradition of multiple use. It was further fueled by the frustration of land users in the public and private sector who saw an opportunity and obligation to develop the energy-rich lands of the West to meet the energy needs of our country.[7]

The "equal footing" doctrine was based on the notion that each of the states came into the Union on the same legal basis as the thirteen original colonies. The colonies got to keep the federal lands in their states, so to the extent that the state of Utah didn't own its lands, we were on unequal footing.

This possibility of a lawsuit to determine ownership of the federal lands was suggested during my 1976 campaign. There were individuals in the Democratic party and in industry who thought it was a very hot political argument, and encouraged me to make it a major priority in my campaign. One of the attorneys for a local utility had initiated a detailed study by a major Utah law firm analyzing the constitutional and equal protection arguments under which Utah might proceed to claim the public domain.[8] I reviewed the material carefully, as did my eldest son, Scott, who was my campaign manager, and a few others. We reached the conclusion that while it was attractive in many respects, it was not an issue I wanted to make part of my campaign for governor. I had established my campaign themes by that time and decided there was no strong incentive for me to introduce a new, major policy initiative.

The legal analysis done by the local law firm was given to Utah Attorney General Robert Hansen in 1977. He presented it to the Western Attorney Generals' Litigation Action Committee. They also analyzed it and came to the conclusion that the "equal footing" doctrine would not prevail and made no recommendation to proceed with the concept. However, during the summer of 1978, Richard Dewsnup, one of the attorneys in the Attorney General's Office, began to get interested in the issue. Dewsnup and Dallin Jensen were the assistant attorneys general I dealt with on most natural resource issues. Dewsnup exchanged letters with Leo Krulitz, the solicitor for the Department of the Interior, regarding problems the state was having in gaining access across federal lands for the development of the school lands.[9]

The state of Nevada then assumed leadership in the Sagebrush Rebellion fight, adopting a bill in February 1979 declaring that Nevada owned the land within the public domain.[10] Dewsnup wrote a memorandum to Attorney General Hansen, evaluating the Nevada bill and alternative approaches to it.[11] While both Dewsnup and Jensen found the analysis of the "equal footing" argument unpersuasive, they both liked the objective of the argument and were looking for other legal ammunition they could utilize in asserting state rights.

By the summer of 1979, the Sagebrush Rebellion was in full bloom and would be an issue I would have to address. U.S. Senator Orrin

Hatch (R., Ut.) jumped aboard the bandwagon with his S. 168, the Western Lands Distribution and Regional Equalization Act. Hatch had not discussed the legislation with me, but I am sure that he was convinced that it was a good political horse to ride. Before anyone had completely analyzed the full impact of his legislation, he had several cosponsors, including influential Republican and Democratic senators, Paul Laxalt, Barry Goldwater, Jesse Helms, Dennis Deconcini and others. I was interested in the Nevada bill and the potential lawsuit. But I thought that Utah should keep its options open, so did not publicly support the Sagebrush Rebellion. I had an opportunity to support Hatch's bill on August 20, 1979 before the Senate Interior Appropriations Committee regarding public lands. However, I thought it was pointless to support the Hatch bill, and I had little confidence in the legal arguments of the Sagebrush Rebels. In any case, Senator Hatch's bill seemed doomed from the very beginning. There were not enough votes in the West to get such a bill passed. It was simply a matter of counting noses. By that time, I was interested in trying to find an alternative which would benefit the state of Utah by giving us some voice in the management of the federal lands in our state.

By the fall of 1979, a counterattack developed from those opposed to the transfer of title of the federal lands to the states. The timing of the Sagebrush Rebellion was so quick, and it had captured the imagination of so many, that it touched off a kneejerk reaction of support before anyone did adequate analysis. When the idea began to take root, environmental organizations came out strongly opposing the idea of wholesale transfers of land. Many of them were concerned that what we were really talking about was the transfer of public lands to private ownership. There was also a great deal of suspicion about the ability of the states to manage all of the lands in the public domain.

In addition, some of the special interest groups and even county commissioners who had been vocal opponents of the Bureau of Land Management suddenly decided that maybe they didn't want the state of Utah telling them how to use the lands either; maybe they would rather deal with a known than an unknown.

During 1979, there was an ebb and flow of views on the Sagebrush Rebellion. Of course, I knew it would be one of the bills which the 1980 legislature would consider. In fact, the bill (S.B. 5) was pre-filed by State Senator Ivan Matheson in the fall of 1979 and was essentially a copy of the Nevada legislation.

I remained skeptical. I knew that the legal, constitutional and political solutions proposed were not likely to succeed; but I was interested in taking advantage of the Sagebrush Rebellion effort to get the West "back in the driver's seat" in terms of federal land issues.

Even though there was some editorial opposition in local papers to the Sagebrush Rebellion, the public attitude in Utah seemed generally to support the idea. 1980 was an election year, and my political advisors were concerned that I would take a political drubbing if I opposed Senator Matheson's S.B. 5.

I decided we needed to amend the Utah bill to postpone its effective date until the Supreme Court of the United States sustained Nevada's position on the constitutional arguments. I was also concerned that we restrict the transfer to BLM lands and recognize the existing land use constraints developed by the federal government. So we asked that the legislature amend the bill placing those conditions in it. I indicated that if they were willing to make those amendments, I would sign the bill; otherwise, I would veto it. The amendments, conceived and drafted by Dewsnup, were inserted into the legislation. Thus, the legislation, the U.S. Land Reclamation Act of 1980, became primarily symbolic.

Because I was able to sign the bill with the amendments, it was never a prominent issue in my 1980 campaign for reelection. Some of the environmental groups were displeased that I had signed it, but it apparently didn't cost me their support.

President Reagan and the Sagebrush Rebellion

During the 1980 campaign, Ronald Reagan had proclaimed himself a Sagebrush Rebel, so when he was elected, I was interested in how he would handle the issue. I was also considering more legally viable options the state could take with respect to the Sagebrush Rebellion. Frank Gregg, former director of the BLM, had made a presentation at the University of Arizona in 1980 in which he pointed out that there were provisions in FLPMA and other federal legislation involving the management of public lands which allowed the states a major role in working with their counterparts at the federal level if the state and local governments were willing to get involved in joint planning efforts.[12] I was already moving in that direction. We had, by this time, signed cooperative agreements with all of the federal land managers and had developed a committee for review of wilderness proposals, so I felt we could achieve a lot of what we wanted to accomplish through administrative approaches.

Early in 1981, the support for the Sagebrush Rebellion seemed to be dwindling. Several senators backed away from Hatch's bill, and at Jackson Hole, Wyoming, during a meeting of the Western Governors' Conference, newly-installed Secretary of the Interior James Watt proclaimed, "We have won the Sagebrush Rebellion!" Of course, we hadn't won anything substantively in terms of the legal issues. What he meant was that there was a clearly-defined change in attitude in the Reagan

Administration, one that would cooperate with state and local governments in managing the public lands within their jurisdictions. Overall, I would say that the Sagebrush Rebellion experience did some good. It dramatically increased public involvement in the public land planning process at the state level. We had a significant turnaround in the way we dealt with federal land managers, and the attitudes of those land managers also changed. Toward the end of the Carter Administration and the Reagan Administration, we dealt with federal land managers who were sensitive to state interests. They were willing to sit down, cooperate and work closely with their state counterparts. In that sense, then, the Sagebrush Rebellion was helpful.

My Support for Jim Watt

Early in 1981, when James Watt had been nominated for Secretary of the Interior, I was asked if I would support him. My political advisors were deeply split. Watt had earned a reputation as being an antienvironmentalist when he was with the Rocky Mountain Legal Foundation. Yet, the state of Utah had some very positive experiences with him while he was in the Department of the Interior in earlier years. He had been in charge of the distribution of funds to improve state and local recreational facilities. On one particular issue involving the acquisition of Johnson Beach, which is now a major component of Bear Lake State Park, Watt cooperated fully. We would never have acquired the beach without his help.

There was also another important factor. Any governor who serves in a western state that has as much federal public land as Utah can ill afford to have a negative relationship with the Secretary of the Interior. I was interested in establishing and maintaining a close, cooperative partnership between federal and state land managers, and Watt was advocating the same thing. Among other things, I wanted to have input into the appointment of the new Bureau of Land Management director. We were in the process of developing a new proposal to deal with state lands, which we were calling Project BOLD, and I knew it would require the active support of the new Interior Secretary if it was going to be successful.

Watt championed many Utah causes before his nomination and while he was secretary. Even after he was asked to resign, I felt that in terms of his relationship with the state of Utah, he was one hundred percent positive. In all of the time he was Interior Secretary, he never crossed me on any issue. He made a major effort to see that the state received its in-lieu and indemnity selections, he supported Project BOLD, and he went to the White House on behalf of Utah's point of view on a number of issues. I do not regret having supported his nomination to Interior.[13]

I had my first meeting with him at a breakfast the day I testified for him on January 8. He was cordial and friendly. Our discussion covered the gamut of public land issues affecting Utah and his responses were reasonable and supportive.

During my involvement with Secretary Watt, I found that his word was always good. Nevertheless, I never felt good about Watt's stridency with the environmental groups and his unwillingness to consider their concerns. I also felt that he was overzealous in inflicting his personal views into Interior management decision making.

Project BOLD

I was invited by my brother Alan, who was dean of the Arizona State University Law School, to speak before their alumni, and I decided the forum would be a good place to launch the Project BOLD concept.[14] Dewsnup had prepared a detailed memorandum outlining a number of grievances the state had regarding the authoritarian manner in which our public lands were managed. They included our complaints about the in-lieu selections, the legal issues surrounding the beds of the Great Salt Lake and Utah Lake, coal leasing in the Alton coal fields, and other concerns. Dewsnup, the "father" of Project BOLD, saw it as a way to solve all of our problems, and his memorandum suggested a wide range of alternative solutions.

We circulated the memorandum to Secretary Watt and his aides, and I met with the secretary on February 10, 1981. I told him that my principal concern was the idea of blocking up the scattered state sections into consolidated holdings that would make some management sense. While I was in general agreement with the Dewsnup memorandum, I saw it as really just a starting point of negotiations. The career staff in Interior, however, worried about the implications of the proposal and its precedent-setting nature. They warned Watt's office and drafted a response for him saying that the Interior Department would have to give the proposal further study. However, Watt had already agreed with the general concept of blocking the lands in a telephone discussion we had had in early March.

The contents of the Dewsnup memorandum were then apparently leaked by Interior staff to members of the New York and Washington news media, and as part of a long article on Jim Watt appearing in the May 4, 1981 *New Yorker*'s "Reporter At Large," Elizabeth Drew took the proposal apart, making it appear that we were out to steal lands of great value from the federal government and turn over a bunch of worthless state lands in the exchange process. This was not what we had in mind at all. Rather, we were concerned that the regulations established for land exchanges in FLPMA were too cumbersome in their detailed analysis of value to make it possible for any large-scale swap of land as we proposed.

Frankly, I was surprised that Project BOLD stirred up as much controversy as it did. I didn't think anybody outside Utah and those immediately affected would be very interested at all. That was clearly a mistake, and we should have done a better public relations job with the critical editorial writers in Washington and New York before we officially advanced the proposal.

I have always shared all information with anyone who had decision-making responsibility and, therefore, I had no problems "floating" the Dewsnup memorandum, even though it contained specific concepts that I knew Interior would not agree with and about which I personally had doubts. So, our initial effort on Project BOLD was something of a fiasco. We created a lot of adverse publicity, and we learned that the issue commanded enough national attention that my initial perception of its public interest value was inaccurate. Many people viewed the Utah proposal as a possible precedent for other public land states.

Developing BOLD

While state officials recognized that the proposal represented a sweeping change from historical practice, there was little comprehension of the difficulties inherent in developing an acceptable legislative proposal which would meet the simple objectives of improving management and eliminating potential ownership conflicts.

It soon became apparent that the statewide exchange proposal would involve much more than identifying and evaluating parcels of land to be exchanged. Skeptics suggested that the approach was too novel, too bold, to ever be considered seriously by policy makers in Congress and that it was too great a departure from the traditional exchange and acquisition procedure to be accepted by land user groups. Initial discussions of the proposal generated criticism from users of state and federal lands who were concerned about possible disruption of their rights and privileges. Environmental groups were concerned that the proposal was simply a backdoor approach to another Sagebrush Rebellion.

Local elected officials in Utah criticized the proposal. They condemned state land management policies under jurisdiction of the State Land Board and argued that the state was a poor neighbor on its existing lands. The county commissioners sent me a clear signal that "Before you're going to get anywhere with Project BOLD, you've got to do something with the State Land Board."

The state determined that an acceptable legislative land exchange proposal could be developed only with the full cooperation of local governments, state and federal agencies, land users and conservation groups. In the spring of 1981, I named a project steering committee, chaired by Dewsnup, charging it with overall management responsibility for the effort. The Board of State Lands and Forestry, which is statutorily empowered to manage state lands (including leasing, sale, exchange and acquisition) retained a primary policy-making role. There was some initial grumbling that we had bypassed them, and we had to do some fence mending there. I named Ralph Becker, a young attorney, as full-time project coordinator of the steering committee. We were fortunate to have Becker, because in late 1981 Dick Dewsnup was stricken by a heart attack and died. He was one of the most knowledgeable natural resource attorneys that I had met, and a real public servant. His loss to me and the state of Utah was enormous. Project BOLD became his legacy.

The Project BOLD steering committee designed an evaluation and review process modeled loosely after the EIS requirements of NEPA. Monthly steering committee and Land Board meetings were open to the public, and we encouraged public discussion of the exchange concept. In the fall of 1981, a series of seven public "scoping" meetings were held to inform Utah citizens about the project, to identify primary concerns and to solicit suggestions for lands to be exchanged.

The first product was a series of draft issue papers, focusing on these key concerns identified through scoping: land management, minerals, land values, local government concerns and criteria for land selection and disposal. Those papers and materials describing more than thirty separate possible land "blocks" were published in *Project BOLD: Alternatives for Utah Land and Consolidation and Exchange* in September 1982.[15]

The document, the procedural equivalent of a draft EIS, was the subject of another round of public hearings and comments, as well as the focal point of numerous informal meetings with ranchers, the mining industry, local governments and environmental groups. The publication of a public review document convinced former skeptics that the state was serious about pursuing the proposal.

The process also increased the involvement of the Utah legislature. Following the review of the document and many meetings with key legislators, the 1983 general session of the legislature adopted two important measures supporting the statewide land exchange and consolidation proposal and amending the State Land Code to modernize the Board of State Lands and Forestry. The statutory changes for the State Land Board were in response to specific concerns raised in the early phases of Project BOLD; they were designed to provide assurances for land users and to give expanded management authority to the state. It required the board to manage state lands in accordance with multiple-use, sustained-yield principles, to develop comprehensive plans and policies for the management of existing land blocks and to assure protection for public land users in state-federal exchanges.[16] Finally, in 1984, I created a State Land Law Review Commission to review all state land statutes. A consolidated and recodified statute was later presented to the Utah legislature in 1985.

A preliminary draft of federal legislation for BOLD was prepared and distributed to interested parties in May 1983, and, in June, yet another public meeting was held by the Board of State Lands and Forestry. During the summer of 1983, the board considered and acted upon a set of detailed principles for federal legislation.

Following positive action by the Land Board, the Project BOLD staff worked with Utah's congressional delegation to finalize draft legislation. A number of drafts were prepared and circulated. Members of Congress, their staffs, user groups, public interest groups and the Interior Department were consulted as the legislative proposal was refined. In March 1984, S. 2471 was introduced by senators Jake Garn and Orrin Hatch and H. 5229 by Congressman James Hansen.

The state believed that the Project BOLD legislation represented a careful, competent effort by federal and state experts to balance land values based on the best available information and analysis. But introduction of the bill was not the end of the discussion and revision. Specifically, additional measures were added at the suggestion of the Interior Department to insure that both state and federal interests were protected. With the departure of Secretary Watt and appointment of Secretary William Clark, we had to convince a whole new set of actors. Sometimes the negotiations were painful, but I believe we ended up with a better product as a result of these compromises and discussions.

The Project BOLD Legislation

An essential element in the development of the exchange proposal, including the review document, dealt with the criteria by which land selections would be made. Specifically, the lands selected by the state were to enhance land management capabilities of both federal and state governments, eliminate state inholdings within federal reservations, avoid conflict with federally-protected lands (such as wilderness study areas), reflect consistency with local plans for use of public lands, increase the return to the school trust fund from state land revenues and maintain the integrity of current land uses. Obviously, each of those objectives could not be met in each specific parcel of land, but they were met in the general, statewide land consolidation plan.

For example, by trading its scattered Rich County BLM lands for state sections elsewhere, BLM could focus its management effort in a smaller area, increasing management effectiveness and efficiency. In two other instances, the state proposed to eliminate current state holdings within areas requiring special management for unique wildlife populations — for the desert tortoise in southern Utah and for buffalo in the Henry Mountains — in exchange for logical management units of equivalent resources outside the critical wildlife areas.

Several of the proposed state blocks provided opportunities for recreational development, wildlife management and grazing improvement. These types of investments are impractical for the current inventory of scattered sections. They are only possible when dealing with units of land of sufficient size to justify the required planning and development.

One of the principle motivations in seeking congressional action on a statewide exchange was the difficulty in concluding exchanges of state and federal lands under current exchange procedures. Therefore, an essential element of the proposal was the development of a more flexible, but still credible, basis for achieving fairness and equity in the exchange.

A state-federal task force classified the lands and resources in Utah into categories of high, medium and low resource potential for each major mineral resource. The task force agreed that the best way to insure equivalent value determinations was to divide the state into geographic provinces according to resource type, quality and market conditions. Lands proposed for exchange reflect approximately equivalent values for each resource within each of these provinces. For example, if the current inventory of state lands includes fifty-five thousand acres of medium quality coal in central Utah, the exchange proposal would leave the state with fifty-five thousand acres of medium quality coal in central Utah, though in a different configuration.

The legislation also addressed the protection of current uses, interests and agreements associated with both federal and state lands. Specific provisions address grazing use, mining claims and rights under the general mining laws of the United States, other mineral rights and leases, rights-of-way, special use agreements and water rights.

Finally, the legislation addresses one other important concern. As noted earlier, the lands involved in the exchange were granted to the state under the provisions of Utah's Enabling Act. The land grant provisions, as interpreted by the courts and by the Utah Attorney General's Office, require that the state receive fair market value for all school land uses. Local governments in Utah often receive free use of federal lands for public uses such as roads, water storage tanks, waste disposal sites and parks, and provide community land grants at a nominal cost. The state is unable to provide free public use of its lands and must require market value reimbursement to the School Trust Fund for such uses. The Project BOLD legislation amends the Enabling Act to clarify the intent of the original land grant, to permit the state to allow public purpose uses of state lands at less than fair market value.

The Future of Project BOLD

Project BOLD faces an uncertain future. The congressional delegation has indicated its willingness to reintroduce BOLD legislation. Secretary of the Interior Donald Hodell has indicated, both to me and to Governor Bangerter, that he supports Project BOLD and feels that it is an important initiative in the management of federal and state public lands.

There remains, however, strong opposition from some quarters, including Cal Black, a very vocal county commissioner from southern Utah who was appointed to the State Land Board and may influence the new administration. If that happens, I think the state will miss a major opportunity to initiate a process of public land exchanges which would rationalize the mosaic of federal-state ownership patterns in Utah.

After a lengthy review in 1985, and a private debate between Ralph Becker and Commissioner Black before Bangerter, the governor has indicated his support of BOLD. But his enthusiasm to push a major piece of federal legislation is lacking. With Utah's enormous education finance problem, BOLD offers hope for increased school revenues. Delay is inexcusable.

CHAPTER 11

Wilderness: Who is to Say

THERE is probably no more contentious public lands issue than the establishment of wilderness areas. In some ways this is ironic, because much of Utah and the West is de facto wilderness, where access is limited to backpackers or horseback riders. But *wilderness* has taken on the connotation of federal preemption, or locking out the states from legitimate land uses; the term has become a code word for those who oppose certain actions of the federal government that appear to infringe upon their "rights."

For me, wilderness represented an essential national policy. For others, wilderness was a threat to economic livelihood. The challenge was to find a way to inform the public about the value of wilderness and still protect essential state concerns; that required constant negotiations. At times it seemed we would take two steps back for every step forward.

The Wilderness Act

The 1964 National Wilderness Preservation System Act created, for the first time, a policy of Congress "to secure for the American people of present and future generations the benefits of an enduring resource of wilderness."

Wilderness is defined in the act as "an area of the earth untrammelled by man, where man is a visitor who does not remain." To qualify as wilderness, an area must have one or more of the following characteristics as spelled out in the act: "(1) Generally appears to have been affected primarily by the forces of nature, with the imprint of man's work substantially unnoticeable; (2) Has outstanding opportunities for solitude or primitive and unconfined type of recreation; (3) Has at least 5,000 acres of land or is of sufficient size to make practical its preservation and use of unimpaired condition; and (4) May also contain ecological, geological or other features of scientific, educational, scenic or historical value."[1]

The act required the Secretary of Agriculture (for the National Forest Service) and the Secretary of the Interior (for the Bureau of Land Management and the National Park Service) to inventory their lands and make recommendations to the President and to Congress with respect to recommendations for wilderness. While the designated lands would be managed in such a way as to protect their wilderness character, there were several specific exemptions to the strict provision. For example, private land inholdings were protected in terms of access and use; existing mineral and grazing rights were also protected. The ability of the state and the Forest Service to manage the watershed and reservoirs, transmission lines and "other facilities needed in the public interest" were protected and state water laws were to be enforced. And while the general use of motor vehicles was prohibited, an exemption was made for their use in emergencies involving the health and safety of persons within the area. Thus, there was no "lockup" of wilderness areas as opponents would claim during the wilderness debates.

While the issue of wilderness was not a major 1976 campaign issue between my opponent, Vernon Romney, and myself, it was very much on the minds of environmental groups. They pushed hard for me to take a strong, pro-wilderness posture in my campaign. I was unwilling to take a position on the specific areas or acreage but simply indicated that I was open to the concept of wilderness and believed it was an appropriate part of overall state land use. Most candidates were antiwilderness or refused to take any position.

Shortly after my election, I received a letter from Regional Forester Vern Hamre, of the U.S. Forest Service, notifying me of his agency's ongoing efforts to study and designate wilderness areas within Utah as part of their Roadless Area Review and Evaluation (RARE II) process.[2]

One of the early issues I faced in 1977 was a recommendation by the Department of Agriculture that the Lone Peak area in the Wasatch Mountains above Salt Lake City be designated a wilderness area. This was actually contrary to the recommendation made by the Forest Service which suggested designation as a scenic area. However, the Carter Administration was very keen to move the wilderness process forward.

Lone Peak, in isolation, was clearly wilderness. But its juxtaposition with a major metropolitan area made many people raise questions. How would we protect the state's watershed? If wilderness areas are designated as Class I under the Clean Air Act (i.e., virtually no air quality degradation allowed), how would that affect development in Salt Lake City?

At that time Utah was the only state in the nation that had no wilderness designations. I felt that it was important to find the management answers to the Lone Peak issue and go ahead with the wilderness designation. Working with Congressman Gunn McKay's office (D., Ut.), we were able to accomplish that objective. The Clean Air Act, as amended by Congress in 1977, did not require that all new wilderness areas be automatically designated as Class I; rather, they were to be designated as Class II, with the ability of either the state or the federal land manager to initiate a tougher standard.

The Lone Peak area piqued the enthusiasm of wilderness proponents. Various environmental organizations, including the Utah Wilderness Association, relentlessly pushed the state and federal land managers to make wilderness designations.

Even with the issue of the clean air amendment settled in 1977, there was a great fear that all of the areas designated as wilderness would eventually be redesignated Class I, as had occurred with wilderness areas designated before 1964. A local research company, under contract from business interests, prepared a map of the state showing all of the proposed and potential wilderness areas in the national forests, on public lands managed by the Bureau of Land Management and in the lands under the jurisdiction of the National Park Service. Drawing a circle around those geographical areas presented a picture of most of the state being precluded from development if all of these wilderness areas were designated Class I.

I believe it was this issue that led to a strong reaction among many county officials and business people against further designation of wilderness in Utah. They felt wilderness designation would endanger the state's ability to grow economically. It was an impression with which both the state and federal land managers would have to contend all through the wilderness review years.

Each of the federal land agencies had its own wilderness review process, and my state planning coordinator, Jed Kee, and others were concerned about the uncoordinated approach to the wilderness study. In a 1977 memorandum to me, he suggested the creation of a State Wilderness Committee, under the auspices of the State Environmental Coordinating Committee (a state NEPA-type organization created by executive order in 1974 by Rampton). Among the options suggested was the coordination of state input and the development of the state's own wilderness alternative. I opted for this course of action, and while the idea of creating an overall state wilderness plan became somewhat unmanageable, the principle that we should view wilderness proposals as a total package and not in isolation made a great deal of sense.

The state's first Wilderness Committee was composed primarily of representatives of the major state departments and divisions affected by wilderness proposals and was chaired by Paul Parker, of the State Planning Coordinator's Office. I later added five local county officials: Commissioner Calvin Black of San Juan County, Commissioner George Buzianis of Tooele County, Commissioner Albert Neff of Daggett County, Mayor William Levitt of Alta, and Mayor Roy Young of Milford. I also added a representative from each of the members of the congressional delegation, recognizing that any wilderness proposal must eventually be adopted by Congress.

In addition to Lone Peak considerations, the Wilderness Committee made detailed recommendations concerning the National Park Service Wilderness recommendations, which were being finalized in 1977. I was concerned that the Park Service's management plans for each of the individual parks was not coordinated with the wilderness proposals of the Forest Service and the Bureau of Land Management. Thus, my tendency was to react very cautiously towards wilderness designations until we had the whole picture.

Out of a total of 2.3 million acres of national parks and monument areas in the state of Utah, the Parks Service Draft Environmental Impact Statements (DEISs) were proposing 1.3 million acres, or approximately fifty-nine percent, designated as wilderness. The Wilderness Committee's analysis of the Park Service proposals, in a February 14, 1978 memorandum, noted that formal wilderness designation would "have minimal impact on local economics or resource development opportunities because current park service management will change little through wilderness designation. The majority of park lands are presently being managed as wilderness."

"Although most local residents are aware of this," the memo concluded, "they are still apprehensive if not totally opposed to wilderness designations. They fear greater restrictions as a result of such designations. Besides a general misunderstanding as to what wilderness is or is not, there exists a certain amount of distrust for federal agencies."

While I was willing to agree to some of the Park Service recommendations, I continued to be concerned about the lack of coordination between their recommendations, the ongoing RARE II study of the Forest Service and the expected Bureau of Land Management Wilderness reviews.

Adoption of a State Wilderness Policy

The state of Utah had not yet adopted a specific policy statement to guide its actions in wilderness determinations. Therefore, one of the first actions of the Wilderness Committee was to adopt such a policy statement. Given the amount of anti-wilderness feeling, it was significant that the statement was adopted unanimously. The statement, approved on January 27, 1978 by the Wilderness Committee and later officially endorsed by my sub-cabinet on Economic and Physical Development and by me, declared it to be the "policy of the state of Utah to secure the benefits of an enduring wilderness resource for present and future generations."

The policy statement defined wilderness values in very much the same terms as the 1964 Wilderness Act had, but noted that "the need to preserve and protect our wilderness resources must be balanced with the need and value of public lands for present and future resource development."

One of the most important concerns of state and local officials was how wilderness areas would be managed. The policy statement concluded with the following comments:

> Because the management of federal wilderness areas affect both state and private lands, the state of Utah, and affected local units of government, should participate in the development of management plans for all designated wilderness areas within Utah.[3]

While the policy statement was adopted unanimously, the ability of the Wilderness Committee to function effectively was constantly tested as individual wilderness proposals were drafted by federal land agencies and submitted to the state for review.

In an April 1978 briefing on wilderness issues, Paul Parker presented an updated overview of the status of each of the land management agencies. The Forest Service in RARE II had studied 130 roadless areas — almost three million acres — in Utah. Disregarding an "all or nothing" alternative, their proposals for wilderness ranged from a low of 125,000 acres, or four percent of the roadless inventory, to a high of 687,699 acres, or twenty-three percent of that inventory. A DEIS was scheduled for release in June 1978, with public comment due in October. The Bureau of Land Management was still circulating wilderness review procedures for public comment. We felt that the state would have the most impact in the BLM procedures; Park Service recommendations were basically complete and already before the President and Congress. Parker noted that most of rural Utah opposed wilderness designations in contrast to national public attitudes and members of Congress, who were more preservation-minded. He argued that the state position would lose all credibility in Congress and on the national scene if we continued to unjustifiably oppose a majority of wilderness proposals.

Responding to RARE II

In addition to attempting to formulate an overall state wilderness strategy, the Wilderness Committee's immediate responsibility was to attempt to develop a state response to the RARE II DEIS being developed by the Forest Service. The DEIS was attacked on all sides: by industry, by environmental organizations and by elected officials.

In an August 8, 1978 letter to Rupert Cutler, assistant secretary for the Department of Agriculture, I sought to extend the comment period to give the state adequate time to consider the overall ramifications of wilderness designations in the state, and I suggested that a supplemental study was required to analyze issues not effectively dealt with in the

DEIS. Our congressional delegation supported the deadline delay. They particularly desired to have the state response come out after the 1978 elections. Their concern over wilderness was reflected in a letter of August 24, 1978 to me from Utah Representative Gunn McKay, in which he concluded that "I understand the Utah Association of Counties is going to take a position of opposing further wilderness areas in the state . . . it represents, to my mind, a good starting point for wilderness discussion." McKay was facing a difficult congressional race (one he would lose to House Speaker Jim Hansen). The public attitude in Utah was generally anti-wilderness and regardless of his sympathies, he didn't want to make it a political issue. It was not a courageous stand but an understandable one.

From July through September, the State Wilderness Committee met to determine a possible state response to the RARE II DEIS. Their recommendations called for the designation of thirteen areas as wilderness representing approximately 684,000 acres, and four areas for further study representing 123,400 acres.[4] While this was far less than the acreage desired by various conservation and wilderness groups, it was a substantial figure. However, the five local officials represented on the Wilderness Committee voted against the proposed recommendations and immediately swarmed to my office to protest. They were downright livid and indicated that the counties might accept somewhere around 300,000 acres of wilderness but no more. They were also infuriated by the committee structure because locally-elected officials were outnumbered by staff who represented state departments. They were right about the committee structure; I had stacked the membership. In the meantime, I was getting letters from Utah sheepmen's and cattlemen's organizations and agricultural interests opposing any wilderness designation at all.[5]

In October, the Governor's Advisory Council on Community Affairs (GACCA—composed of mayors and county commissioners) recommended wilderness totaling about 440,000 acres.[6] During early October, I met with key staff members to decide how the state was going to respond to the RARE II DEIS. Initially, a letter was prepared for my signature which recommended the State Wilderness Committee position with some reductions. I was concerned, however, that we were facing a deeply divided political situation, with the county officials extremely negative towards any sizable wilderness recommendation and antagonistic towards the process as well.

Accordingly, in a letter dated October 13, 1978 to Regional Forester Vern Hamre, I concluded that a decision by the state of Utah on the extent of Forest Service land suitable for wilderness "must wait upon the completion of the Comprehensive Wilderness Plan that is presently being completed by the state, and which must necessarily consider the wilderness proposals advanced by the National Park Service that are virtually complete and those by the Bureau of Land Management which are just beginning." I did submit, to the Forest Service, the analysis by the State Wilderness Committee, along with their recommendations and the recommendations of the Utah Association of Counties, as input into the decision-making process, but not as an official state position.

In addition to the political ramifications, I was concerned about an announcement that the Park Service had made a week earlier which asked for the reclassification of six national monuments in primitive areas of Utah from Class II to Class I air standards under the provision of the Clean Air Act. In effect, we were seeing the realization of the fears of those who opposed further wilderness designations.

I received some personal criticism from individuals who thought the state should take a position. The *Salt Lake Tribune* editorialized, on October 16, "better piecemeal wilderness input than none at all." But I knew we needed greater consensus if we were to get any proposal through Congress.

In late 1978, in order to get a fresh review as well as to remove the structural inequities of the committee's makeup, I dissolved the first Wilderness Committee and established a new one composed of five state department heads and five representatives of local counties and cities. Those representatives were appointed by the Governor's Advisory Council on Community Affairs to make local officials feel they had a vested interest in the decisions made by that group. I made it clear to the elected officials that they were free to take positions different from those of state department heads, but that I hoped they would work together, hold joint meetings and, if possible, come up with a recommendation for the state concerning Forest Service lands that we could submit to the Department of Agriculture and our congressional delegation.

During 1979, I began intensive coordination with our congressional delegation, particularly with Senator Jake Garn (R., Ut.), the senior member. Garn was well-briefed on congressional wilderness politics and I was equally cognizant of state and local attitudes. Our joint efforts were invaluable in the ultimate success of the wilderness legislation. In a letter of March 8, 1979, Garn indicated to Vern Hamre that his intent was to develop legislation on his own in connection with me and other members of the congressional delegation.[7] While it would draw heavily on the Forest Service recommendations under RARE II, it would attempt to anticipate some of the findings of the Bureau of Land Management and the total wilderness picture in the state. Garn's efforts throughout the deliberations on wilderness were important in keeping the congressional delegation together.

On March 9, 1979, the new State Wilderness Committee recommended an official state position on RARE II.[8] They had taken testimony from local elected officials, associations of governments, resource development corporations, environmental and conservation groups, individual citizens and staff from various federal and state agencies. They were able to reach a unified position, but they noted that half the state members and possibly more could have supported additional wilderness, and that a majority of the local officials would have advocated less wilderness than the consensus position. Nevertheless, the consensus position adopted March 9, 1979 represented a total of 592,273 acres of proposed wilderness and areas designated for further planning. This contrasted with a recommendation of 907,288 by the Forest Service in their final EIS.[9]

The new committee was successful in making local officials feel that they were on equal footing with top-level department heads. In addition, the old committee had to start out with 130 areas under review by the Forest Service to make their final cut. The new committee started out with fewer than twenty, and had time for more specific and more detailed negotiations between the environmental organizations and the county officials concerned.

The major difference in the wilderness recommendations had to do with the High Uintas, Utah's most spectacular range of mountains and the only major national mountain range which runs east to west. Much of the Uinta Range, which was already designated a primitive area, was de facto wilderness. Yet, the acreage designated for wilderness became sort of a psychological threshold for both proponents and opponents of wilderness. A number of different acreage figures were suggested.[10] The existing Forest Service primitive area of 267,000 acres was the acreage supported by Summit County officials and a few others. In 1967, the Forest Service had proposed a 323,000-acre wilderness area for the Uintas, and this was the official position in 1979 of the Uinta Basin Association of Governments. The State Wilderness Committee had proposed 408,000 acres which, informally, the Uinta Basin Association of Governments had agreed to accept. It was also a boundary proposal that both the timber and energy industries could live with.

The Forest Service, under RARE II, had proposed 511,000 acres, which was higher than an initial planning figure of 469,000 acres. Finally, environmental groups proposed 655,000 acres of Uinta Wilderness, which may have been a strategic position on their part, and they probably would have accepted the Forest Service proposal of 511,000 acres.

From my standpoint, the two important proposals were the 408,000-acre figure developed by the state and local wilderness committees and that of 511,000 acres proposed by the Forest Service. Neither boundary would affect the completion of the Central Utah Project or any other related water development. Neither boundary represented a conflict with oil and gas or minerals. Grazing conflicts were not significant. Timber interests were affected marginally more with the higher figure, although the affected timber resource was of low quality.

I was perfectly willing to support the higher number for the Uintas but felt that it was important not to break up the state and local coalition. There would also be further negotiations during the legislative process. On March 13, I officially submitted the state and local Wilderness Committee recommendations, as a state position, to Agriculture Secretary Robert Bergland.

The one addition that I made to the Wilderness Committee recommendations was the Pine Valley Mountain area near Cedar City. I included 50,000 acres for further planning purposes, a decision that met with anguished cries from locally-elected officials who felt that they had a previous commitment from me to take the Pine Valley Mountains out of the wilderness study area. I was convinced, however, that an analysis of the Pine Valley area demanded, at the very least, further study. As the legislation eventually went through Congress, we were able to negotiate a satisfactory solution with the Washington County Commission. But at the time, its chairman, Murray Webb, stated that he thought it was a "sad state of affairs when elected officials, regardless of how high their station, failed to respond to the voice of the people."[11] But I had heard other voices from the area.

Walking A Tightrope

The wilderness debate, from March 1979 until final legislation was adopted by Congress in 1984, amounted to a tightrope walk in an effort to keep the principal elected officials in the counties reasonably content over the state's position, to persuade the environmental groups that while the Utah proposal was not all that they wanted, it was at least a good first step, and to get the congressional delegation to draft and push the legislation.

The wilderness issue was a very emotional experience for county commissioners. It was necessary for us to go through the process of examining the characteristics of wilderness and to make clear what one could and could not do in wilderness areas. Once local officials understood these facts, it was possible to decide which lands went into wilderness, and we could begin to look at specific boundaries. I felt it was important not to preempt local decision-making, but at the same time

I knew we had to put a credible wilderness proposal before Congress if we were to avoid having the issue taken out of our hands.

There was a lot of gut reaction against wilderness, with some county commissioners saying, "I don't want to talk about that. This is our land, and we are going to use it for any purpose we wish or for any purpose we can get away with, whatever it is." Of course, it was not their land. It was the public's land, and this attitude sorely tested my commitment to deal with locally-elected officials in solving public problems affecting their areas. They were tough, touchy negotiations, but in the end we were able to find ways to accommodate most of the commissioners' concerns and get them to support the acreage figures cited in the legislation.

I argued to the Utah Wilderness Association that they could make a case for greater wilderness acreage; however, without their cooperation, a wilderness bill would certainly fail in Congress.

It was difficult to get the congressional delegation to push a Forest Service RARE II bill. They were aware of the lack of consensus in Utah on the issue, as well as the congressional paralysis regarding wilderness. However, in an October 22, 1982 decision, the U.S. Ninth Circuit Court of Appeals, *California v. Block* (690 F.2d 753), indicated that the RARE II EISs were deficient under the National Environmental Policy Act. The Reagan Administration announced, in February 1983, that it planned to conduct a third roadless area review and evaluation, a RARE III study.[12]

The spectre of a new RARE III process was more than any of us could stand. Suddenly there was an incentive to introduce legislation, get a consensus and declare that for purposes of the Utah Wilderness Act, the RARE II EIS was sufficient under the NEPA legislation.

In the summer of 1983, the Utah congressional delegation and I held four public meetings and countless smaller meetings around the state to test the waters for a wilderness bill. The Utah Wilderness Association, and other conservation groups, got out the troops to support wilderness, and legislation was finally adopted in late 1984.[13] In total, more than 700,000 acres of wilderness were included in the 1984 Utah Wilderness Act. It includes some of the most scenic and rugged areas in the state and sets a good precedent for dealing with the wilderness proposals of the National Park Service and the Bureau of Land Management.

With the 706,000 acres in the Utah Wilderness Act of 1984, the 30,000-acre Lone Peak Wilderness area and the 22,500-acre BLM Wilderness along the Arizona strip, Utah has approximately 760,000 acres of formal wilderness. The National Park Service has recommended another 1.3 million acres of Utah Wilderness, and the Bureau of Land

Management is currently studying an additional 3.2 million acres for possible inclusion.

In developing our wilderness legislation, we succeeded in providing for an exchange of state land inholdings out of the designated areas, protecting grazing privileges, recognizing state water resource management programs and calling for state and local government involvement in development of site-specific management plans for wilderness.

Certainly, the Utah legislation represented a compromise. It didn't please everyone. Yet, I think the long period of negotiations, the state-local Wilderness Committee process and the 1983 congressional hearings produced a bill that virtually everyone could accept. It was a unique intergovernmental success, involving federal, state and local deliberation and needing substantial input from affected citizens and interest groups. I was personally pleased to see the legislation adopted during my last year in office.

Conclusion

Managing the public domain, both state and federal lands, takes a coordinated, cooperative effort among federal land managers, state officials and local government, particularly in terms of major initiatives such as Project BOLD and wilderness. It also requires action by the federal administration and by Congress. The issues are always complex, and the interests of the affected parties are very difficult to sort out. Utah has no statewide land use planning program and, therefore, must rely upon ad hoc solutions to land management problems. We have probably been more successful than we deserved.

It is clear that an overall effort to develop a statewide master plan for the utilization of our land would make the ad hoc solution unnecessary and provide an overview for a more consistent approach to public lands management. Unfortunately, land use planning still bears a stigma that dictates, to a degree, how public officials must proceed. This is particularly true in Utah and, to a lesser extent, throughout the West. In fact, we have probably accomplished more by ad hoc arrangements than we could have by the watered-down version of the state land use planning law that was adopted by the legislature in 1974 and later repealed by the people in a public referendum.

As a state, we must recognize that land use planning becomes an important part of the way in which the state controls its destiny and its development. Whether we default that control to the federal land managers, exercise control in an ad hoc fashion or attempt to do it in a coordinated fashion is really our own decision.

CHAPTER 12

Water: Federal Preemption or Partnership

THE winter of 1976-77 saw Utah and many other western states grappling with the worst drought since the days of the Great Depression. Water resource managers, farmers and elected public officials had been directly involved in an increasing struggle for more than two years, and their attitudes had changed from worry to grave concern.

Democratic governors from Montana, Wyoming, Idaho, Colorado, New Mexico and Utah, the western states hardest hit by the drought, had scheduled a meeting for February 21, 1977 at the Denver home of Governor Richard Lamm (D., Colo.) to discuss the crisis with newly appointed Interior Secretary Cecil Andrus. We hoped that as a former governor of Idaho and former chairman of the National Governors' Association, Andrus would be sympathetic and helpful.

When I arrived at Stapleton International Airport, I was met by reporters who wanted my reaction to President Carter's announcement that he was eliminating funds in his 1977-78 fiscal year budget for a number of major water projects in the United States, including the Central Utah Project (CUP). Rumors about the President's plans had circulated in January and early February, but the governors were not warned in advance that the administration had singled out specific Bureau of Reclamation projects for elimination. I was shocked and could say little to the press other than I simply did not believe the President had all the necessary facts before making his decision.

As we reached Lamm's residence, we were more concerned about the President's water project "hit list" than with the drought. In our states, water project funding spelled the difference between healthy economic growth and crippling stagnation. The President had blindsided the West and its governors, and we vented our frustrations on Secretary Andrus.

Andrus had been stunned himself to learn of the President's water project hit list, and by the time he arrived at Lamm's residence, he was defensive. He had come to discuss the drought, but the hit list announcement had changed the agenda. I am sure it was not pleasant for the new Interior secretary, a former western governor well-acquainted with western water needs, to face intense crossfire from his former colleagues. We all had long-standing respect and feelings of friendship for him, but we were angry, and we spent most of the meeting hammering the Carter

Administration for what we felt was an insensitive, ill-informed decision made without our knowledge and participation. Andrus had not been forewarned or included in the decision. During the transition period after the 1976 election, President-elect Carter had decided to use a small circle of trusted people in his top-level decision-making processes rather than relying on the more traditional cabinet approach. Andrus was not in the circle. I'm sure this irritated him, but to his credit he tried to play a mediating role between the governors and the President. However, he never succeeded in having a major influence with Carter on water policy.

The Carter announcement and the governors' subsequent reaction to it triggered a lengthy and painful reevaluation of the nation's water policies. It elevated those policies to the forefront of national political debate in the states and in Congress. Unfortunately, the issue is still unresolved.

The debate provided a forum for my involvement in national political issues which allowed me to work with many other governors and with a variety of federal officials. I feel these factors led, in part, to my eventual selection as chairman of the National Governors' Association (NGA). It also sharply focused the extreme difficulty of developing a national water policy to serve states with widely divergent approaches to water management.

The meeting in Denver also served to illustrate, once again, that many issues can't be contained within state boundaries, and that governors working in regional groups often have more success in getting the attention of the federal government.

Defending the Central Utah Project

In his February 21 press release, the President reminded the nation that two of his campaign promises were for "prudent and responsible use of taxpayers' money and protection of the environment." He admitted that water projects had played a critical historic role in developing the national economy, but he now felt that a changing economic picture and new environmental policies had rendered many of them unnecessary.

There were nineteen projects on the hit list, and the total reduction in the budget the first year would amount to $289 million; the potential savings was $5.1 billion. The President assigned Interior Secretary Andrus and Secretary of the Army Alexander to work with the Office of Management and Budget (OMB) and the Council on Environmental Quality (CEQ) to evaluate the nineteen projects — and all other water resource projects — as well as to develop comprehensive national policy reforms based on those evaluations. Four criteria were used to determine which projects the President would recommend dropping:[1]

1. A CEQ determination that the project has a major adverse environmental impact;

2. An OMB determination that remaining costs exceed benefits when calculated at current interest rates;

3. A low proportion of sunk costs (i.e., money already spent which would be lost if the project was abandoned) relative to total projects costs; and

4. Potential safety hazards.

While the President had indicated in his release that he was simply asking for a project review, his deleting funds in his budget for the nineteen listed projects had clearly thrown down the gauntlet. As might be expected, that action touched off a storm of protest, not only from the governors, but from western senators and congressmen, public utility companies and other water interests. Environmental leaders, however, applauded the decision, heralding it as a positive action "aimed at wasteful, unnecessary spending on the projects that would destroy valuable natural resources for the benefit of a few special interests."[2]

At the February 21 meeting, Secretary Andrus promised to conduct public hearings on the nineteen hit-list projects. This would allow each state to present its case. From a state perspective, the secretary played a very positive role. He realized that President Carter had whacked a hornets' nest, and he knew just how angry we all were. I personally believe that despite his sense of loyalty and responsibility to Carter, he believed the President had made a significant mistake.

I was not an expert in Central Utah Project history, so directly after the Denver meeting I immersed myself in a series of meetings with the key figures involved in the project. Together, we planned our strategy for defending the project.

As we prepared the case we would present to Congress and the Interior Department, my frustration over the President's decision mounted. My feelings were reflected in remarks I made on March 11 before the Monticello Chamber of Commerce. I noted that Congress, in adopting the Colorado River Storage Act some twenty years before, had laid the foundations for the Central Utah Water Conservancy District. The project was designed to serve Utah's growing population centers and agricultural interests, insuring an adequate water supply to the year 2020. We had faced court tests and compromises, and we had met all the criteria set by Congress and the Bureau of Reclamation, but now we faced the toughest test of all: a potential death sentence for the CUP which would shrivel the dreams and goals of our lifetimes.

In my Monticello remarks, I noted that President Carter's hit list had brought the CUP to a screeching halt. In just two weeks, we would have two hours to rejustify the work of a generation. I said: "I suspect our major confrontation will be over environmental issues. We're lining up the best, most able spokesmen to present our case. The situation is critical. We have planned no alternative method of delivering water. All our eggs are in the Central Utah Project basket." I was convinced that Carter had made an ill-informed decision and was confident that we could reverse it in Congress.

Andrus set our hearing for March 25, 1977. It was conducted in the Interior Department auditorium in Washington, D.C. I had also arranged with the secretary to conduct an information meeting on March 23 in Salt Lake City. That meeting allowed us to present more in-depth testimony than we could at the March 25 hearing and provided an opportunity for the Utah public to get more information on the critical nature of the CUP.

CUP Environmental Issues

In addition to describing the project's benefits, we challenged the grounds — most of them environmental — on which the President had decided to scuttle it. Although the Bonneville Unit of the CUP was started in 1967, it was an ongoing project and therefore subject to the requirements of the National Environmental Policy Act (NEPA) of 1969. The part of the unit already funded and under construction was in compliance with NEPA. The Sierra Club and other environmental groups and individuals had challenged the adequacy of the Environmental Impact Statement (EIS), but the Tenth Circuit Court of Appeals ruled that the EIS was in full compliance with NEPA, and that the Secretary of the Interior had, in good faith, properly considered the environmental consequences in making his decision to go ahead with the project.[3]

From the beginning, Congress knew of the environmental consequences of the project. All of the President's concerns were discussed in the EIS.[4] For example, the final EIS states that the "Bonneville Unit separately would have only a minor effect on the salinity increase" in the Colorado River (EIS, p. 658). With respect to trout fishing, the EIS stated that the "Bonneville Unit would not be expected to significantly . . . deteriorate . . . existing populations of either game fish species or non-game fish species in either the Upper Bonneville Basin or in the Sevier River" (EIS, p. 349). Furthermore, it noted that the Bonneville Unit would produce 20,000 surface acres of reservoir area that did not exist before, providing habitat for an estimated 3.6 million fish each year (EIS, p. 484).

The Bonneville Unit would also assure minimum flow in some streams that historically dried up during the late summer months or in periods of drought. Fish in those streams would no longer die for lack of water. Our answer to the allegation that the project would limit or destroy wildlife habitat areas was that the unit plan called for the establishment of three new wildlife management areas by the Utah Division of Wildlife Resources.

The project, of course, had some adverse environmental impacts, but we knew what they were, and mitigation measures were included in the plan (EIS, p. 442-68). Furthermore, the EIS determined that doing nothing (a "no action" alternative) would probably lead to haphazard land development around Strawberry Reservoir and erosion problems in the Diamond Fork area (EIS, p. 488-627). It was simply not logical to conclude, on the basis of the environmental studies, that we should dump the project.

Neither could the administration claim that the project's cost-benefit ratio did not meet federal requirements. The legal foundation for those requirements is essentially a single phrase from the Flood Control Act of 1936 which authorized projects "if the benefits to come to whomever they may accrue are in excess of the estimated costs . . . " Since 1936, a number of changes in the rules of the game have occurred but, essentially, the original cost-benefit philosophy remained. In the case of CUP, we were always able to prove that its benefits exceed its costs.

Our defense was well organized for the Salt Lake City hearing on March 23. We had full support from our congressional delegation, and Representative Gunn McKay (D., Ut.) was the first witness. Our case was presented at the official Washington hearings two days later, and I testified before the Senate Appropriations Subcommittee on Public Works on April 4. To the crucial nuts and bolts technical information needed to make a strong case, I added a pointed, philosophical note:

> A whole new generation now exists which has come to rely on the availability of water as an automatic provision in their lifestyles. It is not automatic. It is limited. It is linked to the foresight of men and women who were able to conceive of developments like the Central Utah Project and were able to win the battles and create the atmosphere for the completion of the project. We are a water-poor state, on the verge of massive development and population growth. We are at a juncture which will require our people to be wise with water, to conserve, to alter their way of life in a way that will allow them to survive and compete with the limited amount we have.

I knew that Utah, by interstate agreement (Colorado River Compact), had an entitlement of approximately 1.4 million acre-feet of Colorado River water, and that the CUP was designed to help us use it. We had negotiated contracts in good faith with the federal government, and we were confident that the federal government would not renege on its agreements. I urged Congress to restore funding for the Central Utah Project, and through a well-organized, cooperative effort with the congressional delegation, we finally won.

The President, in reality, did us a favor. He forced a public debate on the CUP and we educated a whole new generation of Utahns. We ended up more unified and much more effective in ensuing budget hearings. In subsequent years the President actually supported increased funding for the project.

Some Historical Perspectives on Western Water Policy[5]

The early riparian doctrine of water rights was primarily governed by Old English common law. It allows anyone along a stream of water the right to use that water and then return it to the stream. So, if you are along the bank, you are entitled to use the water. That works well enough in areas like the East where water is plentiful.

Western water policy, however, reflects the harsh realities of our arid region. Water rights are precious, and western history is sprinkled with tales of water feuds, water crime, water politics and a plethora of both humorous and sobering water lore. The old-timers claim that, in the second-driest state, our values are water, gold and women, in that order.

Water rights are acquired only by beneficial use of water, and the determining principle is, basically, "use it or lose it." Under the western appropriation doctrine, the first person on a stream or river to make beneficial use of water has first right to use it. Even if a second user enters upstream from the first, the original user still has first priority. This doctrine enables the state, through definition of "beneficial use," to prevent waste and mismanagement of its water and vests the state with broad control over its water. Congress passed the 1902 Reclamation Act to encourage development in the West. As with earlier acts, western congressmen secured provisions that gave the states broad control over water resources. Section 8 of the act provides:

> . . . nothing in this Act shall be construed as affecting or intended to affect or to any way interfere with the laws of any state or territory relating to the control, appropriation, use, or distribution of water used in irrigation, or any vested right acquired thereunder, and the Secretary of the Interior, in carrying out the provisions of this Act, shall proceed in conformity with such laws . . .

Thus, the act established a true partnership between nation and states; the federal government would build and operate reclamation projects, and the states would control the acquisition, distribution and use of water. In implementing that policy the Department of the Interior and most presidents really did not have much of a role. The real player historically has been the Congress.

The Reclamation Act was one of the most significant public policies ever adopted and, in my opinion, we owe the economic viability of the West to it. Western agriculture, mining, energy development and population growth are dependent on states' abilities to secure and make use of their water supplies.

The current problem is that, though we have built most of the best and least costly of the nation's water projects and have reaped their benefits for years, the West continues to grow, and we need more water projects to support that growth. Today's projects are more difficult and more expensive to build, and the rate of return on them is not as great.

In 1977 the President and a number of eastern congressmen began to argue that the old Reclamation Act projects were no longer justifiable—that they were boondoggles and that the East was not getting its share of water money. Those changing attitudes were what triggered the national water policy debate. In Utah, we were successful in convincing Congress that our cause with respect to the CUP was just. But each year the funding question was open to debate, and each year I would go back to Congress to testify and reargue the issues. It was time-consuming and very frustrating.

Nevertheless, President Carter was right in initiating the debate. Most members of Congress were becoming increasingly skeptical of the old pork barrel politics of water financing and good projects like the CUP were debated with the bad.

With the current federal budget dilemma and with changing attitudes we have probably seen the end of new large-scale water project financing at the federal level. In 1985, however, the House did adopt a Water Resources Bill that provides for both reform and new funding authorizations. The Senate passed a different bill and the two bills are in a conference committee.

A National Water Policy

Congress received a major environmental message from President Carter on May 21, 1977. He requested that the Secretary of the Interior develop a national water policy. Some feel the decision was made to counter the broad, adverse reaction Carter had received when he announced his water project hit list. Personally, I do not agree with that analysis. As a governor, Carter was well known for his environmental philosophies, and after he was elected president, it was easy to predict that he would design an agenda that included water policy reform.

Secretary Andrus knew the President was in trouble on his water policy and suggested that he meet with western governors to discuss the issues. A meeting was scheduled for October 22 in Denver; western governors attending were Dick Lamm (D., Colo.), Ed Herschler (D., Wyo.), Tom Judge (D., Mont.), John Evans (D., Ida.), Dick Kneip (D., S.D.), Mike O'Callahan (D., Nev.), Jerry Apodaca (D., N.M.) and myself. By that time, the President was aware of the hostile attitude that existed among western governors, congressional delegations and water managers, and he knew he was politically at risk.

It was apparent, at the meeting, that the President was not willing to abandon a national water study, but he was certainly willing to see what he could do to repair his relationship with western governors. He agreed to delay his recommendations to Congress and promised that any national water policy would recognize the preeminence of traditional state water jurisdictions. Nevertheless, the hit list and the manner in which he launched the national water policy debate hurt him badly in the West when he ran for reelection in 1980. He never recovered politically. I think he simply wrote off the West in the 1980 election.

The NGA Subcommittee on Water Management

Just prior to his nomination as Interior secretary, Andrus was NGA chairman, and he urged me to get involved with the NGA's Natural Resources and Environmental Management Committee. I had also met with a number of NGA staffers, such as Dave Johnson, director of the Natural Resources Committee, who told me some controversial water issues were coming up. He said there was no subcommittee on water management, and that there was considerable interest in creating one.

The subcommittee was not formally created until the NGA's annual winter meeting in February 1978, but by the time we got to Washington, D.C. for the meeting, its structure was set, and it was decided that I would be its chairman. I was excited about the prospect of chairing the subcommittee and having an opportunity to directly affect national policy.

I had a strong background in water issues. Rampton had appointed me to the Utah Water Pollution Committee in the 1960s, and I had become acquainted with water quality problems and the relationship of the state and the federal governments under the Water Pollution Control Act. I was involved with the 1972 amendments to that act, with disbursement of wastewater facility construction grant money and the decision concerning the state's taking primacy in managing water pollution control programs.

I had also done some private legal work in water matters and, as general solicitor for Union Pacific Railroad, I had extensive experience in the area of water rights protection. By the time I became chairman of the NGA water subcommittee, I was well acquainted with Utah's water appropriation system and had gained both public and private experience in the field.

I knew the future of energy development in Utah depended largely upon having adequate water, and I commented on that fact in one of my campaign position papers. I had spent a great deal of time during the 1976 campaign looking at the public policy questions associated with development, public use and protection of water, and I placed those goals high on my list of gubernatorial responsibilities.

Water was a major agenda item in early September 1977, at the Anchorage, Alaska Western Governors' Conference meeting during which we formally organized the Western Governors' Policy Office (WESTPO). All of the WESTPO governors strongly supported my decision to develop, independently of the President, a set of principles which could guide us in our federal negotiations. We would continue to discuss the issue with the President and his team, making certain that we had input on the process. At the same time, we decided to develop a parallel structure, getting the governors on record first as to what national water policy should be.

Several factors demanded that course of action. I was tremendously concerned about the nature of the President's national water policy process. As I reviewed it, I became convinced that he wanted a federal program rather than a true federal-state partnership. I sensed that Carter wanted to limit the states to an advisory role, with the decision-making process becoming the responsibility of the federal government. Since the federal government was moving away from financing water projects, the state role was obviously critical. Therefore, if we were to be effective partners, we needed a strong political base from which to operate. And the only way to build it was to formulate independent national water policy goals and to commit ourselves to them as an ongoing basis for discussion, with or without the administration's support. This approach was adopted after a very short discussion and triggered a tremendous cooperative effort among the states.

By February 1978, we had developed a set of principles to guide the governors in articulating a national water policy. We briefed Secretary Andrus on February 3. It became clear to the administration that the governors had their act together, and that we were exerting a major influence on the national water policy process. During the briefing, Andrus stressed that there was not a predetermined Carter water policy, and that he was not proposing a "federal policy." He emphasized that they needed our input.

Carter had just threatened to veto a water appropriations bill because it contained funding for the Tellico Dam, which threatened an endangered species, the snail darter. I noted to Andrus the prophetic irony that the year of Aquarius (1977) dawned with the "hit list" and ended with the snail darter.

NGA Principles for a National Water Policy

At our February 1978 mid-winter meeting, the National Governors' Association approved a detailed set of water principles embodying five policy concerns:[6]

1. Any new water policy should be the result of a cooperative national, not primarily federal, effort;

2. The new policy should recognize the states' primary role in water management;

3. The new policy should strengthen the states' capabilities to manage water policy;

4. The federal government must be more flexible in its response to states; and

5. Management should recognize different hydrological systems among the states.

We believed the integration of concerns for water quantity and quality were essential to any national water policy, and we suggested that the policy recognize regional differences in water management needs and the insurance of flexibility and equity in future federal water investments.

Our proposed policy advocated state primacy in water management. This was a critical jurisdictional point that we had to settle before we could even talk about how to distribute and manage the resource. We wanted to maintain the integrity of the states' roles.

I do not wish to imply here that the federal government should not play an important role. For example, with respect to navigation, flood control and environmental issues, there is an essential federal role, but we did not want the federal government to decide exactly how specific programs should operate in every state. We defined what we felt was the proper federal role: (1) to establish a framework of national objectives and criteria developed in consultation with the states, (2) to provide assistance to the states in the development of programs to meet state needs within such a framework, and (3) to be consistent with such state programs to the maximum extent possible when undertaking direct federal actions pursuant to national interests.

Arguing for greater flexibility in the entire federal support system for water management also became very important to me and was a part of our policy statement. I draw the analogy with the federal government getting into the field of interstate commerce. In doing so, one needn't define interstate commerce so broadly that state roles are eliminated. Flexibility was, therefore, important so that we could have a pragmatic way of solving local problems and have some diversity without preempting all local initiatives with a national water policy.

NGA policy also agreed that federal project-financing, cost-sharing and cost-recovery policies should be reviewed and simplified to eliminate inequities and inherent biases toward specific solutions to water problems. It should promote equal consideration of structural solutions (such as dams) and non-structural solutions (such as conservation). This amazing consensus to consider cost-sharing on major projects ran contrary to the history of water development, and it occurred even before the large federal deficits further suggested realignment of program responsibility. It showed a willingness among the states to enter into some cost-sharing agreements on water projects and to recognize that the federal government was not going to continue to pick up the total cost.

President Carter's National Water Policy Message

During the spring of 1978, the Interior Department, the CEQ and the OMB submitted their recommendations to the President. The governors were successful in persuading the Interior Department to accede to our views on the majority of critical issues.

The President invited the NGA water subcommittee to meet with him on May 17 to discuss his proposed policy. Five other governors attended the meeting, and the major topic was cost sharing. The President proposed that the states share at least ten percent of the cost of new water projects. He also proposed that projects already under construction would be given "grandfather" status and not be required to pay a share. I was generally encouraged by the meeting, although the President was noncommittal on any of our suggestions. It was clear that his upcoming water policy statement would no longer include the more radical proposals initially suggested by his staff, such as changing the discount rate and requiring full cost recovery.

In his June 6, 1978 White House message to Congress, the President proposed water policy initiatives designed to accomplish four objectives:

1. Improved planning and efficient management of federal water resource programs to prevent waste and to permit necessary water projects which are cost-effective, safe and environmentally sound to proceed;

2. Provide a new national emphasis on water conservation;

3. Enhance federal-state cooperation and improve state water resource planning; and

4. Increase attention to environmental quality.

Reactions to the Carter Initiatives

Carter's first objective was to improve federal planning and management. It included initiatives to institute specific procedures for conducting cost-benefit analyses of water projects. It also provided for a separate review by the Water Resources Council to assure planning compliance with these requirements. These initiatives would apply to "all authorized projects (and separate project features) not yet under construction."

Along with this planning objective, the President proposed cost-sharing legislation which would "allow states to participate more actively in project decisions." Cost sharing would be mandatory on projects not yet authorized or those in the Bureau of Reclamations' authorized backlog which, alone, amounted to $32 billion. Voluntary cost sharing by a state on authorized projects would result in a priority for executive branch funding. I viewed the idea of voluntary contributions to accelerate water projects as one of the keys to the President's priority-setting criteria.

While the NGA supported the general concept of cost sharing, I was never able to get the association to take a position on what percent was appropriate, or whether and how it should be retroactively applied. I think there was a certain delusion among western water interests. They thought that the old rules in the 1902 Reclamation Act would continue to apply, and that they would be able to continue to get Congress to appropriate funds for existing and new projects. In contrast, I believe there was a mounting change in attitudes within Congress toward federal water programs. Congress never looked at water financing as a federalism issue — one of determining what was appropriate for the states and for the federal government. Rather, its attitude reflected eastern legislators' concerns with a continued subsidization of western population and economic growth through water project financing.

The second major goal of the Carter Administration was a new national emphasis on water conservation. To implement this objective, the President directed all federal agencies having programs affecting water consumption to encourage conservation.

He outlined a number of specific directives, which included:

1. Making community water conservation measures a precondition to a water supply or wastewater treatment grants or loans from the Environmental Protection Agency, the Department of Agriculture or the Department of Commerce;

2. Integrating water conservation requirements into the housing assistance programs; and

3. Requiring development of water conservation programs as a condition of contracts for storage and delivery of municipal and industrial water supplies for federal projects.

I continued to have concerns with the President's water conservation initiative. Water conservation is not the same as energy conservation. While wasted energy is gone forever, "wasted" water may simply return to the system for use at another time and in another place. The administration also regarded conservation as merely a reduction in demand, not storage of water from the spring runoff for subsequent use. The omission of water storage as a valid and viable conservation practice was a major disappointment for western governors, and I believe it was a major political and technical weakness of the water policy review.

The President's third objective was to enhance state-federal cooperation and to improve state water resources planning. Initiatives in this area included increasing planning grants for the integration and implementation of management programs which emphasize water conservation.

The President also proposed steps to "promptly and expeditiously inventory and quantify" federal and Indian Reserve water rights. Reserve water rights claims, largely unquantified and indefinite, render uncertain the fate of state authorized appropriations on the streams arising from or flowing through Indian reservations and other federal lands. Western states were naturally concerned, because sixty-one percent of the total surface water runoff in the eleven contiguous western states comes from federal lands.

The final objective of the President's new policy was to "increase environmental quality." No one really objected to that, and I support the recent trends to strengthen state control over water management. A further step, perhaps requiring legislative changes, would focus federal law on establishing acceptable levels of pollution, leaving to the states the task of determining how best to meet those goals. This would limit EPA's responsibility to reduce water pollution without undue interference with state economic development strategies. The states would then have the flexibility to experiment with pollution control strategies suited to local areas.

Instream flows were also a major part of the President's plan, and in his message he called for increased attention to maintaining and protecting them. "The states have the principal responsibility for the protection of instream flows," he said. Nevertheless, options considered by Carter agencies seemed insensitive to state prerogatives, including:

1. Improving the efficiency of federal water project use, making the same water available for instream purposes;

2. Amending legislation for specific projects to provide minimum flows for downstream uses; and

3. Including provisions and amending legislation to restrict project diversions during periods of critically low stream flows.

The issue of instream flow is an important and complicated one in the West. Vested water rights are property rights protected by constitutional due process. They cannot be taken, impaired or destroyed without just compensation.

Where water supplies are limited, there are usually accompanying tradeoffs involved between a consumptive use and the maintenance of suitable instream flows. These tradeoffs are best determined at the state level. While I supported the objective President Carter had in mind, I also recognized a need to maintain a cooperative effort between the federal government and the states.

The Carter water policy initiatives raised many problems but solved few of them. They opened a dialogue on water project funding, an issue that was simmering then and one that still needs extensive discussion. Probably the most significant byproduct of the Carter debate was that it strengthened the arguments for strong state policy. It forced disparate interests to come up with a single set of principles that, I think, can serve the governors of the states well in future debates.

Certainly, the downside of the policy was that even with this tremendous effort by the President, by the states and by the water associations, no constructive legislation or policies of any great significance were adopted. Thus, many people viewed the effort as an exercise in futility. I think it proved that if you want to make a dramatic change in public policy, you simply cannot ram it down everyone's throat. Rather, policies should be developed carefully, using solid, long-range due process principles. Neither President Carter nor President Reagan have used that approach on water matters.

As President Carter began to get involved in other areas of domestic and foreign policy, his interest in changing public water policy waned and eventually disappeared from his list of priorities. There was no real effort to push his water program into legislation.

The Development of a State Water Plan

Although water policy was not an issue during my 1976 campaign, it was high on my list of priorities, particularly because of the drought of 1976-77. In my first budget message to the legislature, I asked for an appropriation of $5 million for emergency water-related construction to help farmers, stockmen and cities cope with depleted water supplies.

The drought and the effort to create a national water policy convinced me that we would have to increase our water development efforts.

I sensed that the cost-sharing issues were with us indefinitely, and that we had to be more self-sufficient about managing our water resources for future planning. Through Utah's planning efforts, I was aware that many worthwhile water conservation projects were not built because no front-end money was available. The Construction Fund and the Cities Water Loan Fund, supervised by the Board of Water Resources, were simply not adequate for major projects.

In late 1977, I decided to establish a $100 million revolving fund for larger scale projects which could not be financed from the two existing funds. The legislature was not fond of general obligation bonding, but water development had become increasingly recognized as a legitimate function of government in Utah. In 1978, I asked the lawmakers to authorize the sale of $25 million in general obligation bonds for large scale water projects. Ten were selected for consideration, and they would pay for themselves through power generation and/or water sales. The bonding legislation established a Conservation and Development Fund, which contained the bond proceeds, all interest on unexpended bond revenues and all repayments from water and power sales.[7] In 1980, I sought, and the legislature approved, another $25 million in bonds for additional water projects. In 1983, I was able to secure authorization for an additional $20 million, primarily for water storage.

Today, the Board of Water Resources administers over $125 million in cash and repayable loans, which will revolve back into the fund for future developments.[8] The Board of Water Resources has built projects in every county in Utah. Most have been associated with irrigated agriculture; many have had municipal, industrial, fish and wildlife and recreational values. The board now has three major funds to work with: the initial revolving Construction Fund, the Cities Water Loan Fund and the new Conservation and Development Fund for larger projects. In its twenty-eight years of existence, the board has invested $100.5 million in more than 725 water projects. The list of projects includes dams, canals and canal linings, pipelines, sprinkler systems and municipal and domestic systems.

There are some who question whether or not it is advisable, or even good state policy, to subsidize agricultural and mining interests through tax-exempt, general obligation bonding for water projects. My view is that the development of our state and most of the West is intrinsically tied to the development of its water. We must continue to make available the necessary capital resources for water projects, but we must do it only after carefully examining our priorities.

One of the problems with Utah law is in the allocation process: "first in line, first in right." Both Rampton and I attempted and failed to get legislation to allow the state water engineer to utilize public interest factors in the allocation of water. Changing traditional water policies is a slow process, but we must keep trying, and my view is that wherever we invest our money, it must be done in the public interest.

Future Water Policy Options: Facing the New Realities

There is little doubt in my mind that President Jimmy Carter was right in launching a reevaluation of the nation's water policy. The fact that the process was flawed and the results inconclusive does not lessen the realities of our current water problems. Periodically, reports initiated by the news media have heralded the issue of how to make sure there's enough good water and have asked whether or not water is the nation's next resource crisis, replacing the energy crisis of the late 1970s. The "water crisis" is related to three issues: A growing shortage and/or a maldistribution of water throughout the United States, the problems of the aging infrastructure delivery systems (particularly in the East and industrial Midwest), and the continuing concern over water pollution.

We must learn to manage water in an age of scarcity. As a nation, we have not been very good at conservation until the price of a given resource has induced a change in behavior. Over the past thirty years, the United States has doubled its annual consumption of water to about two thousand gallons for every person in the United States.[9] Despite the apparent abundance of water in certain areas of the country, we know that water is not a limitless resource. A major problem facing the United States is the depletion of some of its major aquifers. The Ogallala, the world's largest aquifer, stretches for 800 miles beneath eight states: South Dakota, Colorado, Kansas, Wyoming, Oklahoma, Nebraska, New Mexico and Texas. It once contained an estimated 650 trillion gallons of fresh water, but today there are indications that the water table is dropping in the Ogallala Aquifer as it is drained by more than 200,000 wells in those eight states.[10]

In the eleven contiguous western states, water is the principle limiting factor for future prosperity; yet indications are that through the year 2000, the population of the West will increase at a rate more than twice that of the rest of the nation. Most of this population will be located in urban areas and will need additional water.

In the East, much water is lost from an aging infrastructure. In recent years, Boston has pumped forty percent more water than it can account for in its customer billings. Leakage through its water system is considered a major cause of the problem. In 1983, the Associated General Contractors of America, a Washington-based industry organization, estimated a price of $138.6 billion on necessary reconstruction of water supply facilities.[11] While a number of bills have been introduced in Congress to address infrastructure issues, Congress has reached no solution and is unlikely to do so in the face of current federal budget deficits.

Pollution of our streams and aquifers is also becoming an increasing problem. Fertilizers and pesticides run into the streets, then into the storm sewers, and from there to our rivers, or they filter through the soil to our aquifers. Many of the nation's wastewater treatment plants are not doing the job for which they were intended. Despite the expenditures of more than $30 billion by the federal government in the last decade, and even more than that by local governments and the private sector, it is estimated that more than $500 billion is necessary to develop the wastewater treatment facilities needed to deal with the quality aspects of water supply.[12]

Coping with these three problems—supply, distribution and quality—will require state and local governments to provide the initiative in leadership, perhaps on a regional basis. I draw this conclusion because of the paralysis that gripped the Carter and Reagan administrations and Congress over the development of a new national water policy. In my view, it is necessary for state and local governments to face five realities:

1. The abandonment of water project financing by the federal government;

2. The continual shift of water rights from agricultural interests to municipal and industrial uses;

3. Continuation of federal environmental regulation without accompanying financial support;

4. The failure of the federal government to settle the reserve rights doctrine; and

5. The inevitability of market factors having a primary effect on water policy decisions.

With the Reagan Administration, the trend towards federal abandonment of financing will likely continue. The abandonment is not an announced definitive policy on the part of the administration, it is simply a turning of their backs on the problem. There has been no affirmative plan of action on a national basis to substitute for the abandonment of the federal role. This opens up a major role and responsibility for the states who have already assumed responsibility for the costs of most small and middle-sized projects. Utah significantly accelerated its funding of water projects during my administration, and that trend is visible in other states.

I think we're also going to see a dramatic privatization of both water development and wastewater treatment facilities. Local mayors and county commissioners may well have to deal with national financial firms in the future instead of the Bureau of Reclamation, the Corps of Engineers and the EPA. The cost of such privatization will be passed along in one way or another to the customers and users of the water, either through hook-up fees imposed on developers or additional water and sewer user fees. State governments may well become the guarantors of projects for water supply and wastewater treatment, thus assisting localities with a subsidized interest cost.

A second reality we must face is the dramatic shift of water uses and water rights from agricultural interests to municipal and industrial interests. Cities and towns are buying up whole agricultural water districts substituting municipal use for irrigation. This is clearly a product of the enormous population growth throughout the West. The market has shifted. Two hundred to three hundred dollars an acre-foot for water is too expensive for a farmer, but it is not expensive relative to the total cost of delivering that water (including the power, operation and maintenance costs) for municipal and industrial use. The CUP was primarily conceived to provide agricultural water, with some municipal and industrial use as a secondary priority. But now it is clear that the municipal and industrial uses are making the repayment of the Central Utah Project possible. It is truly a case of the tail wagging the dog.

In the West, we have to ask ourselves whether the elimination of agricultural lands is good public policy. Efforts have been made by states through greenbelt legislation and other protections of water rights to look out for agricultural interests. But I suspect that the farmer would not allow us to tamper with his rights to sell his water for municipal and industrial purposes if he can get a high price for that water. In many cases, the value of the water is seen as retirement income for today's farmers.

The third reality is that states and localities must learn to live with environmental regulations. These regulations have become more pervasive and preemptive, and we must learn to cope with them in a practical fashion. The only policy that makes sense to me is for the states to assume primacy, or management responsibility, for the environmental programs and try to urge more federal flexibility in those programs.

The fourth reality is the difficult problem of federal reserve water rights. Although the Supreme Court has been very helpful to the states in defining those rights in a manner I feel is appropriate, federal agencies continue to manufacture new water rights theories. States must continually fight against unreasonable interpretations of the federal reserve rights doctrine. Because this issue remains unsettled, states, municipalities and regions will find it difficult to find logical long-term solutions to the financial demands of water planning.

Finally, I believe that market factors will soon determine water policy in the United States. Water prices are still not a big enough cost factor in most municipal areas to force conservation. But increased utility fees and potential utility taxes to finance additional water projects or wastewater systems may well provide the impetus for water conservation, just as the oil embargo and higher prices provided the incentive for energy conservation.

Market forces will also push the states to reconsider the practice of hoarding "their" water. In 1982, the United States Supreme Court, in deciding the case of *Sporhase v. Nebraska* (458 U.S. 941), held that the United States is one nation and that to forbid the exportation of water across state lines, under almost any conceivable circumstances, places an unpermissable burden on interstate commerce and is, therefore, unconstitutional. One state, South Dakota, has proposed the permanent sale of some of their water outside of the basin.

The traditional water managers and water policymakers at the state level are strongly in opposition to the idea of interstate sale or leasing of water, because they are concerned that they will have no control over the process. However, it is certainly something that states like Utah will have to consider in the future.

Unfortunately, the concept of leasing water allocations brings with it a lot of risks, including whether or not such practices are legal under the Colorado River Compact and a number of other legal and practical considerations. What is needed is for the governors of the seven upper basin Colorado River states to sit down and discuss the leasing concept and come to a common understanding. It is more of a political problem than a legal problem, and it's a problem that must be managed on a regional basis to avoid potential lawsuits.

There is, I think, a growing recognition of the problems the nation faces with respect to water. But there is paralysis at the national level in solving these problems, and a vacuum within which the states could emerge as the leaders in developing appropriate solutions. The rules of the game are changing, and governors who do not realize it will not be making the decisions necessary for the future of their citizens.

We may well have made a mistake in not taking advantage of President Carter's 1977 initiative to develop a new national water policy. But the time was not right, the old water forces too strong and the Carter process too blunt. It will take a new president, leadership from the NGA or a regional governors' organization and a solution to the federal budget deficit to find the answers and forge the coalitions needed to confront the problems and realities of our water needs.

CHAPTER 13

Natural Resource Development and Environmental Quality

DURING the past twenty years, protecting the quality of Utah's outstanding physical and sociological environment while developing its valuable natural resources for the benefit of our citizens became a top priority in the governor's office. I learned very quickly that no proposed project involving the development and use of any of our natural resources could ignore environmental questions. It was always the classic question of balance, the need to maintain and improve Utah's economic health without compromising its unique and appealing environment.

We faced many development issues during my eight years in the governor's office, and they were all challenging. But in terms of sheer size, overall impact and opportunity to learn from experience, the siting of a mammoth electrical power generating plant was the issue that caused us to dig deepest for answers.

Shortly after I announced my candidacy for governor, I received a call from David W. Evans, a very influential man in the business community and in the Mormon Church. His firm, Evans Advertising Company, was representing a group of California utilities, led by Southern California Edison Company, which wanted to build a large, coal-fired power plant on the Kaiparowits Plateau in southern Utah. The Kaiparowits project had been the subject of intense debate among public officials in federal and state agencies, private companies and environmental groups.

Evans was calling to ascertain my views and solicit my support for the Kaiparowits project. I replied that I would not take an official position until the completion of the Environmental Impact Statement (EIS). I was therefore not prepared to endorse the project during the campaign. Apparently, that was not the answer he wanted. He vowed to do everything in his power to see that I was not the next governor of the state of Utah. As a first-time candidate for public office I was not only impressed, I was intimidated. But he didn't change my mind.

I was familiar with the Kaiparowits project and the intense feelings it generated on both sides. I had been active in the Utah State Bar and was its past president prior to the time I considered running for governor. During one of our annual meetings, they asked me to put together a panel discussing the merits of the Kaiparowits project. I arranged for Rampton to come in and defend the development side of the issue,

William Gould to speak for Southern California Edison, and a number
of competent and well-informed people from the environmental community to oppose the project. We drew an incredible crowd of lawyers
and had a rousing, thoroughgoing debate.

All of the national environmental organizations lined up against the
project, which would have been the first power plant to operate within
the so-called "Golden Circle" of national parks, monuments and forests in northern Arizona and southern Utah. Within the twenty thousand square miles of southern Utah (bounded on the west by Interstate
15, on the north by Interstate 70, on the east by the Colorado River,
and on the south by the Arizona state line) lies a more diverse and
beautiful country than in any other area of its size on earth. Some of
our greatest national parkland treasures are within this area: Zion,
Bryce Canyon, Capitol Reef, Arches and Canyonlands National Parks,
Cedar Breaks National Monument and Glen Canyon National Recreation Area on Lake Powell. Much of the remaining area of rugged
desolation is thought, by many, to deserve wilderness status under the
1964 Wilderness Act.

The area about which I speak was my early home and, in a sense, will
always be my home. It still provides renewed inspiration upon my increasingly infrequent return visits. The solemnity of each unique scene, at
any given hour of the day or night, gives it a spiritual quality that sets
it apart from all other places.

In describing some of the country near Capitol Reef National Park,
Wallace Stegner wrote, "It is a lovely and terrible wilderness, such a
wilderness as Christ and the Prophets went out into; partially and beautifully colored, broken and worn until its bones are exposed; and its
great sky without a smudge or taint from technocracy; and in hidden
corners and pockets under its cliffs, the sudden poetry of its springs."[1]

In this same area lie some of the state's greatest coal resources, some
of which developers could easily and economically strip-mine. In addition to coal, large deposits of tar sands underlie parts of Glen Canyon
National Recreation Area near Canyonlands Park. Uranium is also
abundant in the area. During the mid-1970s, the nation was facing a
severe energy crisis, a crisis which called for a number of projects including coal gasification, tar sands liquification and, most importantly, coal
development.

Many environmentalists had simply drawn a line and said that no
one was going to defile this part of the United States. But those who
favored the Kaiparowits project saw it as critical to the nation's energy
independence and essential to the economic well-being of southern Utah.
After I announced my candidacy for governor, I was fed information
and influenced by groups on both sides. It was like talking about abor-

tion; every discussion was emotional; there was no middle ground, no room for compromise.

The environmental review of the proposal consumed nearly five years. By the time that the Environmental Impact Statement was published in mid-1976, the cost of the plant had swollen to $3.5 billion from the original estimates of $500 million for a plant half the size originally planned.[2] In April 1976, the utilities, led by Southern Cal Edison, still needing 220 permits and authorizations from 42 federal, state and local agencies, decided to quit. While the public reason was the intense opposition and potentially lengthy litigation over the project, there was also a reevaluation of electrical power demand studies in southern California.[3] Combined with the intense public scrutiny of the project, the California utilities threw in the towel.

In June 1976, Rampton appointed eighteen state officials and citizens to join with fourteen legislators in establishing a Joint Legislative Committee on Energy Policy to attempt to analyze the defeat of the Kaiparowits project and seek ways for Utah to foster prudent development of its abundant energy resources. Simultaneously with the committee's deliberations, eight energy policy seminars, conducted by the University of Utah, Utah State University and Brigham Young University, were held throughout the state. One hour of each of the eight seminars was telecast by KUED Public Television Station, enabling viewers in all parts of Utah to share the information. Extensive coverage of each session was provided by state daily and weekly newspapers and by both public and commercial television and radio stations.

The Kaiparowits debate, the project's eventual demise and the discussions of the Committee on Energy Policy focused my attention on the procedural, legal and political difficulties in developing the state's energy resources. There were some who thought that the best way to handle Utah's development was to divide up the state into two areas, designating the area south of I-70 as pristine and not available for development and the area north of I-70 as suitable for development.

One of the most significant position papers I developed during the campaign was *On Energy and the Environment*.[4] It became a blueprint for actions that I would later take as governor. In the position paper, I argued that Utah can have an important role in national efforts to assure needed energy for future generations. I recognized that energy conservation was a vital element in any energy policy and supported efforts to develop a state conservation plan. But I supported the development of Utah's energy resources as long as the development contributed to the public interest and welfare, improved our standard of living and provided a means of upgrading the quantity and quality of local public services and facilities.

I argued for an end to state energy policy fragmentation and supported the concept of a permanent energy policy council. I also believed that the state could have both clean air and energy development, and that belief has not changed. My position paper asserted that Utah must preserve its ability to develop energy resources in an environmentally sound manner, and that careful planning would be required to insure that all energy development would be in the public interest.

I said that we could have our energy cake and eat it too if we took positive and aggressive steps to determine which air quality classifications would prevent significant air quality deterioration while allowing us to meet both our economic and environmental needs. Once those determinations were met, I maintained, we must then be prepared to forcefully present our case to the federal government. At the bottom line the issue was, and still is, a question of balance.

Because state land use planning was a very sensitive issue, I proposed that local governments have the primary role for site-specific planning for industrial development, land use regulations and the management of community services. The state needed to concern itself only with those issues having a statewide impact, with coordinating actions with federal land managers, with assisting local government in assessing needs and with financing solutions to area problems. I proposed the development of a community impact account, financed through the state's share of mineral lease royalties from the federal government, to assist local government in those financing needs.

I remain convinced that Utah and the United States could develop our energy resources while maintaining a quality environment for ourselves and future generations. It was an ongoing battle, and people on both sides of the spectrum might still argue whether or not I achieved an appropriate balance while governor. I feel that I did. In striking that balance, it was necessary to deal with federal legislation and federal agencies, consider the decisions made by federal courts and listen to the desires and wishes of locally elected officials. Often, their views were irreconcilable.

From the beginning, I developed a very open process of information and debate which served to dissipate much of the hostility that existed between environmental organizations and resource developers. Undoubtedly, some of that hostility remains, but I am still convinced that legitimate debate, open process and reasonable good will can lead to solutions for most problems.

Shortly after I became governor, the proposed Intermountain Power Project, labeled the "Son of Kaiparowits" by many environmental organizations, was the first real test of my ability to balance developmental needs with environmental concerns.

The Intermountain Power Project

The Intermountain Power Project (IPP) was conceived by the Intermountain Consumer Power Association (ICPA), a non-profit, cooperative organization of consumer-owned electric utilities. It was composed of twenty-three cities throughout Utah that had developed public power as an alternative to the private sector power supplied by Utah Power & Light Co. Faced with a projected shortage in electric power, the ICPA began in early 1970 to look at the possibility of constructing a major, coal-fired power plant.

IPP was designed as a 3,000-megawatt plant, which would have been the largest coal-fired installation in the world. In supplanting thirty-five million barrels ($800 million) of foreign oil a year, it would also support the nation's effort to switch from oil to coal as its primary electric power energy fuel. As with Kaiparowits, IPP was slated for location south of the I-70 corridor at a site called Salt Wash, close to Capitol Reef National Park.

My first exposure to the IPP proposal was early in the campaign. I was invited by the sponsors to discuss the project at their office in Sandy, Utah. Members of their board and their executive director, Joe Fackrell, were present. Rampton had not been a great supporter of public power, and they wanted to know where all the gubernatorial candidates stood on the concept of public power. I had some exposure to the public power concept previously and had no serious philosophical difficulty in supporting it. I indicated to the group that I was willing to support IPP.

As IPP was initially conceived, it would provide employment for 2,000 construction workers, 2,000 coal miners and 550 plant personnel. In-lieu property, sales and use taxes would provide state and local governments with additional revenues of $30-40 million annually. The project would supply three-fourths of the electrical needs of five participating Utah cities and over one-third of the needs of the five participating California cities, serving a total population of 3,700,000.

The plant was designed to utilize the best available control technology (BACT), including electrostatic precipitators, which would remove 99.5 percent of the fly ash and flue gas, and desulfurization scrubbers, which would remove ninety percent of the sulfur dioxide and fifty percent of the remaining fine particulate matter (ash) not removed by the precipitators. While the plant would provide a relatively clean source of energy compared to other coal-fired power plants, a large amount of emissions were still expected to be put into the airshed, including 8,000 tons per year of sulfur dioxide, nearly 1,200 tons per year of particulates and 68,500 tons per year of nitrogen oxides.

An extensive study by project sponsors covered engineering feasibility, economics, coal and water availability and environmental effects at several sites. Salt Wash was determined to be the best alternative. That particular site is an arid, undeveloped region approximately eight miles northeast of Capitol Reef National Park and sixteen miles northwest of Hanksville in Wayne County, Utah. A mesa surrounds the site and isolates it from nearby communities and the highway. Construction of railroads to haul coal from the central Utah Emery coalfields would cause little adverse impact on the region and little visual intrusion. Transmission lines could also be favorably situated.

The Fremont River and an underground aquifer in the Navajo Sandstone in the vicinity would provide 55,000 acre-feet of water per year for the operation of the plant. The project sponsors proposed to construct a reservoir to receive water diverted from the river and pumped from the aquifer. The reservoir would, in addition to supplying the plant, provide water for local agricultural, industrial and municipal uses.

Although the site was only eight miles east of the northern end of Capitol Reef National Park, emissions from the plant would seldom affect the park. Prevailing winds, blowing to the northeast, would substantially disperse the plant emissions and carry them away from Capitol Reef toward the San Rafael Swell.

The developers were thoroughly committed to proceeding with the plant at Salt Wash. At the time they developed the site proposal in the early 1970s, it met all existing environmental laws and regulations.

The Clean Air Act Amendments of 1977[5]

Under the Clean Air Act of 1970 and subsequent regulations adopted by the Environmental Protection Agency, states were required to develop air quality implementation plans for "non-attainment areas" which did not meet minimum acceptable air quality standards as defined in the act. However, because the act required the promotion of a general policy of clean air, environmental groups brought suit to force the EPA to disapprove all state air quality implementation plans which did not contain procedures for preventing significant deterioration in any portion of the state where air quality was superior to national standards.

On June 11, 1973, the U.S. Supreme Court affirmed district and circuit court judgments upholding the environmental organizations.[6] The EPA was required to promulgate regulations to prevent significant deterioration for any state that did not take adequate measures. The EPA regulations announced on December 5, 1974 called for establishment of classes of allowable, incremental increases in total suspended particulates and sulfur dioxide.

All areas of the country where air quality was better than national standards were initially designated Class II which would allow for a modest increment in air quality degradation. Provisions were also included to allow states, federal land managers and Indian governing bodies to request redesignation either to a more strict Class I designation, allowing very little additional air quality degradation, or a more relaxed Class III designation. I felt the regulations would encourage state and local initiative by providing state and local governments the flexibility and responsibility for reclassifying areas.

In 1977 Congress amended the Clean Air Act to require states to include provisions for preventing significant deterioration (PSD) in their air quality implementation plans. The amendments also required adoption of classification systems similar to the one provided for in former EPA regulations.

The statute classified national parks and other specified recreation areas as mandatory Class I areas. All other areas with air cleaner than the national ambient air quality standards were initially classified as Class II. According to established procedures, a state could redesignate, as Class I, any area except Indian lands and as Class III, any area other than mandatory Class I areas, Indian lands and certain other federal lands.

I had preferred the regulatory approach, and during the debate over the legislative amendments, I sought some flexibility by which state officials could determine what was meant by "significant deterioration." I noted that relatively minor deterioration of the aesthetic quality of the air may be "significant" in areas where great value is derived from clean air. In areas with high unemployment and little recreational value, the same level of deterioration may be considered "insignificant" in comparison to the favorable impact of new industrial growth with resulting employment and other economic opportunities.[7]

While I was pleased that Congress had provided some role for state governors in their redesignation process, I was not happy with the inflexibility of the particulate standards. Implementation of the PSD policy would clearly have far-ranging impacts on the development of the energy industry in Utah and throughout the West.

IPP and Clean Air Amendments

Because it was clear that the PSD regulations and 1977 legislation would have an impact on the siting of the Intermountain Power Project, extensive air quality monitoring was undertaken by the project's sponsors. Air quality monitoring data indicated that emissions from the Salt Wash plant would not exceed the Class I annual increments for sulfur dioxide and particulates nor the twenty-four-hour allowable increment for particulates in Capitol Reef or in any of the other nearby Class I designated areas.[8] However, due to short-term, ground-based inversions and transitions in wind and thermal stratification, studies conducted by the sponsor and BLM indicated that maximum concentrations of sulfur dioxide might exceed the twenty-four-hour and three-hour Class I increments in Capitol Reef during an estimated fourteen to eighteen days per year.[9] Part of the Class I clean air debate also involved visibility and aesthetic concerns. Under optimal conditions, visibility at Capitol Reef extended a distance of approximately eighty-seven miles, although naturally-occurring haze and windblown dust often reduced visibility in the area to less than forty miles. The studies estimated that IPP would reduce the visibility distance in the park by approximately five miles, two to three percent of the time.

IPP's plant siting problems were brought to the attention of Congress when they considered amendments to the Clean Air Act. In the passage of the Breaux amendments, Congress allowed a procedure by which the federal land manager could provide a variance to the strict Class I standards.[10] The governor was also permitted to initiate such a variance procedure, and if there was a disagreement between federal and state officials, the matter was referred to the President.

The benefits of IPP at the Salt Wash site were weighed against the detriments to Capitol Reef in lengthy and detailed debates on the House floor.[11] With the passage of the Breaux amendments, there was a feeling among the project sponsors that Congress had implicitly endorsed the plant construction at the Salt Wash site, subject to the discretionary approval of the appropriate federal land managers.

Interior Secretary Cecil Andrus, the designated federal land manager for the Bureau of Land Management, met with Joseph Fackrell, IPP's executive director, in July 1977, to discuss siting plans. Andrus was opposed to any grant of variance despite the Breaux amendments. In a letter to Fackrell on August 2, Andrus articulated his concern.

> The problem that must be resolved goes beyond the design and engineering of IPP. There are some treasured natural resources in the United States, many of them units of the National Park System, in which by policy and by law, this Department is sworn to uphold existing standards of environmental integrity. If, even after the best and most sincere application of control technology, those standards would still be degraded, it is my duty to protect the integrity of these areas as I indicated in our meeting.

> I urge you to consider that the evidence available points to the possibility that another site may be necessary in order to protect the air quality at Capitol Reef and Canyonlands National Parks.

> I've instructed the Assistant Secretary for Land and Water Resources to direct the Bureau of Land Management and the Bureau of Reclamation to initiate, in cooperation with the state of Utah, an immediate effort to expeditiously determine the likelihood of water availability and to begin gathering other environ-

mental information that will be useful in evaluating alternative sites north of Interstate 70.[12]

Even before additional air quality data would indicate that IPP might not meet air quality standards with a variance (a finding that IPP sponsors would refute), Andrus told me, after a lengthy and often heated discussion, that he was not going to permit any degradation of Capitol Reef National Park from a standpoint of air quality. He urged me to look for an alternative site for IPP.

To Switch or Fight

During the 1976 campaign, I supported the creation of a permanent energy council. Legislation enacting that concept was approved by the legislature in 1977. The Energy Conservation Development Council was created with both legislative and executive branch appointments. I had preferred not to have legislators on the council, believing that it was a violation of separation of powers; but it was the only way that I could get the legislation adopted. Senator Ed Beck, the sponsor, was appointed to the council and became chairman. In keeping with my policy of trying to get diverse views on such organizations, I appointed attorney Lee Kapaloski, a strong environmentalist, and San Juan County Commissioner Calvin Black, a southern Utah pro-development proponent, on the council, among others.

The majority of the Energy Council, including Beck, were supportive of the Salt Wash site and of the need to provide development for Wayne County. They were unhappy about the fact that Andrus opposed the site and that the law had been changed after the site had been selected. In my opinion, there was some legitimacy to their argument. They wanted to stay with the existing game plan and fight a move to an alternative site.

I rejected the request from some members of my staff that I appeal Andrus' decision directly to the President. Even if I had successfully secured the President's overruling of the Secretary of the Interior, the fact that some air quality models indicated a clear violation of the federal law, even with the variance, made the likelihood of a legal challenge almost a certainty. I also knew that the President was a very strong environmentalist. It was clear that he was going to support Andrus' decision to maintain the pristine air of Capitol Reef National Park.

Power plants are not planned overnight. If we had been forced to litigate IPP over the issue of the variance, we estimated it would have taken three years and perhaps the project would never be built because of inflation. It was Kaiparowits revisited. I was convinced the logical thing to do was to find an alternative.

I discussed the IPP dilemma with my press secretary, Mike Youngren. He suggested throwing the siting decision to the Energy Conservation and Development Council with some outside appointments to be added to a task force. While not giving up on the Salt Wash site, I could indicate to the council that I wanted them to explore alternative sites that could be reviewed in the course of the EIS process. The solution seemed simple. We could continue to support the Salt Wash site, indicating that we felt that it was a reasonable decision and, at the same time, initiate a parallel process to develop acceptable alternative sites. I indicated to council chairman Ed Beck that I wanted the council to play a lead role in an interagency siting task force.

Beck, and a number of council members, had serious concerns with the idea of overruling the developer on the Salt Wash site. They questioned whether or not the role of the Energy Council was to find appropriate sites for power plants. After all, it was only three years after the people of Utah had overwhelmingly rejected an attempt to create a very modest state land use statute. Accordingly, there was a great deal of political concern as to whether it was a good step for the Energy Council to get involved in power plant siting. Beck personally expressed those concerns to me. However, I indicated that it was my interest to find a suitable site for IPP that would allow the development to go forward. The council reluctantly accepted the assignment.

After securing a commitment from Secretary Andrus that federal officials would participate even to the extent of voting in the selection of alternative sites, I named an advisory Interagency Task Force on Power Plant Siting in the fall of 1977, which included the sixteen representatives of the Energy Council, seven other locally elected officials (two of whom were on the council) and five federal officials.

The timing of the interagency task force coincided with efforts by Utah Power & Light Co. to determine the effects of the Clean Air Act amendments of 1977 on their own future power plant siting. They had initiated detailed air quality modeling throughout the state and had come up with a number of proposed sites that they felt were acceptable under the Clean Air Act standards. They were seeking prequalification of those sites from the Energy Council. It was apparent that Utah Power & Light Co. was attempting to reserve all of the acceptable sites for themselves. Ironically, however, their data, and data put together by the state's Bureau of Environmental Quality, were used to isolate six alternative sites for IPP, the public power project, all north of I-70.

The task force examined the socioeconomic impacts associated with development of a large project at each of the proposed sites. The availability and cost of water, potential damage to the environment, land use compatibility, construction and operating costs and competition for airshed space with other proposed developments were all considered. A complicated matrix system was developed and the sites were ranked according to the information determined by task force-initiated studies. While the task force's overall recommendations showed a slight preference for a site at Lynndyl, a second site at Hanksville was also highly ranked. Therefore, the task force recommended that the two sites, not in priority order, be considered as alternatives to the Salt Wash site.[13] The Hanksville site was located in Wayne County, as was the proposed power plant at Salt Wash. There was a strong interest on the part of the local officials from that area to see consideration of a plant site remain within their county. While IPP still indicated a preference for the original Salt Wash site, they committed to me that they would respond to the task force recommendations and, thereafter, file appropriate applications with federal agencies for the necessary permits.

In a letter of November 25, 1977 to Secretary Andrus, I said that I wanted to discuss with him the need "to expedite the environmental review and permit process for the project. The sponsors of IPP argue forcefully and reasonably, I believe, that some concrete commitment from the state of Utah and the federal government is needed before they can ask the municipalities they serve to put up several million more dollars for a comprehensive environmental review (i.e., of an alternative site)." I emphasized that I wanted "a commitment to expedite the required EIS and permitting process, not a commitment to circumvent environmental review."

In his response of December 21, 1977, Secretary Andrus praised the work of the Interagency Task Force on Power Plant Siting and my leadership in bringing together the diverse interests involved. He also promised that there would be no needless or unreasonable delays which would add to the cost or uncertainty of the project. To this end, he "directed the Bureau of Land Management, the National Park Service and the Bureau of Reclamation to continue to give top priority to working, in cooperation with IPP, to expedite the consideration of alternative sites for the project."

In an oblique reference to the fact that the proposed alternative Hanksville site in Wayne County was relatively close to the Capitol Reef National Park and might have some infrequent impact on the park's visibility, Andrus indicated to me that he had informed Fackrell that "from the perspective of my responsibility to protect the pristine quality of the air of the National Parks, air quality must be of the utmost importance in considering a potential site. The Department will not approve a site which would degrade National Park air quality to the

extent that a variance under the Clean Air Act would be required if a comparable alternative site that does not require a variance is available."
It was not hard for IPP to read his clear message, and on February 28, 1978, they issued a statement agreeing to begin scoping and planning work for a site near Lynndyl in Millard County, Utah.

The IPP EIS

While the EIS provides detailed information on the primary proposal and much less detail on alternative proposals, we had a concrete alternative site for IPP and a clear indication that the primary site was unsuitable from the standpoint of the federal land manager. Therefore, the IPP EIS contained the same level of detail on the alternative Lynndyl site as on the Salt Wash site so that enough information was available to the permitting authorities to proceed immediately with the alternative site if that was the selection of the federal officials.

The draft EIS (DEIS) was issued in July 1979.[14] It described the project and the two alternative sites, noting that construction was scheduled to begin in 1981, with commercial operation of the first units by July 1986. The three additional 750-megawatt units were scheduled for operation at one-year intervals thereafter. The plant would occupy approximately 4,600 acres of public land, administered by the Bureau of Land Management.

With regard to the Lynndyl site, the DEIS noted that the project would require a maximum of 45,000 acre-feet of water annually. Water would come from the Sevier River via an 11.5 mile pipeline from an existing reservoir. Surface water rights would be obtained by purchasing water shares in five existing water companies in the area. Ground water, 5,500 acre-feet per year, would be used to supplement the surface water supply.

The generating station would require an average annual coal supply of 7.78 million tons, or 296 million tons over the projected project life. A railroad spur, approximately ten miles in length, would be constructed from the generating station to an existing Union Pacific mainline near Lynndyl, Utah to transport coal. Sponsors were looking to the Wasatch Plateau and the Book Cliffs coalfields as the primary location for coal. Approximately 1,350 miles of new power lines would deliver power to Utah, Nevada and California. The DEIS also indicated that all air and water quality standards would be met by IPP at the Lynndyl site.

At the peak of construction, the work force would reach 2,520, and about 630 workers would be required when the plant was in full operation. Expansion of existing communities in the Delta-Lynndyl area were proposed to accommodate the increase in population resulting from the construction and operation of IPP at the Lynndyl site. This would require additional water and wastewater treatment capacity and additional school capacity for an expected 700 students. About 460 new permanent housing units and 1,750 temporary units, such as campers and trailers, would be needed for the project development.

The most controversial part of the Lynndyl siting decision was the diversion of water from agricultural use to the power project. In order to meet its water needs, IPP negotiated (at a handsome price) the necessary water from local water districts and, assuming that none of that water would come back into agricultural use, the DEIS noted that the project would remove about 7,500 acres from agricultural production.

On September 6, 1979, I filed the state's official comments on the DEIS with Secretary Andrus. I commended the Bureau of Land Management for the comprehensive and expeditious manner in which they assembled the document and also noted my appreciation for the effort that the Secretary had made to work with me to find a mutually agreeable location for the project.

In my letter, I stated, "As you know, it has been the state of Utah's position that the Salt Wash location provided an adequate site for the plant. However, I appreciate the responsibilities you face in deciding where to grant permits for the location of projects on public land. As the environmental statement shows, Lynndyl offers a desirable alternative site to construct IPP. If the decision is made to proceed with the construction at Lynndyl, all levels of government — especially BLM and the state of Utah — will need to work closely with the project sponsors to mitigate the adverse socioeconomic impacts from the plant on Carbon, Emery and Millard counties."

In a response to me on October 19, 1979, Secretary Andrus assured me that the Interior Department stood ready to cooperate with the state of Utah, local governments and project proponents in identifying and mitigating any adverse impacts which might result from the development.

On December 19, 1979, IPP scheduled a dinner at the Hotel Utah to honor the individuals who had worked successfully to find a location for the project. At that banquet, Andrus announced the go-ahead for the Lynndyl site. He also read a letter from President Carter to me[15] citing IPP as a major achievement for our nation, an example of our determination to bolster our economy and our national security through reliance on America's own natural resources.

The President noted that the approval "could not have been reached without the exceptional degree of good will and cooperation evidenced in this effort . . . The approval of the site at Lynndyl demonstrates the possibility of developing major energy facilities without sacrificing community values, agricultural interests or the beauty of our environment." Carter added some personal thanks for my leadership in putting together the interagency task force. "To unite our people and to bring interests together in recognition of the shared purposes that turn diversity into strength are important and sometimes very difficult responsibilities. Meeting these responsibilities with a commitment to integrity and progress is an accomplishment which exemplifies the effectiveness of our democratic system of government," said President Carter.

In his remarks, Secretary Andrus said that the "confidence, fairness and dedication displayed by all of you as you refined the IPP proposal has brought about more than the approval of one major energy product. If we have not yet created a model, we have provided an impressive example. People all over the country have watched this process, and the observers have learned almost as much as the participants."[16]

Secretary Andrus also indicated the federal government, following the President's stated policy, was going to demonstrate an "absolute commitment to protect the social and economic integrity of communities that are affected by energy projects such as this."

On my advice, and with strong support from Interior and the White House, Farmers Home Administration agreed to help the Utah counties of Carbon and Emery, adversely affected by coal development for IPP, as well as Millard County, where the plant would be built.

Mitigating the Impacts of IPP

Along with the creation of the Energy Conservation and Development Council, one of the other major legislative goals I achieved in the 1977 legislative session was the creation of the Community Impact Board and Community Impact Account. The board, made up of representatives of local officials and state agencies, assisted state and local governments in prioritizing projects that needed state assistance because of large-scale energy developments. Rural local units of government, where most of the energy development was occurring, are incapable, both politically and economically, of providing all of the necessary resources for that kind of major impact. The state has the capacity, ability and the personnel to assist. The Community Impact Board and Community Impact Fund were commitments to the need for a strong local-state partnership in these matters.

The Community Impact Board has the authority to provide either grants or loans to communities affected by energy development or to assist communities that have suffered the demise of mineral development or an energy project. During my term as governor, over $100 million was allocated to 306 different community projects. More than one-third of the projects and dollars ($36 million) went to community water needs. Sewer systems were second highest on the priority list at $23 million, followed by schools at $10.5 million and local roads at $9 million. Other funds were allocated for planning, medical needs, fire protection, recreation and other community services.[17]

The Intermountain Power Project mitigation was a special case. IPP, as a group of municipalities, wanted tax-exempt status for their power entity, a status which would save them hundreds of millions of dollars in interest cost payments over the life of the financing of the project. While Utah localities could enter into interlocal agreements, in effect, creating a separate municipal entity to conduct certain mutually acceptable functions, the provision of power was not a permissible function under Utah law.

While I am not a fan of subsidies, I felt that the tax-exempt status was appropriate in this case where a significant part of the power was going to public power entities. However, as a quid pro quo for my support of the tax-exempt status, I wanted detailed legislation, committing the IPP project sponsors to assist the local communities with the socioeconomic impacts of that project. The efforts to achieve that legislation and negotiate the proper contracts and agreements between the project sponsors and the local government officials were complicated and tedious and, at times, very emotional.

By the time the IPP impacts began to occur, however, we had in place a suitable set of agreements and had designed a process of mitigation that avoided the boomtown problems associated with other large-scale developments which had occurred. Rock Springs and Gilette, Wyoming had provided close-at-hand examples of the kind of problems to avoid in a boom situation.

Pursuant to state law, IPP developed a needs assessment and an impact mitigation program for the localities affected by the project. A number of agreements were signed with local, regional and state agencies detailing specific responsibilities. IPP provided $8.2 million to Millard School District to assist in the construction of new elementary and middle schools in Delta and to expand the high school to accommodate a vocational program. Millard County has received $8.3 million from IPP to assist in construction of a new county jail and in the provision of operating and maintenance expenses through completion of construction of IPP. IPP provided $7.8 million to Delta City for planning and administrative purposes, to upgrade the city's water and sewer systems and to share in the costs of a new municipal building.

The IPP construction work force created a significant need for temporary housing accommodations within the two-county Millard-Juab area. Over $25 million was spent for housing, provision of a community center, food services for single workers and other necessary support facilities. $1.2 million was provided to the State Department of Social Services to help alleviate the direct impacts of IPP workers and their dependents on human and social services agencies. Lesser sums were spent in other surrounding communities and school districts. While the total spent by IPP will probably not exceed $100 million in a multi-billion dollar project, the monies provided essential services to the towns and communities directly affected by the project.

Attempting to Create Facility Siting Legislation

Flushed with victory over our interagency task force effort, I attempted to formalize the process in legislation.[18] By 1980, all of the contiguous eleven western states, except Utah, had some type of siting regulations. The interagency task force had been an ad hoc approach to a specific situation, and although we were able to utilize the task force to site two other power plants, it was not a general siting task force which we could utilize for all large-scale industrial developments.

There are a number of reasons for developing siting legislation. The location of a large industrial facility is a critical factor in determining future growth patterns in a state. I also thought that a proposed siting bill should define more than a determination of physical location. It should consist of three principal concerns: first, an evaluation of the feasibility of the proposed project in terms of whether or not development is appropriate; second, consideration of alternative site locations; and third, determination of the optimal strategy to accommodate resource development on the selected site.

Even so, industrial siting is not popular in Utah. The Joint Legislative Committee on Energy Policy created by Rampton could not agree to a siting policy as part of their 1976 report and I eventually failed, in 1981, to get the legislature to agree to the proposal siting legislation.

As I look at our attempts to get formal facility siting legislation and the success of the Interagency Task Force on Power Plant Siting, it would be easy to conclude that the informal approach is the only one that will work in Utah's political environment. One of the positive aspects of an informal approach is the ability to involve elected local and federal officials in the decision-making process. That was certainly one of the keys to our success in the IPP siting process. While local units of government don't necessarily have the capacity to make things happen, they do have a tremendous ability to prevent things from happening if they mobilize for that purpose.

In retrospect, I am satisfied that Utah has not suffered by not having formal siting legislation. But I also believe that for good long-range planning and management the state should, when the politics are right, address the issue legislatively once again.

Energy Development South of I-70

Since environmental organizations were a part of the effort to find an alternative site for IPP and participated in the siting process itself, they really didn't have any basis to object to the siting of IPP at Lynndyl. Most strong environmentalists in the state do feel that growth and development is important to Utah's future so long as it's done in an environmentally safe manner. IPP proves that to be good policy.

Siting a large-scale energy development south of I-70 is, of course, an entirely different objective, and I am certain there would be strong opposition from environmental groups to any development within the so-called "Golden Triangle" of national parks and recreation areas. The Interagency Task Force on Power Plant Siting produced a number of acceptable sites, all north of I-70. That result was not predetermined by me but was the result of their professional study results and based on air quality monitoring.

Environmental organizations are still thoroughly committed to no development on the Kaiparowits Plateau. But I hope the door can be kept open to the possibility of development of energy resources at many appropriate locations in Utah, whether north or south of I-70. We ought to stay flexible and not close doors to important future opportunities. Technology changes things. The technical capacity to help natural resource developers extract resources in environmentally safe ways continues to improve. Therefore, my judgment is that we should neither restrict our developmental planning to any single area in the state nor preclude any single area.

With respect to the siting of IPP, since there was an acceptable alternative north of I-70, I was just as pleased that the power plant went there and not near one of our national parks.

Conclusion—The Process of Balance

IPP was an intergovernmental success where the interests of the nation, the state, local communities and environmental concerns were well served. We easily could have let IPP go the way of the Kaiparowits project— drowned in a sea of opposition, red tape and mutual distrust.

Undoubtedly, there are times when the interests pursuing development of a natural resource cannot be reconciled with those who seek to preserve the environment. In those cases, tradeoffs are painful and require the best judgment of our political leaders who have the responsibility to make those decisions.

I am of the opinion that we can resolve most problems if we approach them in a conciliatory fashion, with a view to finding solutions, not reasons for opposition. What is required is an open process, men and women of good will and mutual trust.

The National Environmental Policy Act of 1969 (NEPA) and its key process, the Environmental Impact Statement (EIS), provide a procedural tool that is critical for decision makers. While the state of Utah has often used the EIS as a shield to protect itself from unwanted events (the location of the MX or the Weteye nerve gas transfer), more often, we have found it an effective sword to pierce through problems and find opportunities for solutions.

IPP, wilderness review, Project BOLD, oil shale development in the Uinta Basin, water projects, mining and road building in Utah have all benefited from the EIS process to provide alternatives and improved decision making.

NEPA and the EIS process are imperfect. Too often, the agency responsible (both federal and state agencies are guilty) views the EIS as a procedural hoop, not a tool for better decisions. Too often, the documents contain too many facts and too little analysis of alternatives to help the decision maker. CEQ has recognized this problem and has attempted to provide guidelines to assist agencies in producing better documents with some limited success.[19]

The federal courts have strongly supported NEPA and its regulations providing for the EIS. Their commonsense interpretations have put agencies on notice of the need to take the process seriously.[20]

NEPA has changed the way in which we attempt to achieve a balance between the aims of development and the need to preserve our environment. Political muscle and influence can no longer ride roughshod over environmental concerns. The EIS does not always guarantee better decisions. But it does open up the process in a dramatic way, a way a democratic form of government should operate when making its decisions.

We can develop our natural resources *and* preserve the environment if we are willing to follow the spirit of NEPA, utilize the EIS or a similar process in making decisions; in so doing we can find the right balance in our decision making. Success or failure will affect both present and future generations in a dramatic way. The extra paperwork and time is a small price if we can make better decisions as a result.

PART IV

The New Governor

CHAPTER 14

Becoming Governor

ON the morning of the general election in 1976, I was asked by one of the television channels to appear live on the 10:00 P.M. news. I accepted the invitation and agreed to meet at the monument at Social Hall Avenue in downtown Salt Lake City just before airtime. The election for governor had been called in my favor just before our appointment. I arrived a minute or two early and watched the crew set up the camera and other equipment. One of them turned to me and asked, "Who are you?" I told him, and he laughed with a wry observation, "We're going to have to start getting used to you." That comment made me a bit uneasy. I'd have to get used to the change myself, I thought.

A week or so later, while driving down the street with Mike Youngren, my press secretary, I stopped for a red light. The driver of the car in the next lane kept staring at me. When we pulled into the intersection, I turned to Mike and asked, "Why did that guy keep looking at me?" He laughed, "You still don't realize you're the next governor of the state of Utah."

Realization came swiftly. While it was difficult to adjust from being a private, unknown member of the community to being the chief executive of the state, I really had no time to worry or to savor. We were moving, and I was aboard.

During the two-month transition and first year in office, I faced many important decisions, selected key staff, and basically set the tone for my eight years in office. While I had a general sense of what I wanted to accomplish, often a particular decision was the product of trial and error. I certainly had my share of opportunities to learn and grow on the job.

Preparing for the Role of Governor

Rarely does one prepare to be a governor. There is no pre-governors' training school. You bring whatever skill and experience you have to that responsibility, and in your first year or so in office, you get on-the-job training. I did bring some management experience with me to the office. And one critical asset I brought with me was my legal background. My law school training, my philosophical views on separation of powers, checks and balances and an open democratic process guided my administration. Basically, however, I relied upon what I learned at home. I took from that environment a set of attitudes and values about working in a democratic system. They sustained me for my entire eight years in office.

My limited management experience was acquired during my last few years with Union Pacific Railroad Company. I managed a number of lawyers in several states and had the opportunity to supervise people and put the budget together each year for the region's legal department. I also attended several management seminars. Union Pacific's policy of supporting its people in acquiring management skills to improve their administrative capabilities proved invaluable when I assumed office.

I've often wondered what the proper mix for an ideal governor might be, what combination of training, experience and skill would best serve the public. Prior experience in public office is obviously valuable, and most governors have either been state legislators or have served in elected positions in local government. However, many governors, including myself, never served as publicly-elected officials before.

A legal background is desirable, and a high percentage of governors are lawyers. Nevertheless, history is replete with records of governors who were non-lawyers. Robert Ray (R., Iowa) and Mike O'Callaghan (D., Nev.) are just two who served with great distinction during my tenure.

Sex is certainly not the test. Our women governors, although fewer in number, have performed equally as well as men. The fact is that governors of states are no different than anyone else. They come in all sizes, personalities and varieties. There is no formula for success.

Many political scientists believe that timing and issues make the real difference. There is substantial merit to that argument, certainly in elections. Incumbents usually win when the economy is good. But timing alone is not the whole answer. The political party process illustrates that. And issues are not always the difference. Ronald Reagan has proven that he can be elected even when a majority of voters disagree with him on major issues.

In the final analysis the best governors, overall, have been men and women who have the right combination of values for quality public service, the courage to stick to their convictions, even when in the minority, integrity by instinct, compassion by nature, leadership by perception, and the character to admit wrong and, when necessary, to accept defeat.

From Candidate to Governor Elect

The citizens of Utah were not particularly excited about the management issues in the 1976 campaign. Instead, they focused on traditional, substantive proposals. For example, we issued white papers on tax reform, economic growth, social services and natural resource development. Public response was generally favorable. I think that, in addition, the compilation of a set of management white papers created a sense that I understood management issues in the state. They were also valuable in helping me focus on what I wanted to do as governor after I was elected.

There is an ongoing debate among campaign managers and candidates as to the value of white papers, or position papers, apart from the one- or two-page blurbs that are submitted as press releases during a campaign. Nevertheless, the real value of position papers occurs after you are elected. They set a certain tone for an incoming administration—an agenda which new staff and department heads can immediately embrace and implement. Thus, the position papers I issued in the 1976 campaign were converted during the months of November and December into our legislative policy initiatives for the 1977 general session. I was able to get out of the gate with a running start. It helped create an image with the public that I was in charge and had a clear understanding of the needs of our state.

The New Governors' Seminar

One of the valuable activities conducted by the National Governors' Association (NGA) is the new governors' seminar, which is held in November, shortly after each general election, to provide assistance to incoming governors. Both the governor-elect and his or her spouse are invited, along with the governor's chief assistant. Norma and I took Mike Graham, who was a very effective participant in my campaign and who became my first executive assistant. I remember going to the new governors' seminar with some apprehension, because it was so soon after the general election and we were totally exhausted. But the purpose of the seminar is to move new governors as quickly as possible from an election atmosphere into a practical transition period and give them an understanding of the urgency of what they must do immediately and during the critical early days of their administration.

The seminar is the best opportunity, and perhaps the only opportunity, for new governors to understand and learn from people who have had the actual experience of serving as governor. The faculty for that 1976 session included Governor Cecil Andrus (D., Id.), who was chairman of the NGA and soon to become Secretary of the Interior under President Carter, Governor Ruben Askew (D., Fl.) and a number of other really outstanding governors who demonstrated a range of different management styles over the three-day period.

It started me thinking about how I would handle the transition in my first months in office. We talked about planning, budgeting, press relations, the first legislative sessions and organization of the governor's office—all of the things necessary for a newly elected governor to do, and to do very quickly.

Among sitting governors, there were many styles of management. Ruben Askew, for example, managed Florida in a very disciplined and structured way. He believed in working only a limited number of hours. It was his view that if you worked more than eight hours a day, you lost your ability to be sharp and make good decisions. He also refused to see anyone outside of his office staff until 11:00 A.M. each workday. During the early morning period, he was dealing with staff and agency heads, both formally and informally. He firmly believed that state management required a hands-on relationship from 8:00 A.M. to 11:00 A.M. every single day to handle both predictable events and emergencies.

A contrasting style was advocated by Governor Julian Carroll (D., Ky.). He advocated the LBJ style of management. He was always trying to find ways to maximize political gain for every decision and to curry favor so that he could later call in the chips when needed. For example, whenever he used the state airplane, he always made sure that it was loaded to capacity with legislators and third parties from whom he would extract commitments for future issues. He was also of the view that staff should never impose information on the governor unless they had distilled it into the essence of the issue. His rule was, "Don't ever hand me a single sheet of paper unless it is important enough for me to read, to understand and to use." Julian was clearly a first-class horse trader.

I never believed in the horse trading style of management. I remember discussing this with Jay Rockefeller, the newly elected governor of West Virginia. At the time, he said that he rejected the Julian Carroll style and was going to adopt a Ruben Askew style of management. Several years later, we were at another new governors' seminar at Sea Pines, Georgia. Both Rockefeller and I were then faculty members. Rockefeller had undergone a complete metamorphosis in his attitude. He said he was no longer a Ruben Askew manager but was now a horse trading Julian Carroll manager. I never did change my views.

My point is not to criticize governors Carroll or Rockefeller but to indicate that governors develop a management style that is comfortable for them, one that provides them with the feeling that they are in command on a daily basis.

I never attempted to organize my office as tightly as Governor Askew did. I liked informality and the ability to roll with punches, because the nature of the job requires that you respond to events on an ongoing basis every day. I also think my legal background heavily influenced the way that I made my decisions. I was comfortable with digesting a large amount of information to make decisions, and I got into the habit of spending many hours learning the components of the government for which I was responsible.

It seemed as though I read constantly. I would review materials while traveling in the car, the airplane, at my residence or wherever I could spend a few minutes by myself.

I believe governors are most effective when they have full knowledge of an issue before a decision-making meeting, so that you rarely have to use notes or refer to material. In that way, you can look people in the eye, ask them questions and get the answers you need. You control the agenda. Those attending the meeting realize the governor is in command of the facts and the issues. It helps you make better decisions and to get others to back those decisions.

The Transition and Administrative Start-up

The gubernatorial transition and the first few months in office are critical for any new state administration. Early mistakes can plague a governor throughout an entire term, and a successful start can lead to a honeymoon with the press and public. A good start provides important momentum to accomplish objectives.

After the new governors' seminar, I moved quickly to select key staff and fill department positions. I thought that the selections of my executive assistants and press secretary were critical in establishing the tone of my administration. I attempted to select people on my personal staff who could operate without my defining the total parameters of the job. I wanted people who were capable. I wanted experience, but I was willing to gamble on people who had innate ability, providing they were willing to make a commitment of time, loyalty and accountability.

It's no secret that I expected a lot from my staff, and I've been fortunate to attract people with a great deal of motivation and who met the characteristics I required. I also thought it was important to maintain some experienced staff from the prior administration. Most important, I wanted individuals who knew me, knew what I was like, and who would sustain my views in the institutional structure of state government.

In terms of department heads, we looked at the qualifications of the people who were there. I succeeded a Democratic governor, and there was no need to undertake a total housecleaning. I certainly wanted to keep good people in office, but there were several who I felt had been there too long. I had to take into consideration the geography of the state as well as the difficulty of getting people to take jobs that didn't pay a salary commensurate with their ability and the state's needs. I had to push hard to find the right people who were willing to make the sacrifice to achieve demanding goals.

For my chief executive, I chose Michael Graham, a person with good political instincts and management skills. Mike was originally hired as a campaign fund-raiser. He was the only member of the campaign team who I put in a key slot in my administration. He was totally loyal and could handle the administrative chores of the governor's office in addition to providing the political buffer that a governor needs.

Kent Briggs was Rampton's federal-state coordinator, and I asked him to continue in that capacity. I had become acquainted with Kent as he briefed me on pending federal legislation during the campaign. I learned that he got up early every morning and went to the office to take advantage of the fact that Washington, D.C. was two hours ahead of Utah. He would make the update calls, get the current information and brief me before I started the day's campaign. He clearly established his intergovernmental skills during that period and proved his willingness to put in the extra effort. Since one of my major themes in the campaign was to increase the state's role in initiating policy with the federal government, I saw Kent's experience as a very major contribution to the success of that effort. He later replaced Mike Graham as my executive assistant and continued to excel.

I was not acquainted with Michael Youngren before I interviewed him for the position of press secretary. He was recommended to me by George Hatch, owner of KUTV-TV, and Mickey Gallivan, who handled the advertising and media effort during my campaign. I talked to several people before the interview, and Youngren was given high marks for his capabilities and his professionalism. As a reporter, Youngren had gone to a lot of Rampton's press conferences, and Rampton told me he didn't care much for Youngren, because he was so persistent in asking tough questions. That actually tended to reinforce my positive view. I found we shared the same philosophical belief that our dealings with the press should be on an open, professional basis. Mike was a strong believer in opening up the decision-making process to the press, and that was an important factor in establishing the tone of my administration. That continued throughout both terms and contributed greatly to my success as governor.

Mike had not had much political experience and had never written a major speech. That, of course, is one of the things that a press secretary simply has to do well. Thus, I hired him partly on instinct, and the first thing I did was to discuss the preparation of a draft of my inaugural speech. A week later, he came back to me and said he didn't know whether there was anything worthwhile in the draft but to look it over and see what I thought. When I read it, I knew we had a winner.

I met Beth Jarman during the campaign. She was running for reelection to the state legislature and had been in the House of Representatives for one term from Davis County, a fairly conservative district. She was very enthusiastic, and impressed me with her intelligence. We talked about a number of the issues we felt were important, particularly the need to bring competent women into governmental policy making and to bring women's issues to the front of the political process. When she was defeated for reelection, I asked if she would come in and serve as one of my legislative assistants. Later she became head of the Department of Community Affairs.

The First Legislative Session

My Inaugural Address on January 3, 1977, was basically an effort to introduce the new governor to the people of Utah, and to give them some degree of comfort in their new chief executive. I knew that after twelve years under Rampton, the change in governors would be somewhat traumatic, especially when his replacement, although another Democrat, was an untried, untested neophyte. Utahns liked and respected Rampton and had been satisfied and comfortable with his style and leadership. They were a bit uneasy about their new helmsman.

I attempted in the address to tie our destiny to traditional Utah values which were simple, understandable and supportable. Of course, those values were also my own. I made an effort to encompass all Utahns within the proper concerns of state government. The address concluded with a brief charting of what I expected for Utah's future and my pledge to carry out the responsibilities of the office. Few, if any, had serious disagreement with it.

My State of the State Address presented to the joint session of the legislature, about a week later, was entirely different. The Inaugural was delivered from the second floor of the Capitol to a crowd primarily located on the first floor. The distance apart made the relationship quite impersonal. Although I was excited and enthusiastic, I felt no real emotion. The State of the State, however, was presented in the House Chamber, with legislators closely packed in around the rostrum. Emotions were high. There was a mix of hostility, antagonism, support, tolerance, loyalty, and forbearance. Those feelings certainly had an impact on my presentation. I was new, naive and nervous. Even worse, the microphone was loose and I was obliged to hold it up with one hand during the entire presentation. At the conclusion, it was a relief to return to the executive chambers to wipe the perspiration from my balding head and brow.

I did, however, outline my legislative program in detail. The specifics basically included the proposals I had developed throughout the campaign and were the product of many long hours of thought and preparation. The immediate reaction was decidedly mixed. The Republican majority in the House was quite critical, a view editorially shared by one of our daily Salt Lake City newspapers. The Democratic majority in the Senate, however, was supportive and complimentary. The political process was still quite predictable.

Nevertheless, the results of our efforts in the 1977 legislature were highly successful. Nineteen of the twenty major policy proposals I presented were ultimately passed in some form. They included funding of my Executive Reorganization Committee, the creation of the State Energy and Conservation Council, the establishment of the Community Impact Board, and the adoption of the "circuit-breaker," a means of allowing senior citizens modest tax relief on their home property taxes.

The Governor and the Legislature

It is reasonably well known that on some occasions I did not have a harmonious working relationship with the legislature. Part of the problem was due to the fact that I had no real experience with the legislative branch of government, had never served as a legislator, and during most of my administration was dealing with the largest legislative Republican majority in both houses in the United States. In fact, the Utah legislature was "veto proof" during my entire second term.

The ability of the policy-making branch to call itself into session and to override a gubernatorial veto with a single party line vote changed the nature of our basic relationship, and the attitude of a majority of the Republican legislators, as well. The net effect was the loss of the traditional checks and balance system in state government. The sole remaining check became the electorate. It responded in 1982 and in 1984 by retaining the veto-proof legislature.

As long as the Utah voter is willing, by design or default, to maintain the current political makeup, there is really no check on the majority party at all, except for traditional constitutional limitations. Therefore, the party in power can, if it chooses, be about as outrageous as it pleases. In my view a healthier environment for policy making is a body without a veto-proof majority in either party, which must vote legislation in the traditional, open way, together with executive branch give-and-take. That mix requires everyone to play by the same procedural and substantive due process rules, and it has served the country well for more than two hundred years.

Nevertheless, and in spite of the foregoing reasons, my personal attitude toward the legislative branch as an entity stems primarily from a strong commitment to the integrity of the doctrine of the separation of powers. I firmly believe that the chief executive officer of the executive branch has an affirmative, constitutional duty to protect the integrity of each branch of the government, and that requires an arm's-length relationship with the legislative body at all times. This is nothing more than a reaffirmation of the fundamental principle expressed by Montesquieu, that the nature of each power is fundamentally different, a principle which sometimes requires criticism, sometimes praise. However, I freely admit my impatience with the tediousness of the legislative process; as a consequence some legitimate criticism has been directed toward some of my comments about the legislature over the years of my governorship. Even so, it was rare indeed for me to publicly criticize individual members of the legislature, in either party, although I submit that just cause often presented itself. And, on a personal basis, I pursued an ongoing effort to work with my legislative colleagues in friendship and cooperation. For the most part, at least informally, we got along quite well. In retrospect, I confess I have forgotten almost all of my legislative battles.

The Gary Gilmore Execution

Gary Gilmore had been convicted of murder and wanted to die. His execution, during my first ten days as governor, affected me more than any other event that first year. My role was limited; yet there was a perception, nationally and in the international community, that I had the power to stay the execution. Most governors have such power, but the Utah governor does not.

In Utah, the jurisdiction over stays and commutations of sentence is in the hands of the Board of Pardons. The governor appoints the Board for staggered terms, subject to the advice and consent of the Senate, and in effect relinquishes his executive authority to the Board. A governor can request a stay of execution until the next regularly scheduled

Board of Pardons meeting. Rampton had done this in December, but the Board had reinstated a new execution date — just shortly after my inauguration.

Since Gilmore's was the first execution in the United States in over ten years, the case received international publicity. I received hundreds of telegrams and letters each day. Religious leaders and other anti-capital punishment groups flew in from all over the world to meet with me at my home in Salt Lake City (I was not yet living in the Executive Residence). We had to have Highway Patrol officers assume security and crowd control over several blocks surrounding my neighborhood — which made life difficult for my neighbors.

We were all tense and our emotions were visible. At 3:00 A.M. on the morning of the execution Gilmore's attorneys called to argue I could issue a new stay until the next Board of Pardons meeting because I was a new governor. That seemed to me to be a distorted reading of the statute. Gilmore was entitled to a stay and a hearing before the Board of Pardons. But, he had clearly already had that opportunity.

An eleventh-hour appeal brought a stay of execution from federal Judge Willis W. Ritter; but the Utah Attorney General flew over to Denver to the Tenth Circuit, rounded up a quorum of judges (using the state airplane) and got Ritter's stay overturned.

There was continual pressure from the national and international press — hundreds of people were involved and helicopters filled the air over the prison. The emotion got to us all. The lawyers and the press were trying to intimidate everyone involved.

Sam Smith, the warden, had been a major target for this pressure. Smith called me at 6:00 A.M., the morning of the execution, distraught. He really needed support. I said, "Sam, I'll tell you what to do. You do your job. You carry out the law. This is our democratic system and you just happen to have the unlucky responsibility of the person in charge." He later told me how helpful that conversation had been. Sam was a professional, and I believe he carried out his duty under great personal conflict.

Smith called me after the execution, "Governor, it's done; it's over." There was sickening feeling — all of us were numb. Youngren came in to my office and said, "There are hundreds of press out there and they want a statement from the governor."

I said, "Mike, I don't have anything to say." But, we moved the press into a large legislative caucus room in the capitol. There was no conversation; the room was quiet. I'm not sure even what I said, except I remember noting that "We have carried out the law; it's over and it's now time for everyone to get back to other things."

After the press conference, I decided to get out of the office. Mike Graham and I went for a long walk on the hill above the capitol. During that walk I first began to feel the total responsibilities of my role as governor. Even though I could not personally affect the outcome, for the first time, I clearly understood that I *was* governor. I'm sure the event helped me mature in the job.

Gilmore's death affected all of us emotionally. We are accustomed to death, in our families and on the highways. Yet for some reason, I guess because of the deliberate nature of it, we were involved in this tremendous emotional tug-of-war. We all sensed it. I remember a particularly thoughtful conversation with Bill Moyers discussing our value system, the rights of society and those of an individual. I became friends with Moyers and learned to respect him greatly. Actually most of the press handled the situation professionally. It was just very difficult to deal with so many of them while trying to deal with personal emotions as well.

The New Governor in Action

As a rookie governor in 1977, I made a number of mistakes. But even the worst of them created a learning opportunity. You can become a more effective governor by learning from your mistakes and experiences. If you're fortunate, and the mistakes are not too disastrous, you can recover.

One that stands out in my mind during 1977 was our handling of a statewide drought crisis. Earlier I mentioned the importance of water and the nature of the drought in the West in 1976-77. I had succeeded, during the 1977 General Session of the Utah legislature, in getting lawmakers to set aside $5 million in a "drought fund" for emergency relief for the summer and decided to appoint a committee of state and local water experts to recommend the best ways to utilize it.

At the time, a number of people on my staff were suggesting that I needed to find a role for the Secretary of State-Lieutenant Governor David S. Monson. Prior to 1984, when the Utah Constitution was changed, the governor and the lieutenant governor ran for office independently of one another. In Utah, the parties split the top two offices. Monson is a Republican, and the office of lieutenant governor really held very little responsibility unless, of course, he succeeded the governor. So at the urging of my staff, I asked Lieutenant Governor Monson to assume the chairmanship of the committee.

The Drought Committee performed admirably. During the spring and early summer, it came up with a set of recommendations for presentation to a special session of the legislature scheduled in July of 1977. Prior to the session, I decided to use what I thought was a lull in activity in the office and take a vacation to Scotland with my family. My eldest son was at Oxford on a Rhodes Scholarship, and it seemed like a good opportunity for the rest of the family to do some visiting in that part of the world. Matheson, of course, is a Scottish name, and we were interested in returning to the homeland of my grandparents.

I had seen the recommendations of the Drought Committee and felt that my staff could prepare for the special session without any great difficulty, and I would be back before the session began. Unfortunately, while I was gone, Monson decided to come up with his own set of legislative proposals to present to the legislature. Undoubtedly, he was hoping to create positive publicity and to promote himself as the leader in the state drought effort.

I returned from Scotland two days prior to the legislative session and found absolute chaos. The legislature had two sets of recommendations regarding the drought, both purportedly from the same committee. I was extremely upset and I foolishly lashed out in a press conference at both Monson and the legislature for playing political football with the drought issue. By chance, I happened to see my sorry performance on television. I looked bad. It was probably the low point of my first year as governor. I vowed never again to say anything in public or make any decision when I was emotionally out of control.

Fortunately, I was able to patch things up with the lawmakers in time for them to consider and adopt the original package as presented by the Drought Committee. However, it was six years before I left the country again on any extended vacation. I suppose I always had a certain insecurity about leaving the state and seeing things fall apart while I was gone. It wasn't until my last few years as governor that I felt confident that I had capable administrators and a staff who could effectively oversee the management of state government without my personal, day-to-day supervision.

The Monson experience was one of many that help you understand the role of a governor. It's important to get off to a good start, but there is a measure of trial and error in learning the ropes. Each year provides another learning experience.

A New Approach to Appointments

One of my first acts after the election was to appoint a SEARCH Committee (an acronym for State Efforts to Attract Responsible Citizen Help) headed by State Planning Coordinator Jed Kee, whom I had asked to remain in that position. The committee was composed of individuals from a wide range of business and interest groups, and of both parties, to recommend and review names of individuals who wanted to serve in government on a full-time basis or as a volunteer to serve on advisory or policy boards. In Utah, there are more than two hundred boards and commissions. Many have fairly limited roles, such as advisory boards concerned with licensing specific professions. Others have major roles, such as the Public Service Commission and the Board of Health. Many divisions have policy boards, and some division directors cannot be hired or fired without their concurrence.

Traditional politics had made the boards the province of the political parties and certain powerful interest groups in labor and industry. Many people had served on boards and commissions for extended periods of time. During the campaign, I developed the idea of trying to get more citizen participation into government. A number of people said to me, "I want to do something. I want to help. I want to be a part of state government, and I don't ever have a chance. I've sent a resume in, or I've called, and no one will listen to me." That was a chronic complaint during the campaign, and I reached the conclusion that appointments had become, pretty much, a closed shop under Rampton.

The SEARCH Committee was designed to change the makeup and method of selections. It placed large announcements in statewide newspapers advertising board and director openings. It made a special effort to attract qualified women and minorities who were not well represented on the boards.

The Democratic and Republican parties continued to have input, but no final selection rights or veto power. Thus began an arm's-length policy with respect even to my own Democratic party and all other special interest groups that in past years had felt that they "owned" specific board or policy appointments.

I had run as a citizen candidate and I was determined to fulfill that pledge. SEARCH was my affirmation of what I viewed were the requirements of a citizen governor—a person who was governor of all the people in the state. Because the policy conflicted with established custom, it drew me into immediate conflict with old party Democrats.

The SEARCH Committee selections were in keeping with the bipartisan makeup that was statutorily required of the various commissions, and I always made certain that the extra person was a Democrat so that the Democrats controlled the policy board. Therefore, I don't believe the party was abused by the SEARCH Committee. What actually happened was that we brought a lot of new Democrats who were not part of the old party structure into state government. That's where I got into trouble with the old party members.

In addition, I think there were some people who felt that the SEARCH idea was simply a mistake. We received thousands of resumes from individuals who applied for various appointments, commissions and committees. People told me that if I had fifteen names for every appointment, then I'd have one happy person and fourteen angry ones. I guess there was a little truth in that. I did disappoint some people, but SEARCH brought some new blood into the boards, and the transfusion was vitally needed. In retrospect, I would do it again.

Setting the Tone for the Administration

Although Mike Youngren was the least political of my appointees, he probably did more to establish the tone of my administration than any other person. Mike was determined that I have an open-door policy with the press and that without some special reason (personnel or finance matters) all meetings should be open to the press. We agreed to try it. Initially, I was a little uncomfortable with all of my meetings occurring in a fish bowl, but it was amazing how quickly that uneasiness evaporated.

Mike also was good at giving me lessons on how to bridge the gap between the private citizen and the public governor. He always argued, "Let the public know what you're doing. Use the press as your ally. Don't get mad at them because they ask tough and penetrating questions. Try and be responsive." He also helped solidify my administration's commitment to an open government. This openness involved the publication of public information, both good and bad, and we got an early test.

I was at home ill one day, and it was about dark. The doorbell rang, and at the door was Republican Attorney General Robert Hansen. He was delivering a document in which one of his attorneys concluded that I had improperly used some of the governor's emergency funds to assist the International Women's Year Conference. He even reached the conclusion that I may have been guilty of committing a number of felonies, although the memo argued these were strictly technical in nature. Hansen had stamped the document, "Draft Only – Not for Publication."

I called Youngren and asked him to come over, read it and see what he thought. He read it, and the next morning put it out to the press without consulting me. To be honest, I was a little miffed about it, and the attorney general was absolutely furious. Mike looked upon that as a critical opportunity to establish a policy of openness in the governor's office, of both good and bad information. Whatever was public material should be published so that everyone could read it and talk about it. In that particular instance, I asked Rampton to represent me in the matter and respond to the memo from the attorney general. Rampton did his usual outstanding job and nothing ever came of the issue.

A second tone that Youngren helped develop was a byproduct of his years as a journalist. He was always probing, trying to look at the other side of the question. He brought a devil's advocate role to the office.

There were no sacred cows. I picked up on that, both in terms of my own questioning of staff and agency heads' attitudes and briefings, but also by encouraging open and adversarial debate on major policy issues.

Those decisions helped me set the right tone during my first year in office. They established processes that reinforced my commitment to an open democratic system, and the bringing in of new people through SEARCH gave credence to my citizen-governor theme.

Despite some mistakes and legislative heartburn, I came through that first year relatively unscathed. I was able to survive several crises and see most of my legislative programs adopted; I began to enjoy being governor.

CHAPTER 15

Managing Crisis

THE management and operation of state government remains the most significant and traditional gubernatorial role. It becomes even more critical in relation to the growing size and complexity of government and the nature of the problems with which it must deal. Governors have also traditionally handled emergencies of one sort or another, such as prison riots or natural disasters.

A governor is perhaps most visible during a catastrophic event, whether it is a prison riot, the closure of a major assembly plant, a strike or a natural disaster of some kind. The public expects the governor to take a lead in addressing the problem. While they don't expect miracles, they do expect competent leadership, and a governor who is found wanting in a crisis situation rarely recovers politically.

I had the opportunity to let the public judge my performance during several major crises that confronted the state of Utah during the eight years I was governor. In 1977, my first year, I faced three major events that affected me both personally and as governor. The execution of convicted murderer Gary Gilmore was the first in the nation in over ten years and occurred during the first month I was governor; the winter of 1976-77 brought the worst drought the western states had experienced since the depression; and, near the end of 1977, a very divisive and potentially explosive coal strike began in southeastern Utah.

During my remaining seven years in office we also experienced gas rationing and the problems of allocating fuel during the oil embargo, a severe recessionary period from 1979 to 1982, and in 1983, after two consecutive record water years, the state experienced the worst flooding in its history, an unusual overabundance in a dry state which would plague Utah throughout 1984, 1985 and 1986.

Each governor has his own rules for an emergency situation. I asked Rampton what he had done. He explained that Utah had a statutorily created Council of Defense that must be called together to formally declare an emergency before the state could officially act. Individual members of the Council lived all over the state. Therefore, with a serious situation, a governor could not wait for a Council of Defense meeting.

"I understand the process, but what do you really do?" I asked. He responded, "You take care of it." I promised myself that if I had an emergency, I would mobilize whatever resources and spend whatever money was necessary to address it. That placed me at some political and legal risk, but I believed that this is what was required of a chief executive in an emergency. I also discovered that Utah had an archaic emergency management system, and we took steps to improve it in later years.

A governor has two critical responsibilities in a crisis. First, he must disseminate complete and accurate information about the nature of the crisis and what is being done to address it. He must respond promptly to rumors and become the main source of factual information about the nature of the situation. Second, he must mobilize all necessary resources at the state, local and federal levels and in the private sector as well to attempt to address the specific emergency. A governor is in a unique position to call upon the resources of the private sector, as well as governmental entities, to assist him. While there may be no legal requirement for compliance, public pressure to comply with the governor in an emergency situation buttresses whatever weak statutory authority he may have. In an age of television, the ability to appeal through the media for cooperation from the public is often critical.

While it is useful to have certain emergency powers and spending authority, it is my view that the governor is responsible for doing whatever is reasonably necessary in the public interest in a crisis situation, allowing the public and the legislature to later judge whether that course of action was correct.

The 1977 Coal Strike[1]

The coal strike in the fall of 1977 was a nationwide action called by the United Mine Workers. In Utah, about half of the coal miners are union, and about half are non-union. Those who were not part of the United Mine Workers organization obviously wanted to continue working on their jobs. That produced some very emotional feelings and animosity between union and non-union members. The union members looked upon their non-union counterparts as weakening their strike effort and having the potential for adversely affecting their overall livelihood.

The non-union mine owners and their attorneys met with me in November 1977 and expressed their concern over the ability of local law enforcement officials to handle the emotions that were likely in the event of a strike. While I did not promise to intervene, I did indicate that we would monitor the situation closely and that we would assist local law enforcement officers if requested to do so. Public Safety Director Larry Lunnen was in constant contact with Carbon County Sheriff Al Passic. He also developed a network within Carbon County that provided the Department of Public Safety with ongoing information about what was occurring.

Well before the strike began, Lunnen sent in people to assess the situation; they became friends with the miners and were prepared to assist in the event of a strike. During November and early December, Lunnen identified eighty-five Highway Patrol officers who could move promptly into Carbon County if needed and who were prepared in terms of training and experience.

On the morning of December 6, shortly after the strike began, Passic asked Lunnen and my office for assistance. Information we received confirmed that there were hundreds of miners and miners' spouses on a virtual rampage in Carbon County. Although it was difficult to ascertain the nature and extent of the trouble, reports indicated excessive drinking, drug use and people roaming the county in marauding bands. Though it was hard to separate fact from rumor, one county bridge was burned, and there was a lot of rock throwing and shouting between the non-union and union individuals. Carbon County people were concerned that the sheriff didn't have the resources to handle a possible escalation.

Sheriff Passic and his deputies had been escorting the non-union miners to and from work, and during the night shift on December 6 two deputies escorting a caravan from one of the mines encountered 200 angry picketers. Rocks were thrown, a bus window smashed, and one person sustained a cut over one eye. The sheriff mobilized all law enforcement officers in the area, including the local Highway Patrol, but the ten officers, who had been on duty for forty-eight hours without rest, were no match for the problem. It was at that point that Passic asked Lunnen to mobilize his reserve officers.

I called a meeting the evening of December 6. In addition to Lunnen, I asked the National Guard Adjutant General Nick Watts to attend, as well as several members from my office including Michael Graham, Kent Briggs and Michael Youngren. During the meeting, there were additional phone calls and reports from Carbon and Emery counties indicating a great deal of unrest, including threats, accusations and intimidations. While I did not want to overreact to this situation, I felt that the state needed to respond to the county sheriff's request for assistance.

The major decision at the meeting was whether to utilize the National Guard or the Highway Patrol. There were certainly pros and cons on both sides of the issue. The National Guard was a well-organized unit and had the necessary support services for mobilization, the capability for food delivery, field hospitals and other support services which the law enforcement agencies did not have. The major concern in my mind was the time required for mobilization. It would take at least forty-eight hours to mobilize the Guard and send them into Carbon and Emery counties. In addition, members of the National Guard were really weekend soldiers trained for a wartime emergency. They had no training for riot situations. The tragedy at Kent State during the Vietnam War protest provides a vivid example of the stress and tragedy that can occur when you have untrained people in an explosive situation. While the Highway Patrol was smaller, we could send twenty-five officers into the county that very night, all of whom had field experience and riot training. One of the Patrol's lieutenants, Frank Whipple, was also born and raised in Carbon County and knew many of the people involved. Captain John Rogers and Whipple were in charge of the men at the field level. Lunnen told me he could have a total of eighty-five men in the area by the next night. I had great confidence in both Lunnen and Watts but felt that the smaller, better trained, more selective group was the appropriate first response to the situation. That turned out to be the right decision.

Sheriff Passic had asked for assistance and, for all public purposes, he was in charge of the operation. That allowed him to retain visible leadership while, in fact, all of the actual shots were being called by Lunnen and the members of the Highway Patrol. They went in on December 6 and by the end of the following night had calmed the situation. Lunnen was to prove his value as Public Safety Director repeatedly during my eight years as governor.

Over the next several days, the Highway Patrol, with their highly visible uniforms, epitomized the law-and-order image I thought was needed. I wanted people to understand that we are not anarchists and that we live by rules. The Highway Patrol didn't take any guff but never overreacted to a situation. As a result there were no further serious injuries during the strike.

Less than a week later, I decided to go down to Carbon County and meet with the mine owners and strikers. Several people encouraged me to go down, thinking there was some chance that management and labor might get together to work out their differences. I felt it was important to indicate the supportive role that the state of Utah would play in preventing violence and helping find a solution to the strike. My political advisors thought it was unwise, and my chief of security was not at all happy about me going down; he considered it an unnecessary risk. But I thought it was important for the chief executive officer in the state to visibly show where the state stood on an issue involving the health and safety of its people.

Out of concern for my safety, Larry Lunnen carried a firearm — one of the few times he did so while he was head of Public Safety. Also, when I wanted to go across the street from the Carbon County courthouse to get a cup of coffee, I was escorted by three armed guards. I thought this was an overreaction to the situation, but I can understand the concern of my security advisors.

I held separate meetings with management and labor and then with both sides together. I wanted to make it clear to them that the state was not going to take sides in the issue, although we were anxious to have them get together and end the strike as quickly as possible. Our principle concern was the health and safety issue, and I indicated strongly that if anyone violated any state rule regarding health and safety, we would do what was necessary to make sure health and safety is maintained in the community.

The Democratic chairman from Emery County was a leader of the labor group. After I made my public statement that I was down there as governor and not to intervene on their behalf, the labor leader turned to me and said, "Since you won't take our side in this case, I want everyone in this room to know that I'm going to do everything I possibly can to defeat you the next time you run for governor."

I thought about that statement for a minute. It gave me a chance to be governor in the full sense of the word. I responded, "I understand what you're saying. But I want you to understand me. I don't care one way or another whether I get reelected. That's not why I'm down here. I'm down here to tell you that I'm enforcing the laws of the state of Utah in this community, and you'd better believe that's the sole reason I'm here."

There was a tremendous atmosphere of intimidation in that meeting. But I felt I did a good job that day, and I left the meeting feeling it was my meeting and their threats did not influence me. That really set the tone for the day and I was able to stick to my agenda, which was to calm things down.

I also went out to meet with the strikers. It was windy and snowy; they were bundled up, huddled around an open fire—angry, tired and cold. I went up to one picket line of about thirty United Mine Workers. I shook hands with every one of them. Two or three didn't want to shake hands with me, but I shamed them into it. The word went out that the governor had visited the picket lines. I think, in general, the strikers were pleased that I came down there that day and tried to get the negotiations moving again.

While I did not help the strikers directly in terms of the settlement, we did assist those miners and their families who were hurt by the strike by setting up emergency programs through the Department of Social Services to provide additional food, medical attention and emergency funds.

The strike lasted 109 days and was finally settled in March 1978. I'm not sure if my visit to Carbon County assisted in the solution, but it did alleviate some of the emotional feelings. With the concern over rioting and individual public safety diminishing, it was a little easier to get back to the bargaining table and solve the specific disagreements. By mid-January, the area was calm enough to recall the Highway Patrol.

The Flooding in 1983[2]

Nineteen eighty-two had been the wettest year in the state's history. And 1983 topped that record. The ground was saturated. The reservoirs and rivers were full. It was clear we were going to have major flooding, and the actual extent of it was phenomenal, creating a crisis of major proportion and heavy national publicity.

Most people remember the flooding of 1983 for the creation of temporary waterways or "canals" down several of the main streets of Salt Lake City to handle runoff which could not be accommodated by the drainage system. It was an effort involving cooperation of the state, county, city officials, church officials and an incredible outpouring of citizen volunteers. While the flooding along the Wasatch Front and at Great Salt Lake received most of the publicity, the major emergency, from the state perspective, occurred at Thistle in Spanish Fork Canyon, south of Provo, Utah.

No one seems to know just when the mud slide began. The officials from the Denver and Rio Grande Western Railroad (D&RG) visited the canyon on April 9 after receiving reports that the railroad tracks were moving slightly. Three days later, a railroad geologist inspected the slide but was not yet concerned. Although no one can pinpoint when the slide first began to inch its way across the canyon, everyone agreed that once it started, it moved dangerously fast.

On April 14, railroad tracks next to U.S. Highways 6 and 89 in Spanish Fork Canyon turned into roller coasters as four million cubic yards of mud from the sliding mountain began pushing around and under the roads and tracks. Crews from both the Utah Department of Transportation (UDOT) and the D&RG Railroad worked around the clock to stop the slide, but to no avail. By Friday, April 15, water from the Spanish Fork River washed over the tracks and roads, forcing the closure of both at 1:00 A.M. By this time, the slide had shifted the tracks ten feet east of their original position and seven feet into the air; approximately fifteen hundred feet of track were under water. The highways had also moved ten feet. Travelers on US 6 were forced to take a one-hundred-mile detour through Fairview and Moroni, while rail traffic moved through Wyoming to Denver, an eleven-hundred-mile side trip. Public Safety Director Lunnen was notified and went to the site. Utah County Emergency Management Officer Gary Clayton set up a command post and communications center at a cafe in Spanish Fork. The two officers would work closely together in the weeks ahead.

On Saturday, April 16, crews from three construction companies fought to keep a drainage channel open to prevent the slide from creating a dam and flooding the town of Thistle. But a thirty-five-foot drainage channel created on Friday had shrunk to ten feet on Saturday and was completely clogged by the next day. The slide, moving about eight inches an hour, pushed the Spanish Fork River up twenty-five feet. Crews gave up trying to salvage the road or railroad as they concentrated on saving the town of Thistle. Lunnen mobilized the state's Office of Emergency Management, talked to the railroad president about possible courses of action and provided a full report to me. He said that despite their efforts, he did not think they could save Thistle.

By Sunday, the Spanish Fork River, backed up by the natural dam created by the slide, flooded the town. Twenty-two families were forced from their homes early Sunday morning, and a fifty-foot lake covered the town. The slide was moving at speeds between six and twenty-four inches per hour.

By Monday, April 18, the massive slide measured one thousand feet at its widest spot and six hundred feet at its base and was about one and one-half miles long. More than one hundred workers were at the site as three construction companies, the Utah National Guard, the U.S. Army Corps of Engineers and railroad officials joined the fight. Attempts were made to relieve the massive pressure building up from the water behind the dam by installing thirty-six-inch pipes, but the pipes broke under the pressure of the slide. By Wednesday, April 20, the slide was moving at about one foot per hour at the lower end and five feet per hour at the upper end. The lake created by the natural dam was now one and one-half miles long and rising at a rate of three inches per hour.

By Thursday, April 21, it was clear that efforts to halt or control the slide would not be effective, and plans were made to mitigate the damages. The railroad officials announced plans to tunnel through the canyon walls and create a new route for its railroad tracks. Utah County officials, realizing the scope of the potential problems, asked the state to assume primary responsibility.

By then, the old Council of Defense had been abolished, and we had organized a new streamlined Office of Emergency Management Services under the supervision of Public Safety Director Larry Lunnen. At my request, Lunnen immediately took charge of the disaster.

On Friday, April 22, I declared Thistle and Spanish Fork Canyon a disaster area. This freed certain state funds available for disaster aid and set the stage for a later Presidential declaration signed on April 30.

The events of that week and of the coming months were to see the state, the railroad and federal officials working around the clock in a race against potential disaster. The southeastern part of the state was isolated economically, cut off from the Wasatch Front cities of Provo and Salt Lake City. Coal trains which normally flowed out of Carbon County were halted. Twenty-two families from Thistle were without homes. Residents of the town of Spanish Fork, downstream from the new natural dam and "Thistle Lake," wondered if the dam would break and if they too would have to flee.

Part of the new legislation that created the Office of Emergency Management allowed me to utilize $2 million in state funds for disaster aid. It was clear that mitigation measures necessary for the Thistle slide, let alone for the upcoming flooding that was expected to occur along the Wasatch Front in June and July, would far exceed the $2 million. I again determined that the best course of action was to spend what money was needed and then go back to the legislature for assistance.

Warm days and rains were bringing additional water down the mountains into Spanish Fork Canyon. The river, having no outlet because of the dam, continued to back up and, throughout April and May, both the height of the dam and the amount of water behind it grew on a daily basis.

During the next several months, Lunnen took the lead in coordinating the efforts of state officials, Utah County officials, officials from the town of Spanish Fork, representatives of the Federal Emergency Management Administration (FEMA), the Corps of Engineers and officials from D&RG Railroad. They had to address a number of simultaneous crises on an ongoing basis. The first was the response to the disaster itself, providing individual assistance to those whose homes were lost under Thistle Lake. Second was the protection of the town of Spanish Fork. This required stabilizing the existing natural dam and figuring out some way to provide an outlet for the water from Spanish Fork Canyon that was building up behind the natural dam. Third was the potential rerouting and reconstruction of US Highways 6 and 89, major routes which joined very near the point of the slide itself and, finally, assisting the railroad in rerouting their track to get the economies of southeastern Utah going again.

We had to decide on a method and begin the construction of a diversion channel from Thistle Lake even prior to an official Presidential declaration of disaster. Eventually, the declaration meant that the state's share of the cost of the diversion and eventual drainage of Thistle Lake would be twenty-five percent, or $4.35 million, and the federal share would be seventy-five percent, or $13.05 million.

Because of the importance of the diversion channel, which would enable the railroad to begin a tunnel, D&RG agreed to share its cost with the state. In order for the railroad to begin its tunnel, the state agreed to set the diversion channel at 170 feet. Utah's Department of Transportation (UDOT) had wanted a channel at a lower level because of a desired road configuration. But experts from Oregon, brought in by the railroad, and our own water officials were concerned about how fast the water was filling the lake. Lunnen made the decision to go with the 170-foot channel.

The water depth reached 170 feet on May 18, the same day the diversion channel was complete, and water began to flow through the overflow tunnel. By the following day, the water depth was one foot above the overflow tunnel, and the water depth of the dam reached its greatest point at 194 feet in early June when it slowly began to subside. Had the diversion channel not been in place by May 18 and had the Corps of Engineers not pumped water out of the lake to the other side of the dam throughout May, it is the conclusion of geologists that water would have flowed over the dam, causing a breach which would have flooded part of the town of Spanish Fork.

Lunnen kept me continually informed throughout the crisis. Whenever he had a problem, I backed him up. When I felt that UDOT was dragging its feet on the road construction because of disagreements with Lunnen or the railroad, I had to knock a few heads together. It was important that one person be responsible and that he should have my confidence and authority. I also made sure that Lunnen had whatever personnel he needed assigned to him from whatever agency that he felt was necessary to get the job done.

While the Thistle crisis was essentially over by early June with the dam holding and the diversion channel operating, Thistle Lake still had to be drained, and the spring runoff was causing flooding throughout the state. The state assumed responsibility for draining the lake, and did so by using a rather complicated series of tunnels that eventually created a bypass of the dam for the Spanish Fork River. We also pushed to reopen highways 6 and 89. Rail traffic began moving through Spanish Fork Canyon on July 24, and new roads were constructed by the end of 1983.

Cities and counties have the primary responsibility for flood control. Thus, in 1983, the state's efforts, except for the Thistle slide, were primarily coordination and facilitation. We coordinated the assistance of the National Guard, which provided a major portion of the large equipment used in controlling the flooding. Their efforts saved millions of dollars.

Under the direction of Lorayne Tempest, our Emergency Operation Center operated around the clock, securing sandbags from all over the country, working with federal disaster personnel and helping assess flood damage. By July 1, twenty-two of Utah's twenty-nine counties were included in the Presidential disaster declaration because of Thistle and other areas.

The state as a whole responded well to the disaster; Salt Lake City's "State Street River" and our great volunteer effort received national publicity and acclaim from President Reagan.

Nevertheless, I knew we had to do a better job of planning for 1984 when another wet year was anticipated. I named Larry Lunnen overall flood coordinator again, and he put together a task force, composed of representatives of all state agencies, cities, counties and major private organizations. Mitigation efforts and planning for the 1983 flooding were critically evaluated. New culverts and drainage systems were installed, rivers dredged, and soil conditions monitored for potential slides.

Nineteen eighty-four was not as serious a flood year as 1983 and with better planning and advanced preparations, the flooding and flood damages were substantially contained. In contrast, the estimated 1983 damage for the Thistle slide and other flooding around the state was $478 million.

Get well and come back soon....we've burned you in effigy but it just wasn't the same... signed the Conservative Republicans.."

Personal Crisis: My 1983 Heart Attack

Governors often have to cope with personal problems or tragedies. Some have gone through divorces, others have faced personal or family illness. The best are able to overcome these adversities. It takes support from family and friends.

In the spring of 1983, I suffered a mild heart attack. The attack came at the end of a very stressful legislative session. It occurred during the constitutional period in which I had to sign or veto bills. Several were on the "moral" issues, family planning and obscenity, and I was getting pressured both ways.

I was also chairman of the NGA that year and had a heavy travel and speaking schedule. I'm sure I was run down both physically and emotionally. Even so, the heart attack came as a shock. While not life threatening, it required immediate attention and care.

I spent one week in Holy Cross Hospital and another three weeks recovering at home in the executive residence. My wife has always played a partner role in my life and work, and she was an active first lady; Norma picked up most of my speaking schedule. Other governors assumed some of my NGA responsibilities. Kent Briggs, my executive assistant, took over the day-to-day administrative responsibilities. Also, since the attack was mild and I was never unconscious, I was able to meet with Kent on a daily basis and with other key advisors as needed.

There was an outpouring of support from the public which I appreciated. And one byproduct of the attack generated international publicity. While in the hospital I had not been shaving. One day a reporter asked Norma how I looked and was feeling and she said, "Fine, except for that straggly beard he's growing."

"...Do NOT stare at the Governor's beard, my dear, it only encourages him."

I hadn't deliberately been growing a beard, but everyone now wanted to see it. The beard story grew in importance and actually overshadowed the heart attack — which was just as well, though not planned in advance.

Well I let the beard grow and said I was going to keep it until the June 24th Pioneer Day Parade. After all, the Mormon pioneers all wore beards. Public opinion was divided; some thought it was distinguished, but one person wrote that I looked like an old sheepherder off the range. The final vote was Norma's — the beard was to go.

Actually, during the summer it was beginning to itch and I was growing tired of it. We made the shaving a public event in the Capitol and it attracted incredible attention, getting picked up by the wire services. For some people, they only found out about my heart attack after seeing my beard in the *International Herald Tribune*.

It was a funny ending to a difficult time for me personally. But by 1983 I really had a competent set of administrators in state government, and state government continued to run in an efficient manner during the months I was recovering.

CHAPTER 16

Creating Excellence in Government

THE public tends to categorize its public officials. Some are policy-oriented and care little about implementation details, others are noted more for what they don't do than for what they do. I was certainly active in creating policy issues and was perhaps best known for my various battles with the federal government, on MX, Weteyes, public lands and others. However, people also judged me a good manager of state government. I took a very pragmatic attitude towards management issues, but during my first term I began to crystallize my own thinking on what it takes to succeed as a public manager. I was never satisfied with adequate service to the public. I always believed we should strive for excellence.

A number of books in recent years have attempted to articulate what makes an organization succeed. *In Search of Excellence*, by Peters and Waterman, is perhaps the best known.[1] While the market for these books is primarily the private sector, some discussion has occurred on how one can translate these concepts to the public sector.[2] Implicit in the discussion is the assumption that public sector managers would succeed if they adopted the principles of hard-nosed business managers, and that failure results when public leaders fail to adopt those principles.

There are, of course, many differences between the private and public sectors; but I've never viewed those differences as an excuse for a lack of productivity in the public sector. In my opinion, the key to success, in creating excellence in both the public and the private sector, is leadership. Here I discuss the concepts or elements that I found helpful on the public side.

First is the personal style you create as governor. I ran as a "citizen candidate" and felt it was important to foster a climate of openness and honesty. The perception of the people toward a public official is basically set during the transition and first year of service. Therefore, it's critical to have a sense of what you stand for and what you want to accomplish at the beginning of your administration.

Second are the processes you design by which you achieve your goals. Some may evolve over time; but the processes that personally contain your stamp often dictate the result. Good processes help to achieve good results.

The third and most critical element is understanding the public. Governors simply have to stay ahead of the curve of public attitudes to provide leadership. They cannot constantly run with prevailing winds, or even run counter to those attitudes after the fact; but with care, foresight and risk, they can shape issues.

The fourth element is the articulation of a set of goals and values understandable to the public. If a sense of your intended direction is clear, it's easier to gain the necessary support — from the state workers, the legislature and the public — to accomplish your objectives. I recommend simply-understood goals, few in number and buttressed with your own value-system.

Fifth is motivation of the state's public employees. Productivity, efficiency and effectiveness are just words if there is a lack of commitment from public employees. That's why I could never understand candidates who run against the "bureaucrats." They can make or break you on too many issues. It helps to remember that those bureaucrats are your next door neighbors and have the same hopes and dreams that you do. They also will still be working in government long after current elected officials are gone.

Sixth is a willingness to promote risk-taking and entrepreneurship in government. Success seldom comes from "playing it safe," and the governor must send out a strong signal that he backs the innovator of good, new ideas. That includes accepting the responsibility for failures along the way.

The seventh element to success is to keep management structures simple and flexible. Government seems to create its own complexity, and success is often dependent upon the governor distilling the essential issues for decision making and finding the right set of actors to get things done.

The eighth element is a sense of urgency. Typical governmental processes are perceived as too slow. Accordingly, a governor must continually work at shifting his administration to a higher gear.

I didn't have a clear sense of these concepts when I ran for governor; they emerged during my first term. I believe that during my second term we had as strong a management team and administrative structure as any state government. And my success as governor was, to a substantial degree, the result of the public perception that I ran an efficient, effective and open governmental operation.

Becoming a Citizens' Governor

In the 1976 campaign, I had run as a citizens' candidate. In my inaugural address, I pledged to become a citizens' governor. I said that I planned "to bring everyone into government, and government to everyone. I will react to the requests of special interest groups, but to different kinds of special interest groups. The miner is as much a part of our society as a mining corporation, a switchman as significant as the railroad, a teacher as important as the education system . . . If a government cannot be responsive to its citizens . . . If the citizens do not relate to their government, then the ideal of democracy will be lost, and we will have failed."

I closed my inaugural address with these words:

> I was a citizens' candidate. I will be a citizens' governor. My administration will be a citizens' administration. My strength comes from people concerned with their government. It comes from the laborer, the businessman, the farmer, the cleric, the teacher, the housewife and the retired. My strength comes from the wide range of people we have in this state. My strength comes from you. You are the human resource I talk about. You have the talent, and the strength, and the courage, and the desire we need. You will be part of this government. It is your government.

The citizen governor image was one I wore as naturally as I did my boots and Levis. It fit my personality, my informal nature and the openness that I sought to encourage throughout my administration.

Whenever I had the opportunity in a speech, I attempted to reinforce that theme. Early in my administration, I included the following in a speech to the Lions Club:

> Citizens who become involved get a chance to meet the problems face-to-face. . . . These involved citizens are the best possible guarantee that government will not become a dehumanized and impersonalized machine. The individual who is involved surely must be a better learner, a better citizen, a more complete person, a more self-respecting person than is the person who doesn't care.[3]

The processes that I initiated during the transition and first year in office, which I described in chapter fourteen, all helped reinforce the image that I wanted to establish. The SEARCH Committee to recruit new talent into government, my open-door policy to the press and my arm's-length approach to interest groups visibly demonstrated this central principle of my administration—that I was in fact a citizen governor. These efforts created the tone for my administration. However, the two processes that most contributed to my management success were the Committee on Executive Reorganization and the development of an effective planning and budgeting effort.

Committee on Executive Reorganization

One of my early acts as governor was the creation of the Committee on Executive Reorganization. It fulfilled a campaign pledge to have an ongoing look at the organization and efficiency of state government.[4] Created initially by executive order and funded by contributions from the state planning office and other state agencies, the committee has received legislative funding since 1978 and has survived through a transition to the new administration of Governor Norman Bangerter in 1985.

The committee has a small research staff capably headed by Helen Goddard, but the key to its success is the involvement of private sector leaders who want to contribute to the efficient operations of government. Because of the prestige of those individuals and its first chairman, Arch Madsen, the committee had a tremendous track record of success with the legislature. Out of twenty major legislative recommendations made by the committee during my eight years, sixteen were adopted.

The committee's vice chairman was Dr. Robert Huefner, a political scientist and director of the University of Utah's Center for Public Affairs and Administration. Huefner had served as the state's first planning director under both a Republican and a Democratic governor, and his understanding of the structure of state government provided an important ballast to the committee. The other members of the committee included a broad mix of private sector business interests, people experienced in state and local government and political scientists.

Although I assisted the committee in setting the agenda for study, I adopted a hands-off policy in terms of their recommendations, and with a few minor exceptions, forwarded all the committee's proposals to the legislature. The Committee on Executive Reorganization achieved a success that will have an enormous impact on the future administration of state government.

Among its most significant accomplishments were a new Personnel Management Act, the creation of a State Budget Office directly under the governor, and consolidations of a number of agencies into three major departments: Community and Economic Development, Natural Resources and Energy, and Administrative Services. The committee also recommended a major restructuring of our health and public service commission agencies. Both were given increased authority to meet the demands placed on them.

The selection of Arch Madsen as the initial chairman was really the key to the success of the committee. The minute his name was suggested, I knew he was the perfect choice. He represented the best of the business community and had been involved in public service all his life. I had a meeting with him, told him that I needed one day a month of his time, and promised that's all it would take.

Madsen was tremendously busy, with his responsibilities as president of Bonneville International (a major communications company owned by the Mormon Church), with Radio Free Europe and with other Church duties, but he said that he would think about it and would talk to his boss about it. His boss was L.D.S. Church First Counselor Nathan Eldon Tanner.

Madsen went over to see President Tanner and relates this story. He explained to President Tanner what I had asked him to do, and said he realized that it was important, but he was really very busy and didn't think he could do it. President Tanner said, "Well, isn't part of what the Church stands for performing public service?" Arch said, "Of course it is." President Tanner said, "Well, why aren't you doing this then?" Arch answered, "I'm too busy. How do I get the rest of my job done?" Tanner reportedly replied, "Arch, that's your problem." So, in effect, Madsen was assigned by President Tanner to take this chairmanship.

Madsen was initially going to stay on for a year, but I was able to keep him as chairman for five years. I know that we got much more than one day a month out of him. He attended all the legislative dinners for years, and he periodically presented the committee's program to both houses of the legislature. He participated in all of the debates and subcommittee discussions, and he really marketed the products of the committee with individual legislators. In 1983, Roy W. Simmons, president of Zion's First National Bank, effectively succeeded Arch Madsen as chairman of the committee. I believe that the efforts of the Committee on Executive Reorganization will be a lasting contribution of my administration.

Understanding the Public

Books such as *In Search of Excellence* advise private sector organizations to stay close to their customers. This is equally true in the public sector, whose customers include direct recipients of government services, as well as taxpayers. One of the most critical things for a governor is to understand public attitudes. This doesn't mean that you take a poll and then react to what the public thinks. Rather, you attempt to understand the concerns and feelings of the taxpayers and the people who receive government services. You attempt to articulate those concerns and find solutions to their problems and needs.

I made regular use of public hearings and town meetings, as well as briefings by selected interest groups to keep in touch with all affected parties. "A public hearing," I once said in a speech, "is a dialogue and not a monologue."[5] For me, the public hearings and town meetings became a way of keeping ahead of public viewpoints, serving as both the catalyst and consensus builder of the citizens of the state on major issues.

A good example of my approach was the proposed deployment of the MX Missile in the Great Basin of Utah and Nevada. In October 1979, local polls showed sixty-nine percent of Utah residents supporting the federal government.[6] Although I had earlier supported the MX, I was becoming increasingly concerned about the impacts of its proposed basing scheme on the social fabric and economy of the state, and, as I mentioned earlier, I chose a military appropriations subcommittee meeting in St. George, Utah in November 1979 to articulate those concerns. During the next twenty-six weeks, I held town meetings throughout the state, leading to the debate on public television that was seen nationwide.

By the time I officially opposed the MX deployment in June 1980, less than half the population supported the MX in Utah. It was nearly a year later, after the Mormon Church issued a statement in opposition to the MX, that other statewide officials joined the opposition. By that time, three-fourths of the state's residents were against deployment of the MX in the racetrack scheme.[7]

I sometimes found it necessary to take positions contrary to the views of the Mormon Church. I did so with respect to the ERA and also with respect to legislation permitting government to censor cable TV programming for "indecent material." I viewed that legislation as an unconstitutional restriction on individuals and a free society. My veto of that bill was overridden by the predominantly Mormon legislature. Yet the polls showed the majority of Utahns were in agreement with me and opposed the censorship bill. My opposition may have made it possible for many Mormons to side with me. Federal courts agreed with my constitutional concerns and struck down the legislation. An initiative offering a watered-down version of the original bill was defeated by the Utah public in 1984 by a two-to-one margin.

Articulating Values

Essential to the success of any organization is the importance of a strong set of central guiding values. In the public sector, we face a complexity and multiplicity of values that, in many cases, conflict with one another. Within Utah's Department of Natural Resources and Energy are divisions with a strong development focus, for example, Water Resources and the Energy Office, and divisions whose missions are inherently contradictory to development, for example, Wildlife Resources and Parks.

The political process itself creates a diffusion of power and responsibility that makes articulation of central values very difficult. There are many actors: the governor, the agency heads, the legislature, the consumers of government services and the taxpayers. The actors often have a vested interest in not recognizing the values embodied in another person's position. While we have to recognize the ambiguity of values existing in the public sector, governors must establish and define policy direction.

In my 1976 campaign position papers and early in my administration, I articulated a set of major goals and objectives. In the last six years, these were explicitly relayed to department heads in annual planning and budget retreats. The budget became my most important management tool to keep agencies in tune with my values and priorities.

The Importance of the State Budget

Because of the time involved in preparation of a state budget, a governor who is elected in November and must present a budget in January has very little time to change what his predecessor has proposed. Even though Governor Rampton had invited me or my representative to participate in budget hearings, the budget I presented to the legislature in 1977, with a few minor exceptions to reflect priorities that I had indicated in the campaign, was pretty much a Rampton budget. I also found out it was totally the product of two men — Rampton, who was intimately involved and knew the details of the budgets of all of the departments; and Budget Director Mel Coombs, who was virtually a one-man show. He kept the decisions and the revenue projections in his back pocket, ready to pull them out at a moment's notice.

This approach may have worked when the budget of the state was in the hundreds of millions of dollars, but Utah's budget was now over one billion dollars. Rampton had served twelve years in the office, had grown up with and actually created many of the agencies. He actually got involved in decisions as to whether individual agencies were entitled to another secretary or another typewriter.

I was not comfortable with the way the budget was presented. There were gaping holes in our analyses, and we really weren't able to defend the budget very successfully before the legislature in 1977. Fortunately, the state economy was very strong, so it was simply a matter of dividing up the pie. We were able to fund most of my priorities.

The summer meeting of the National Governors' Association was in Detroit in 1977, and a number of my key staff went to the conference with me, including Kent Briggs, my federal-state coordinator, Jed Kee, my state planning coordinator, and Ken Olsen, a former state planning coordinator and a government consultant. We talked about the different ways in which governors approach budgeting. Some get heavily involved in all of the decisions; some governors delegate a vast amount of authority to a budget staff or the executive assistant and want to be involved in only the major budget decisions; other governors take an approach somewhere in between.

I remember discussions of the executive budget during the new governors' seminar in North Carolina shortly after my election. One of the new governors, Joe Teasdale (Walking Joe) from Missouri, was listening to the discussion about the budget — the time frames, the value of the budget as a policy and management tool and so on. After we had been talking for at least an hour, he raised his hand and asked, "Does a governor have to prepare a budget?" He didn't even know that. He then thought he would go ahead and just issue the budget his predecessor had prepared. Everyone raised their hands in horror, and the NGA staff ended up going out to Missouri and helping Governor Teasdale fashion his own budget.

The budget determines policy decisions; it allows governors to implement their policy choices. I had seen, during the legislative deliberations in 1977, that my ability to implement my goals and objectives during the first year was heavily dependent on decisions made by the legislature on appropriations. So I decided that during the next go-around on the budget, which really had already begun, I would become more involved and would use my planning office to help set priorities for the budget and relate those to my policy themes.

I also asked my Committee on Executive Reorganization to examine the functions of the budget and planning office and recommend institutional changes that I could advocate before the legislature in 1978. The evolution of a strategy for integrating my policy objectives, the efforts of the planning office and the executive budget took several years to develop. But it would end up as the major administrative process of my administration.

The budget cycle became a year-round effort with the official kickoff each year at a planning and budget retreat with my department directors and key staff. Preparation for these retreats would begin early in the year. The departments were asked to set major budgetary and policy goals and relate them to my policy themes. I established a governor's steering committee, composed of my budget and planning directors, key department heads and close staff to review the materials and suggest modifications or adjustments to my policy themes and directions.

The spring budget and planning retreat centered around discussions of what I hoped to accomplish and how each department could play its role. We then outlined general budgetary guidelines for the coming fiscal planning year. Follow-up meetings were held with each department head and key staff during the summer to review programs and make decisions on legislation, policy and budgets. All of this occurred before the actual budget preparations of the agencies took place in late summer.

The entire planning and budget process, as it developed through the years, enabled me to keep the agencies on track with my priorities. While I permitted agencies to push programs not part of my policy themes as long as they were not counterproductive, the whole effort of my administration was geared to advocate those programs which most contributed to the central direction.

When I first became governor, I didn't really appreciate the significance of the budget and planning process. I soon learned that the budget allowed me to manage all of the administrative processes of state government, and that it's the most important policy tool in the governor's entire arsenal. During the last six years, my administration utilized the budget to manage department heads and all of the programs of government.

In 1981, we developed Utah's first capital budget. It looked at the long-range capital requirements of the state and matched those needs with existing revenues and proposals for bonding. I know that some governors simply don't take the time to learn the budgeting process, but I believe that if you don't know it and use it, you don't manage the system. The budget is the fuel and the rudder to manage state government. There is no doubt that it requires an enormous commitment of personal time.

The department heads and staff pay attention to the governor's time preferences. If you spend your time making sure that the budget and planning process is a high priority, you get people in the agencies to devote their time to appropriate planning and budgeting. It also motivates people to carry out the priorities you have set. I never felt that any of that time was wasted.

The Importance of the Public Employee

I came to the job of governor with a very strong commitment to public employees and to the relationship one has with fellow workers. The more you deal with that relationship personally, the higher your chances are of a good relationship, good public morale and good public performance.

You can do a lot of things in government to increase productivity. But two-thirds of the state government budget is allocated for the people who do the public's business, and most increases in productivity come from the workers themselves. They are the teachers in public schools, professors at institutions of higher education, highway patrol troopers, social workers, prison guards, tax collectors and wildlife officers. Virtually all want to do a good job.

While my first responsibility was to the taxpayer and to the public, we all recognize that the taxpayer gets more for his money out of a positively-motivated work force. So I spent a lot of time speaking to public employee groups over the years, going to their public occasions, meeting with them and participating in awards ceremonies. I always met with their representatives at the front end of the budget cycle, trying to be sensitive to their attitudes and concerns. I worked cooperatively with them through the Personnel Office and through all of the departments. Most important, I was accessible, meeting with them regularly to listen to their issues and problems.

I viewed one of my responsibilities as becoming their advocate before the legislature, both in terms of adequate salaries and promoting policies designed to enhance their stature. There were fiscal years when it was impossible to offer large salary increases, so we would try to find other ways to recognize the outstanding performers.

Whenever I toured the state, I would visit local state offices — the local social services, transportation or job service offices — and sit down to talk with the state workers. I occasionally made unannounced walk-throughs of department offices.

Many state legislators have a negative attitude towards state employees, and the public often treats them as second-class citizens. They're treated as faceless nonentities, and are popularly referred to as bureaucrats. Perhaps there are some people who work in public service who exemplify the negative image which the word "bureaucrat" connotes. I've always felt that the best way to handle that image problem is to try to market state employees as individuals who live next door and go to the grocery store just like everyone else. They go to church on Sunday, to basketball games at night and do the same things that everyone else does. They are no different in their attitudes, habits and concerns than the rest of the public. They are honest, hard-working people who want to make state government function efficiently. When the public employee is understood as your neighbor, the stereotypical "bureaucrat" image evaporates.

I fought hard for new office space for state employees and was successful in completing a new office building in downtown Salt Lake City and in promoting the passage of legislation for a regional office center in Ogden as well as a new building for the Department of Health. Despite some legislative carping at the cost of the Heber M. Wells Office Building in Salt Lake City, one Utah magazine commented that "There is a widely held belief that a beautifully designed, aesthetically pleasing building must be immoderately expensive. The state's new Heber M. Wells office building disproves that theory."[8] Completed well within the allotted budget and three months ahead of schedule, the building was described by a visiting observer as "the finest state building since the State Capitol."[9]

In my mind, the Heber M. Wells building embodies four principles which could easily represent the goals of my administration: quality, economy, efficiency and flexibility. I never felt that least-cost office space made sense for state workers if you expected them to do a good job. I fought for long-range solutions that would put most of the state's work force in state-owned facilities. They are not opulent, but I did attempt to make them state-of-the-art in terms of automation, telecommunications and energy systems. Employee working conditions do affect performance.

I also believe that employee and management training is a critical component to successful productivity. The private sector understands this and makes the necessary investments, but I could never get the legislature to fund training in state government. The agencies always had to find ways in their existing budgets to provide for some management training. We were successful in initiating a management certification program through the Division of Personnel Management and made a major effort to increase "computer literacy."

Even when money was tight, I openly supported the use of bonuses for extraordinary performance and made productivity efforts visible in our state employee newspaper. I appointed a state productivity coordinator, Roger Black, and designated the major management agency, the Department of Administrative Services, as the lead agency for productivity in state government. Jed Kee, the director of the department, and Black pushed management reforms in finance, personnel, data processing and purchasing. I personally supported their efforts in the budget and in meetings with other agency directors.

There are things about the public sector that continued to bother me. The state merit system, while designed to provide valuable protection to the state employees, was often frustrating because of the difficulty it created in removing poor workers. Still, I thought that it was important to work within and not circumvent the public system. I also came in with a strong attitude towards affirmative action and regularly monitored the hiring statistics of the agencies during the budget and planning process to see how they were meeting that goal. As a result, we witnessed a dramatic improvement in minority hirings during the eight years I was governor.

There is an intrinsic value content in public service. The majority of public employees work in government because they support the values government seeks to promote. Therefore, any governor or public administrator who doesn't work very hard to support, enhance and motivate the work force, set the right examples and to disseminate information important to the employee will simply not succeed.

Promoting Risk-Taking and Innovation

Autonomy, innovation and entrepreneurial risk-taking are trademarks of successful private organizations, according to the books promoting organizational excellence. At times, they seem nearly impossible in the public sector. Miscalculations of public sector organizations receive considerable public scrutiny that cannot be buried in overall financial statements. And the media, unfortunately, is ever anxious to accentuate government failures. The opposition party can turn any failure into a rallying cry for a change in administration. Even within those constraints — and they are serious — I think it is essential for a governor to encourage new thinking and ideas and risk-taking among public managers.

One of the things I attempted to do, with some moderate success, was consolidate line items to give managers more flexibility. I urged our financial controllers to avoid second-guessing management decisions. We approved shifting of funds to accommodate automation and other productivity initiatives. When managers found ways to save money, we rewarded them, rather than penalize them through budget reductions.

I think we were successful in encouraging new ideas and risk-taking. State initiatives of which I am particularly proud include health care cost containment efforts that have become models for other states, jobs programs as an alternative to welfare, implementation of an innovative private-public partnership through the federal Jobs Training Partnership Act (to meet the skill needs of new and expanding industries in the state), the deinstitutionalization of youth offenders and mental health cases, and an increase in the use of office automation that has made Utah a leader in integrated, distributed data processing.

Data processing and office automation did not start out as a big success story for my administration. I inherited a bad situation. Rampton was studying the idea of contracting out the entire function to Boeing in Seattle, and a public hearing (which about one hundred angry data processing staff attended) was held to discuss the issue. This was after the election in 1976. Rampton invited me to attend the meeting and, after it was over, turned to me and said, "Well, Scott, I'm going to let you make this decision."

In Utah, the Department of Systems Planning had responsibility for the state's data processing, both controlling purchases and delivering services. Most governors, including Rampton, simply don't want to deal with such technical issues. Unfortunately, the managers of those departments tend not to communicate in a manner that is understandable to most people.

We ended up not contracting out that function, which I think was the right decision. But it took another four years before we began to put a good data processing structure in place. The first person I picked to head that department appeared to have all the skills, but he antagonized state department heads. They viewed him as a policeman regulating how they purchased and utilized equipment. It reached a critical point in 1980. He had alienated almost all of the department heads and was, himself, implicated in potential wrongdoing regarding the purchase of equipment. Although he was cleared of that charge, I found, as I got into the issues, that he was ineffective; I had to make a change. I named Dick Raybould to the position and placed him under the supervision of Finance Director Dale Williams.

The problem with data processing was that most department heads and other people in management positions, including myself, were afraid of computers. We didn't know anything about them. Word processing was an unknown factor. Data processing issues were assigned to subordinates, and when things went wrong, it was easy to blame the central data processing agency. I became convinced that in order for us to succeed in automating state government, all of the department heads and managers were going to have to become more computer literate. I insisted that all department heads attend a computer seminar with me so that together we could learn the rudiments of that mysterious entity — the computer — and begin to bring the state into the twentieth century. We followed up the meeting by organizing a group from throughout state government who spent the whole summer designing a Utah Systems Plan that laid out various automation and management systems that were necessary in state government. David Duncan, chairman of the Tax Commission, took the leadership on the project and did an excellent job.

During my second term, in just four years, we turned a very difficult situation into a very strong productivity factor in state government. We really started to get data processing moving with the creation of the Department of Administrative Services in 1981, which developed a greater service emphasis with data processing. This department did an outstanding job in advocating change. Dick Raybould deserves a great deal of credit for his entrepreneurial innovations and efforts to encourage automation in state government. It's a great story of how to dig your way out of a morass and ultimately turn a big deficit into a big advantage. I consider it a major achievement of my administration.

Overall, I believe that my call for imagination and risk-taking in state government was successful. It allowed the state to continue existing services and to expand services to its growing population with virtually no increase in state employment during the eight years I was governor, a fairly reasonable quantification of increasing productivity.

In fact, Utah has fewer state employees per 1,000 population than any other state in the nation.

The Flounder System: Keeping Things Simple

Some of my political advisors, particularly those whose academic background is political science or public administration, try to dissuade me from talking about my "flounder system." I'm sure that to them it connotes the process of acting clumsily or ineffectively. To me, it represents the natural struggle of government — to move forward and obtain footing in a constantly changing organizational and political climate. In government, size generates complexity, yet success in administration often depends upon a manager's ability to keep things simple.

I always attempted to deal directly with department heads and assign tasks out through them. I found that I was comfortable, however, in dealing with a broader group of individuals under different arrangements. So I made great use of ad hoc task forces and interagency arrangements whenever that seemed the best way to get a job done.

I always kept my personal staff small. This required me to rely on my departmental managers for policy implementation without the interference or bureaucratic layering that a large governor's staff can inadvertantly provide.

I consider myself one who delegates freely. Once I became familiar with an individual, either a department head or staff person, I never hesitated to show my trust in a substantial delegation of responsibility. When I hired an individual, I would deliberately leave open a substantial part of the nature of that job in order for that individual to fill out the remainder of his or her performance. Most people who were so delegated filled the gaps well and broadened their circles of influence, though a few didn't. The more I knew and judged the capacity and ability of the individual, the more I delegated. In return for that, I did ask loyalty and accountability for carrying out my objectives.

It isn't a perfect system. It's a gamble, in fact. You have to rely on your judgment of character and ability. Sometimes mistakes are made, but part of the job of being governor is to live with the performance of the people to whom you delegate. If that person does a super job and gets the results you want, you bask in the sunshine of achievement and success, and we're all happy. If the reverse happens, as occasionally it did, you personally must suffer the pain of having blown it.

Part of this open process requires that one is open with the public, as well as with the department heads, when mistakes are made. If the department head accepted the mistake, assumed accountability and took corrective action, I would back him. Occasionally, that didn't happen. When a problem surfaces, it is critical to know as soon as possible if you've picked a person who simply can't take care of it; and you have to remove that person from the administration as quickly as possible.

The hardest part of any management job is looking an individual in the eye, someone who may have started out with high hopes of achievement, and telling that person that the opportunities you previously discussed and the positive things that you had hoped for are not achievable. You have to make a change. That is difficult to do; but it is something I believe a governor must do personally. It is not something you should delegate to your executive assistant.

One area of constant concern to a governor is corrections. It is rare indeed to find an individual with the necessary special abilities to manage that enormous responsibility well. On one occasion a serious breach of procedure occurred and an innocent party was permanently disabled. The failure of the department head to recognize the obvious predictability of the incident, a symptom of poor management in corrections, was a clear failure to perform his duty. If the department head had come in with an action plan to overcome the situation, I would have backed him. Instead there was no action, only excuses. I had to go to someone else to get my answers. Those answers triggered my request for the department head's resignation.

You have to suffer failures occasionally in order to have successes. You've got to back up risk-takers in order to encourage people to try out new ideas that might succeed. A department head must know whenever he gets out on a limb that if he falls the governor will fall with him. That allows you to develop a mutual loyalty with people. That loyalty factor is not a casual relationship. It creates a lot of emotion, and that's why it's critical to avoid mistakes in the selection process at the front end. I never had much patience for the "play it safe" manager who attempted to minimize failures. Those people rarely have successes.

A Sense of Urgency

Peters and Waterman suggest that the successful private sector company's motto is "Ready, Fire, Aim." Those companies are in a hurry to get things done. Government has a tendency to want to study issues to death.

It is my judgment that there are already sufficient checks and balances in the system — the legislature, the courts and the public — to safeguard the commonwealth. Therefore, a governor must infuse a sense of urgency in the people who do the public's business. Problems must be faced and dealt with. Ideas tried. Changes made.

A governor should give agency directors the freedom to try new methods of solving problems without an elaborate check and balance system within the executive branch. Management agencies, such as finance and personnel, need to find ways to assist, not hinder, public management. Control of the operations of government is best exercised through accountability for results, not through an up-front approval process for every action.

Governors need to recognize that their political longevity is limited. To foster change, a high level of energy is constantly required to prevent inertia from sapping the strength of new ideas.

Conclusion

I believe it's possible for a governor to encourage and create excellence in government. A governor has to do so by understanding the similarities as well as the differences between the public and private sectors. One can't slavishly imitate private sector practices; yet, one *can* look at the kinds of behavior that successful organizations depict and emulate that behavior. I've tried to distill some of those elements here and relate them to my administration. Hopefully, there are lessons for other governors and managers of the public trust.

My administration was not without its problems and failures. But I think we were successful in creating a drive toward excellence in public management. To do so, it was necessary to articulate a set of values and define a set of public goals for state government. It was critical to find the right people and to *rely* on those individuals, and together to motivate the state work force. This would not have succeeded had I not had the backing of the public and the political muscle to get the legislative policy necessary to achieve those public goals.

I regularly worked a sixty-hour week, and seventy to eighty hours were not unusual. I expected and received great dedication from those who worked with me. I think that this commitment enabled my administration to set the tone for the rest of state government. Morale among the state workers stayed at a high level throughout my two terms, and I believe we managed state government well and initiated policy directions that will continue to guide the state in the years to come.

CHAPTER 17

The Emergence of Regional and National Organizations

WHEN I was elected governor in 1976, it was clear to me that along with taking care of Utah's business, I wanted to involve myself in regional and national issues. At the time, I really had no idea of the future extent of my involvement. As things turned out, I spent a great deal of time working with my colleagues to streamline both regional and national governors' organizations. The challenges were formidable, but in retrospect, they were among the most rewarding ones I faced in my entire eight years in office.

I know there are still governors who believe that their responsibilities end at the state line, and that they need only pay superficial attention to regional issues. That attitude, however, is less prevalent today than it was in years past, and most governors depend increasingly on their affiliations with regional and national governors' organizations for the clout they need to deal effectively with regional problems and the federal government.

The reforms we made in our regional governors' organizations and in the National Governors' Association (NGA) were substantive and resulted in greatly improved services and forums for Utah.

My predecessor, Governor Calvin L. Rampton, (D., Ut.) had a hand in sparking the beginnings of a long period of regional introspection that would eventually lead, during my administration, to some extensive revamping of western governors' organizations and, to a certain extent, the focus of the NGA. The seeds for his active involvement were sown while he was in Washington, D.C. testifying, as chairman of the NGA, on revisions to the Federal Highway Act of 1955.

The problem Rampton discovered was an enormous proliferation of multistate organizations and the unaccountability to state chief executives of representatives of state executive branch organizations (EBOs). At the hearing, Rampton was surprised to learn that an official of the American Association of State Highway and Transportation Officials—individuals who should be working with, and accountable to, their governors—took a position directly contrary to the governors on how to use the Highway Trust Fund.

After he examined the problem more closely, he began to understand the serious extent to which EBOs had begun to cut their own deals in the federal triangle consisting of congressional committees, the federal and state bureaucrats responsible for programs and the recipients of program benefits.

The problem Rampton saw was one I would also face, and, as I became aware of just how negatively it affected governmental efficiency, I began to view my role in the western states, and eventually as NGA chairman, as one of trying to reduce the proliferation of multistate organizations and to make the EBOs more accountable to their governors.

The coalition of governors which later became the NGA was first convened in 1907 by a former governor, President Theodore Roosevelt. Governors had never met collectively before that time, and Roosevelt wanted them to back his new conservation program. Obviously, he felt it would be more efficient to get them together in a single meeting than trying to convince them individually of the importance of his program. Governors have met as a national group every year since the Roosevelt meeting.

The multistate organization concept was broadened in 1932 with the creation of the Council of State Governments (CSG) headquartered in Lexington, Kentucky. The CSG was an effort on the part of the states, which were then reeling under the weight of the Great Depression, to pull together interest groups and elected officials in every strata of state government. The initial membership of CSG included the governors, other executive branch elected officials, and legislators. Eventually, the organization became a "holding company" for the National Governors' Conference, four Regional Governors' Conferences, the National Conference of State Legislators and, as time passed, for a number of EBOs such as personnel officers, budget directors, state planners, finance directors, transportation and welfare officials.

Early meetings of the National Governors' Conference and the regional governors' groups were largely social events. The substantive part of their meetings was in the morning, and the rest of the day was spent in socializing. Press criticism of this socializing increased and a number of governors began to work in the direction of a more efficient use of their time together.

The Maturation of State Governments

As I have mentioned, the 1960s and 1970s were a period during which state governments began to mature significantly. Earlier, states had been on the defensive because of the tremendous increases in federal activity that had begun under Franklin D. Roosevelt's administration and accelerated under President Lyndon B. Johnson. The federal government had assumed program after program which the states were either unwilling or unable to handle.

In the mid-1960s more than half of the nation's governors had to run for reelection every two years, and most had very limited power. There were no services at the national level available to assist governors to do the type of job they should do. The same was true of the legislative branch. State legislatures were unstaffed, provincial and virtually none of them, with the exception of California and New York, had sophisticated organizational structures.

State constitutional changes have since increased the terms of most governors to four years and strengthened their budget authority. In addition, the number of other elected officials unresponsive or unaccountable to the governor has been dramatically reduced over the years, and executive reorganizations have created more streamlined state models with fewer officials reporting directly to the governors. Most state legislatures now have full-time staffs and fiscal analysts to assist them both in the legislative and appropriation processes. Legislative auditor generals examine whether or not the executive branch is carrying out legislative intent.

After the Vietnam War and Watergate, the notion that the federal government could or should solve all the nation's problems came under fire. People began to look more to their state governments for solutions. During the 1970s, a new breed of governor was coming into power. The back-slapping politician was replaced by a younger, better educated, more dynamic governor who was more interested in improving the quality of state government than in patronage appointments.

The modernization and improvement in governors, and of the state executive and legislative branch organizations as well, coincided with major growth at the federal level of the federal grant-in-aid structure. Those federal actions, in some ways, created the impetus for reevaluation of the organizational structure of the governors.

Federal "Top Down" Regionalism

President Lyndon B. Johnson's Great Society created 208 new pieces of legislation for grants in aid aimed at state and local governments. This doubled the existing grant-in-aid structure and began to put considerable stress on delivery mechanisms. One of the new programs was the Economic Development Act of 1965. That act encouraged the states to get together in logical regions to work together to solve their economic problems. Funding was provided for a small staff, and grants were allocated to the states from regional commission funds. Within ten years of the act, regional commissions (Title V commissions) existed throughout the entire nation. Utah was a member of the Four Corners Regional Commission, which initially included Utah, Colorado, New

Mexico and Arizona. Nevada, not one of the original Four Corners members, was later added.

In a 1969 executive order, President Richard M. Nixon added another federal layer through the creation of ten federal regions in an attempt to consolidate the regional headquarters of all major federal entities into one location. In the West, there were three regions – one based in Denver, one in San Francisco and the third one in Dallas. While Nixon was attempting to deliver federal services in a more efficient manner, it is interesting to note that his federal regions concept did not geographically correspond with the Title V regional commissions developed by President Johnson in his Economic Development Act of 1965. Thus, within the Four Corners Commission, Utah and Colorado were part of the federal region headquartered in Denver. New Mexico's federal region was in Dallas and Arizona's and Nevada's were in San Francisco.

There is still strong disagreement over whether these regional groupings actually provided any substantive assistance to state and local governments. Many, including President Reagan, argue that they merely created another overlapping bureaucratic layer. Shortly after his election, Reagan eliminated both the Title V commissions and the ten regions created by Nixon.

In one important way, top-down, federally-imposed regionalism succeeded. It forced governors to talk among themselves within a regional context. Soon, they began to sense that there were some serious regional concerns not being met by the state individuals and certainly not by the umbrella organizations created within the CSG framework, such as the Western Governors' Conference.

Western Governors Pull Their Act Together

During the mid-1960s, several new governors were elected who began to look at emerging issues from a regional perspective. They saw what the federal government was attempting to do. They took a look at the decision to develop the Title V regional commissions and decided that, while the federal government had made an initial decision concerning regional boundaries, a different grouping of states might make more sense.

Several western governors wanted to develop the regional idea. The Federation of Rocky Mountain States was created in 1965 by governors Jack Campbell (D., N.M.), John Love (R., Colo.) and Utah's Democratic governor, Calvin Rampton. The federation focused on the commonality of the public lands characteristics of the Rocky Mountain Region. It was also characterized by a private, as well as public, component; it brought governors together with businessmen who were interested in public policy.

The Yom Kippur War in the 1970s and the energy crisis that resulted from it made the energy-rich Rocky Mountain West very attractive to developers. At the same time, there were increasing concerns about environmental policies to guide energy development. Many of the governors who were elected during this period were concerned about the "rape and run" attitude which characterized a number of the emerging developers. Some of these governors, like Richard Lamm (D., Colo.), Ed Herschler (D., Wyo.) and Jerry Apodaca (D., N.M.), were not comfortable with creating public policy in tandem with the private sector when they saw so many of the private sector interests attempting to exploit the West and its land and resources.

In the 1970s governors were attending Western Governors' Conference meetings, Title V regional commission meetings and Federation of Rocky Mountain States meetings. Many were not convinced that any of those entities were going to provide the effective coalition needed to represent the Rocky Mountain region in Washington.

Led in the beginning by governors Lamm and Tom Judge (D., Mont.), governors began to take a hard look at the three regional organizations and ultimately concluded that none of these organizations could serve their needs. The governors were uncomfortable having the private sector in on their deliberations. They recognized the need for a 'governors only' organization. In their estimation, the Western Governors' Conference was too much concerned with the social agenda and not concerned enough with the policy agenda.

Yet another western organization, the Western Governors' Regional Energy Policy Office (WGREPO), was formed in 1975 for the single purpose of dealing with energy development issues. While the energy crisis eventually evaporated, at its peak western governors were planning vast developments in oil shale and coal gasification. WGREPO was formed by members of the old Title V regional commissions – the five states in the Four Corners Commission and the five states in the Old West Regional Commission (North and South Dakota, Wyoming, Idaho and Nebraska), a group of states which, at that time, expected rapid energy development.

There was also a very strong environmental agenda that accompanied the creation of WGREPO. Rampton was initially suspicious of joining this group, because he felt environmental issues would dominate it, and he was a little wary of the new governor from Colorado, Richard Lamm, who had replaced his old friend, John Love.

Lamm had come to public prominence in Colorado by leading the successful effort in 1972 to oppose Denver's proposal to host the Winter Olympics. Nevertheless, Rampton eventually joined WGREPO even though he basically opposed the proliferation of western governors' organizations. Instead of three organizations, there were now four attempting to make some sense out of what was happening in the West.

In 1975, Lamm came to Salt Lake to visit Rampton, who was the leader of the development block in the western states. He was also chairman of the NGA and one of the nation's senior governors. Lamm recognized Rampton's position as senior leader in this region and the validity of his development agenda. But he wanted to find a way to bring some logic to the regional approach. "What's happening is we are getting played off," Lamm said. "The federal government and private interests are playing us off, one against the other, and we won't compete regionally until we can work together harmoniously."

Rampton remained wary but recognized the merit in Lamm's arguments. The Utah governor was an institution builder and had been a leader in strengthening the National Governors' Association. In August of 1976, at an NGA meeting in Hershey, Pennsylvania, the western governors created a task force which had two basic objectives: To stop the proliferation of governors' organizations and to get greater control and accountability over western EBOs.

Sixteen states were represented on the task force, and they reported back to their governors in December 1976, recommending the creation of a new sixteen-state western regional policy organization that would combine the geography of WGREPO with the Pacific Rim. The governors gave preliminary approval to the plan the same month and set the date for final ratification at the Western Governors' Conference meeting the following year in Anchorage, Alaska. Essentially, the proposal was to consolidate the Western Governors' Conference into a larger and stronger policy-making organization, basically run by the governors themselves.

Nineteen seventy-six was an election year, and several strong governors who had been proponents of consolidation were replaced. That was the year I replaced Rampton, and I was committed to the consolidation. I retained Rampton's federal-state coordinator, Kent Briggs, who had been intimately involved in the consolidation strategy. But Cecil Andrus (D., Id.), Dan Evans (R., Wash.) and Tom McCall (R., Ore.) were gone. Jerry Brown (D., Ca.) and several other new governors were not supportive of the consolidation approach.

The staff of the Western Governors' Conference located in San Francisco began to lobby governors to oppose the consolidation and the effort created divided loyalties. They attempted to create the impression that some of the new aggressive governors like Lamm and Judge were trying to grab power. There were also some personal feelings against some of the staff members involved in the consolidation effort. Some of the trouble was plainly due to personality clashes. For example, Governor

Mike O'Callahan (D. Nev.) told Lamm that unless Lamm fired one of his staff persons involved in creating the new organization, he would not join. By the time of the Anchorage meeting, the debate was heated and emotional. Nevertheless, a new organization, the Western Governors' Policy Office (WESTPO), was created at the September 1977 Alaska meeting. I won't forget the haggling we had to wade through in order to create the new entity. Unfortunately, bitter feelings split the governors, and not all of the western states joined.

WESTPO was to serve as a regional forum and to provide a mechanism for its member governors to address and influence important national, regional, interstate and federal-state issues. The new organization, headquartered in Denver, provided a vehicle for collective political expression and influence, an important asset for the sparsely-populated western states. It served as an instrument for policy management, identifying and dealing with issues that crosscut functional areas.

During the Anchorage meeting, I felt sure we had picked a winner in WESTPO, and subsequent experience proved that to be true. With the organization of WESTPO, the Federation of Rocky Mountain States and WGREPO were eliminated. However, because not all of the western states joined WESTPO, the Western Governors' Conference remained active. WESTPO was essentially a high focus, activist entity that eventually brought together thirteen interior states of the Rocky Mountain region.

During the period from 1977 to 1983, there were two western governors' organizations, both claiming legitimacy to represent the West. It was a jumble, and I threatened a number of times to resign from the Western Governors' Conference. But because the WGC and the CSG were the umbrella organizations for a number of EBOs, such as the Western States Water Council, the Western Interstate Commission on Higher Education and the Western Interstate Energy Board, we did not achieve the second objective of our two-part consolidation effort, accountability from EBOs.

WESTPO developed a Western Coal Export Task Force, with me serving as chairman, to look at the possibility of marketing intermountain steam coal to Japan and other foreign countries, and that led me to consider the possibility of trying to include the Pacific Rim states and territories in our organization. The idea was simple: If we were really going to be serious about exporting coal to the Far East, we would have to use West Coast ports. Our staff began to work with their counterparts in Washington, Oregon, California and Hawaii. These discussions began to break down the tensions created with the organization of WESTPO.

WESTPO significantly improved its member states' regional efficiency, but by the early 1980s, it was clear that having two separate governors' groups in the West was counterproductive. Accordingly, with the backing of a few of my western colleagues, I began to work on a consolidation plan. The process was to take almost four years of painful negotiations.

At the November 19-20, 1982 annual meeting of WESTPO in Colorado Springs, Colorado, I was interviewed by Malin Foster, managing editor of a Logan, Utah newspaper and later my press secretary. "We have two governors' organizations overlapping," I told him, "and they both perform valuable services, but the idea of having duplicate entities dealing with the same issues twice amounts to reinventing the wheel too often."

By the time we convened the Colorado Springs meeting, I had discussed the matter with all of the governors involved. Some were very receptive, but many were skeptical. Some of my colleagues were worried that including all the WESTPO states with the Pacific Rim states did not actually constitute a cohesive region. They were concerned that the problems of the Pacific Northwest, California, Hawaii and our Pacific territories were not the same as those of the interior Rocky Mountain region. Others were concerned about the futures of the staff members who were already entrenched in WESTPO and in the Western Governors' Conference.

At this point, I wasn't exactly overwhelmed by support, but the fact that we were arguing about details was at least an indication that the governors were giving the proposal some serious thought. I was still firmly convinced that despite some regional differences, we were still the West, and we needed unity in order to meet the growing challenges we faced on both the regional and national levels.

The proposal gained more support by the time the June 26-28, 1983 annual meeting of the Western Governors' Conference was convened in Kalispell, Montana. Between the Colorado Springs and Kalispell meetings, I had substantially refined the proposal. Essentially, we finally agreed in Montana that we would be far better served by a single, powerful western regional governors' association, particularly on national political issues. Two months later, during the August 18-20 WESTPO annual meeting in Bismark, North Dakota, the WESTPO governors endorsed the plan we had agreed upon in Montana. The next step was to obtain the formal support of the Western Governors' Conference.

I was chairman of the National Governors' Association in 1983 and in that position, I felt even more responsibility to continue my attempts at pulling the western governors together. I could see, as a result of my national activities, how important unity would be in the future.

There was still some convincing to do before we could formalize the merger of the two organizations, and one of the key steps I took in 1983 was to write a long letter — it could almost be called a white paper — to Oregon Governor Victor Atiyeh, who was then chairman of the Western Governors' Conference. I suggested that we ought to try to set an example in the West and consider an NGA model.

When a governor is elected, he is automatically a member of the National Governors' Association. At that time, however, when a western governor was elected, there was a battle for his participation in both the Western Governors' Conference and WESTPO. Of course, that made no sense. I therefore asked Atiyeh to continue an open review of the issue. I suggested that we continue our negotiations, but that we do so on the condition that we would make no decision as to where the headquarters of the new organization would be located, what its name would be or who would staff the new entity.

The process culminated in February 1984 at the midwinter meeting of the NGA in the formal creation of the Western Governors' Association, which now encompasses states from Nebraska to the northern Mariana Islands. I was elated. The bitter divisions and the complications of having two duplicating organizations were behind us.

What we gained in this new entity — composed of eighteen states and the Pacific territories — was a commonality of focus similar to WESTPO. There remains concern that California, which is so large and diverse it is almost a nation in itself, does not really fit in any region. And size is always a factor in operating efficiently and cooperatively. However, I feel the advantages of an entire consolidated West in terms of policy clout clearly offset those disadvantages.

Reform in the National Governors' Association

At the same time we were wrapping up the restructuring of our regional organization, there was strong sentiment for reform in the National Governors' Association (NGA).

Through the years, most states had developed their own ways of dealing with the federal government, but the only organization that gives state chief executives a chance to argue in a unified voice remains the NGA. In 1965 the National Governors' Conference was a creature of the Council of State Governments (CSG). Governor Dan Evans (R., Wash.) was chairman of the conference in 1971-72, and along with Rampton and other senior governors, led the move to strengthen the National Governors' Conference. The first step took place in 1966 when the governors established an office for federal-state relations in Washington under the auspices of the Council of State Governments. This was a full-time governors' lobby, funded by annual appropriations from the states.

Governor Evans argued that governors needed to shed the CSG, which could not engage in lobbying. The final disaffiliation came in 1975. The governors created a separate, non-profit Center for Policy Research and Analysis to serve as their think tank.

In 1975, the National Governors' Conference (NGC) also approved the concept of consolidating several state offices and other state lobby groups scattered throughout the city into one building called the "Hall of the States." The move provided central coordination of state efforts for the first time. Two of the governors' major staff support groups — the budget directors under the auspices of a National Association of State Budget Officers (NASBO), and the planners, under the Council of State Planning Agencies (CSPA) — also left the umbrella CSG organization and joined the NGC.

At their 1977 annual meeting, the governors changed their name to the National Governors' Association, because the word "association" reflected the full-time, active nature of the organization. Currently, the NGA has its own multi-million-dollar budget, employs a complete staff of professionals and is directly managed by an Executive Committee of nine governors, a significant departure from the 1960s when they had four employees and were beholden to CSG.

The Decision to Seek the NGA Chairmanship

During the time I was working on my opposition to MX deployment in Utah, I had several opportunities to informally talk about the NGA with my MX Project Manager Ken Olsen and with my federal-state coordinator Kent Briggs, who would later become my executive assistant. Both had done significant work with the NGA — Olsen as a special advisor to Evans during the reorganizational efforts in the early 1970s, and Briggs as the federal-state assistant to Rampton when he was NGA chairman in 1974-75. The chairmanship alternates between Republicans and Democrats. George Busbee (D., Ga.) was the current chairman, and the incoming chairman was Richard Snelling (R., Vt.). The political arms of the NGA, the Democratic governors and the Republican governors caucus, make the final selection. With Olsen and Briggs, I laid out a strategy for nailing down the necessary support to succeed Snelling as NGA chairman.

Winning the chairmanship required a personal relationship with every other Democratic governor. I spent countless hours on the telephone with each, and over the years had innumerable personal contacts. The key to my success was the investment of close association with most of the governors over the early years of my membership. Loyalties were in place by the time the campaign began and basically assured my election. And, like any good politician, I knew how to count the votes early. One of the perceptions I had was that the NGA staff was too wound up in the affairs of Washington, D.C. and didn't pay enough attention to what was going on in the states. I thought NGA could do a better job of supporting the governors in their efforts to become more efficient and could provide a structure for innovation and dissemination of information. I also had made dramatic improvements in the data processing and communication capacity in my own state and knew that the NGA was simply not equipped, in a technological sense, to deal with its modern role.

I was also concerned with the tendency of the governors to continually go to Capitol Hill to seek more funding without providing any overall framework for legitimate federal support to states and localities. While NGA had become a strong lobbying force on the Hill, its credibility was often suspect. As federal deficits grew, the governors continued to argue for more money and to avoid program cuts. That approach was neither realistic nor in the public interest.

After election by the Democratic governors' caucus as chairman-elect in February 1981, I met with Snelling to get his authorization to head up a group of governors from the executive committee who would look at the future of the NGA. He agreed this would be an appropriate thing for me to do.

I put together a committee which I called the Agenda for the Eighties. In addition to myself, the other members included governors George Busbee (D., Ga.), Bob Ray (R., Ia.) and William Milliken (R., Mich.). All three had served as NGA chairmen, and Ray and Milliken, who were retiring in 1982, had each served more than fourteen years as governor. While I had some perceptions of what was needed, the perspectives of these governors and their staffs heavily influenced the final report, which was approved by all of the governors at the NGA annual meeting in the summer of 1982 when I took over as chairman.

From my perspective, the Agenda for the Eighties dialogue resulted in a number of positive changes for the organization. One of my major goals was to enhance the professional services to the governors, and one of our efforts was to improve the new governors' seminar, affectionately labeled "charm school." In 1982, we held the new governors' seminar in Park City, Utah. We made a concerted effort to increase the caliber of programs presented to new governors on how to govern effectively and provided them with technical information on what they needed to do to enhance their budgeting efforts, develop their legislative programs, select their personnel, handle appointments, handle crises, etc. The faculty for the meeting was composed primarily of sitting governors. We had a program for spouses which focused on the special problems they would face, such as dealing with the executive residence, their own appointments and deciding to what extent they wanted to participate in the administration. The NGA now provides follow-up technical assistance to any governor upon request.

I also wanted to strengthen the state services side of the NGA staff. That proved to be more difficult, partly because of budget concerns and partly because of organizational inertia within the NGA staff.

NGA's executive committee provides the overall direction for the organization, but it also had a separate committee on executive management and fiscal affairs that handled many of the crosscutting issues dealing with the states and the federal government. We decided that we needed to assign those crosscutting issues directly to the executive committee. That decision, along with selection of a new executive director of the association, were instrumental in getting the governors involved in the debate over the federal budget in 1982.

A third response from the Agenda for the Eighties was the need to bring the organization into the modern world of information systems. We found that about half of the states didn't have even rudimentary computers in the chief executive's office. In fact, one or two governors refused to have them. We recommended a central telecommunications and data processing system for the Hall of the States, run either by NGA or the central services organization of the building. This was an extremely difficult and painstaking effort due to the complex nature of the equipment selection process. A number of states had companies that wanted to receive the bids, and some states had a wide range of different systems, many of which were incompatible with one another. After negotiating for more than a year, we finally agreed on a system which is now fully operational.

Part of my personal agenda was to replace Steve Farber, the executive director of NGA. Farber had been director for a number of years, and he deserves credit for developing a professional NGA staff and providing more visibility for the governors in Washington, D.C. Farber's credentials as an advocate for the states and the governors were not the issue; I believe we needed new leadership that would aggressively push the governors forward on national issues. After I became chairman elect, I sounded out other governors on a possible change. Steve has many friends among the governors and discussions concerning a new director were spirited. However, the executive committee supported my views and Farber gracefully resigned.

The new executive director, Raymond Scheppach, who was deputy director of the Congressional Budget Office, was selected in the fall of 1982 after an extensive search by the NGA executive committee. Mr. Scheppach represented the opportunity for us to take a more aggressive stance before Congress, to improve the quality of our staff work and become more effective in lobbying our positions on the Hill. He pressed the governors to take stronger and more responsive stands on major policy issues and utilized us very effectively in lobbying states' positions on the Hill. With these actions, our earlier credibility problems were basically overcome.

Another effort in the Agenda for the Eighties was to again attempt a better integration of EBOs to support the governors' efforts. One success was in a new relationship with the National Association of State Budget Officers. They had also selected a new executive director, former Michigan Budget Director Jerry Miller, who increased the ability of that organization to provide budget and fiscal information for the governors. Over two or three years, a new institutional relationship has developed which, in effect, has made Mr. Miller a significant staff support for the governors on fiscal and budget matters.

I attempted, while I was chairman, to get all of the major EBOs to sign affiliate agreements with the NGA indicating they would not take policy positions contrary to the governors and that they would provide staff support to the various governors' committees. I was only moderately successful in this effort because of a great deal of foot-dragging by the EBOs. They had countless reasons why they thought the affiliation agreements would not work effectively. When my successor, Governor Jim Thompson (R., Ill.), did not show the same enthusiasm for corralling the EBOs, the matter was dropped, and today they remain basically independent.

The NGA as a Policy Maker

During the last several years, the governors have gained new credibility with Congress through their effective and persuasive lobbying efforts. A number of specific efforts, including discussion of a national water policy, opposition to the Emergency Mobilization Board (which the governors were able to kill), continuation of the wastewater construction grant program and the governors' position on the federal budget policy have served to enhance our credibility.

We were particularly effective in working for the passage of the Nickle Gas Tax in the fall of 1982. Secretary of Transportation Drew Lewis had proposed the tax to provide additional revenue for the federal government and the states for completion of the Interstate Highway System. But we were in a serious recession, and the states needed the money. This was a way to get the necessary funding out to the construction community as well as enhancing the economies of the states and the nation. The President approved of the proposal, and Congress went into a lame duck session in the fall of 1982 to consider the issue.

Representing the governors was the NGA Committee on Transportation, headed by Governor Bob Orr (R., Ind.) and very capably staffed by Charilyn Cowan. She was so knowledgeable on the intricacies of the federal highway policy that she was able, in a single weekend, to take all of the concerns that Congress had raised with Secretary Lewis's initial proposal and redraft all of those into legislation to the satisfaction of the Transportation Committee, Bob Orr and myself. She met with Drew Lewis on Sunday morning, and the administration agreed to the bill. It was presented to Congress the next week, and it passed.

Secretary Lewis said after that occasion that the NGA made the difference in getting the bill through. That pleased me a great deal; the states were very much in need of the additional funds, and it really showed, in a dramatic way, how governors could effectively influence an important piece of legislation.

The Future of NGA and WGA

To a large extent, the effectiveness of organizations like the NGA and WGA are dependent upon the capability of the staffs involved, but, even more importantly, that effectiveness depends upon the leadership of those who steer such organizations. Poor leadership can only result in the paralysis and eventual demise of these organizations.

The chairman must be willing to spend much of his personal time on the business at hand; staff members simply do not have the necessary influence on other governors and on federal and congressional leaders. In order for these organizations to grow and to develop the clout we want them to have, the leaders must continue to have a deep personal commitment.

If the states are to reassert their proper role in the federal system, the governors must become stronger players in the congressional process. It will not only take a strong resolve on the part of the governors to see it happen, but it will require continual lobbying efforts, bringing the states' case before a reluctant Congress. The NGA will also have to develop coalitions with representatives of local and county governments if it is to continue to gain credibility and the reputation it needs to be effective. Governors sometimes tend to be impatient with local governmental entities, but we must all realize that any major restructuring of our federal system will not occur without their active participation.

On the regional front, leadership is also the key to the long-range success of the Western Governors' Association. I still believe that regional organizations can provide easy access to vastly expanded resources for governors. They are easy to use, but, unfortunately, they are too often the least used. Governors need to focus more attention on regional activities.

We have the regional vehicle, and it offers states the resources and the focus to work together on a wide variety of issues in a large, potentially powerful regional bloc. Bringing the Pacific Rim states and territories into the association, for example, has opened the door to new opportunities for economic development in the areas of high technology, tourism and trade. The WGA has a responsibility to cultivate these Pacific ties, even though it may appear that the day-to-day issues of the interior states do not always have much relation to what's going on in Hawaii and beyond. The future success of the West is heavily dependent on economic expansion in the Pacific, as well as our recognition that western unity from Micronesia to Nebraska is essential in the competitive regional environment of the 1980s.

CHAPTER 18

The Governors Debate the Federal Budget

ONE of the toughest challenges the governors took on during and after my term as NGA chairman was the federal budget deficit. That experience was not completely successful, but it proved once again that if governors are united in a common cause, they can have a significant impact on national governmental policy.

In his interview for the position of NGA director, Ray Scheppach was blunt with us. He told us that if we wanted to have policy impact on Capitol Hill, we would have to develop a defensible position on the federal budget. We could not simply come in every year and ask that federal dollars going to state and local governments not be reduced by Congress while cuts were occurring in other places.

It had been difficult for governors to take a substantive position on the federal budget, because very few had detailed knowledge of most of the complex issues, particularly those concerning defense. In addition, we shared a philosophical concern about whether or not we should take positions on the federal budget apart from those areas directly impacting state and local governments. Scheppach, the former deputy at the Congressional Budget Office, gave us the capacity to articulate an effective overall budget position. In addition, a number of young Democratic governors assumed office in 1983 in the midst of a deep recession. Faced with the prospects of cutting state services and raising taxes, they were more militant in their views of the national economy and the impacts of the reduced federal budget; they effectively prodded the NGA into deliberations over federal budget matters.

It was the governors' view that the deficit was hurting state and local governments. In the past, deficits of $50 to $60 billion were considered unthinkable, but we were now looking at projected deficits of $200 billion or more. The deficits were fueled by poor economic growth in the country, and a permanent mismatch of revenues and expenditures as a result of the 1981 tax cuts. The high interest rates that existed during this period were hitting some industries — agriculture, automobiles and housing — very hard and slowing overall capital expansion.

Even though the constitutions or statutes of forty-nine of the fifty states require balanced state budgets, six states would close fiscal year 1983 with year-end deficits, and five more with zero balances. During 1982 and 1983, forty-four states increased taxes, and forty-three others initiated various cost-cutting measures. When looking at the size of the state tax increases versus the federal tax decreases, governors had to ask themselves whether or not the net effect resulted in any real savings to the taxpayers.

Early in 1983, with the support of Scheppach and several key NGA executive committee members, I proposed that we consider and adopt a comprehensive position on the federal budget. As I saw the condition of the states and the federal deficit problems plaguing the nation, it was clear that discretionary federal aid to states and municipalities would again be a target for cuts by the Reagan Administration. Federalism negotiations had broken down. The President was under pressure to reduce the deficits. The governors needed to develop a strong bargaining position to respond to whatever the administration proposed.

The NGA Winter Meeting, 1983

The budget resolution presented at our 1983 winter meeting was essentially drafted by Governor Richard Lamm (D., Col.), NGA Vice Chairman Jim Thompson (R., Ill.) and myself with strong support from Ray Scheppach. It was Thompson's job to hold the Republicans together on a budget resolution; for that to happen it couldn't appear too anti-Reagan. Nevertheless, we wanted it to have some teeth when we went to Congress. During the debate over the budget, we had credible testimony from both congressional sources and private individuals concerning the importance of driving the budget deficit down.

Congressman Jim Jones (D., Okla.), chairman of the House Budget Committee, Senator Pete Domenici (R., N.M.), chairman of the Senate Finance Committee, Peter G. Peterson, former Secretary of Commerce and then chairman of a bipartisan group of business leaders organized to balance the budget, and others were unanimous in their views about the general direction that was required. They all felt that despite the President's pledge to hold fast to the 1981 tax cuts, some combination of budget reductions and tax increases would be necessary to drive the budget deficit below $100 billion.

Both Jones and Domenici were totally committed to a balanced budget policy. Neither were timid about facing up to the hard choices in budget reductions and new taxes to achieve the goal of a sane national fiscal policy. I told them during the meeting that I would be perfectly willing to have them jointly design the federal budget and would be comfortable in supporting it sight unseen.

During the days leading to the final NGA vote, each word in the budget resolution was carefully scrutinized. Several compromises were made on both the Democratic and Republican sides in order to get a consensus position. Although I was chairman of a bipartisan organization, it was difficult for the Democratic governors to resist confronting the Reagan Administration's budget policies, "Reaganomics" and the impact of the recession on their state programs. Several alternative Democratic governors' resolutions were floating around, and they were much more strident in their anti-Reagan approach. Some of the governors, like Anthony Earl (D., Wis.) and Toney Anaya (D., N.M.), wanted to turn the budget discussion into a full-fledged Reaganomics debate. Earl, in particular, was very effective.

The NGA staff and Scheppach, however, felt the issue was so divisive that it would be impossible to get consensus. Many of the governors' staff members were concerned about the political implications; they worried about how a resolution cutting the budget, potentially raising taxes, and calling for social security reform would play back home. In fact, several staff members informally asked that I withdraw the resolution.

My approach, however, was to allow free debate and give all governors a chance to vent their feelings. During the Democratic caucus prior to the closing Plenary Session, I told the Democratic governors that I had never attempted to advise any governor on how to vote on a particular resolution, and I wasn't about to begin. I recognized there was a wide divergence of views, but I also stressed the fact that the budget resolution was a critical step in our efforts to increase our credibility as an effective governors' organization. It was also clear to every Democratic governor that the chairman was somewhat "out on a limb" on the budget issue, and that without their support the effort would fail.

In my opening remarks to the March 1 NGA Plenary Session, I said we were participants in a historic meeting, because for the first time we were wrestling with the full weight of the federal budget. I noted that many governors believed the current deficits were the "tip of an enormous iceberg which threatens to tear apart the strained superstructure of state and local government financing. These past few years, we have nervously eyed this iceberg, hoping to navigate around it by raising taxes and cutting budgets. But the projected deficits—whether we use projections of the administration or the Congressional Budget Office— are unacceptable and pose a clear and present danger to our ships of state."

I knew that it would be a disaster for the NGA to be split by partisan differences. Accordingly, I concluded, "When we act as an association of governors, we leave party labels at the door, bringing only the concerns of our citizens and our states to this table . . . As governors, we can play a strong role in shaping the congressional budget response if we can reach a substantive consensus here. While I expect the debate to be spirited, I hope you will not forget our goal—to restore hope and prosperity to every state in this country."

The debate *was* spirited and often heavily partisan. Staff from the White House, including Rich Williamson, lobbied against the resolution, but in the end, Thompson was able to get all but one Republican to support it. A majority of the Democratic governors went along with the consensus resolution, voting against several stronger Democratic alternatives. Governor Dick Riley (D., S.C.), was particularly effective in a floor speech on behalf of the resolution. I considered the successful outcome a major first step in making the governors active players in the budget debate, and the experience proved a perfect example of what the NGA can do, as long as its members are unified. As chairman, I had also passed a major test.

NGA Budget Policy

The governors supported the Social Security reform recommendations of the bipartisan commission appointed by the President. This included delaying the cost-of-living adjustment (COLA), a fifty percent tax for high-income individuals and an increase in the payroll tax.

On nondefense discretionary spending, which included grants to state and local governments, assistance to business and commerce, veteran's health care, environmental regulations and other general government programs, we recommended that Congress restrict the fiscal year 1984-1988 increases to three-fourths the rate of inflation.

We urged full funding for income-based entitlement programs, including AFDC, Food Stamps, Medicaid, Child Nutrition and SSI, noting that budgets for these programs had already been significantly cut during fiscal years 1982 and 1983.

Regarding entitlement programs not based on need (non-means tested entitlement programs), we suggested significant reductions, including the various medical insurance, disability and retirement programs funded by the federal government.

In national defense, we argued for a growth rate of between three and five percent in real terms over the 1984-1988 fiscal period. We noted that defense had increased almost fifty-seven percent over the 1981-1983 period and felt that we should modernize our defense system but slow the rate of increase. We were supported in this view by several former secretaries of defense.

Finally, while we did not endorse any specific revenue proposals, we indicated that revenues would have to increase enough to offset the remaining portion of the deficit to reach a goal of two percent of GNP. By fiscal year 1988, the projected deficit of $267 billion (CBO's projection) would be reduced, under the governors' plan, by $177 billion, leaving a remaining deficit of $90 billion, or about two percent of GNP. While the $90 billion was higher than most governors would have wished, it was simply not possible to devise a scheme acceptable to everyone that would reduce the deficit any further. At $90 billion, the so-called "structural deficit problem" would be eliminated, which meant that if we had full employment, we would actually balance the budget.

It was clear that the governors' actions had some impact on the congressional deliberations. The large budget cuts proposed by the President for aid to state and local governments were not enacted. In remarks I made closing my year of chairmanship of the NGA on July 31, 1983 in Portland, Maine, I noted the maturity of the governors in advancing their cause in Washington:

> The dynamics of our federal system in the past ten years have thrust governors into the Washington scene, whether they like it or not. We have pressed our case before Congress and the administration on issues ranging from water policy to health care, and it was a measure of our ascending influence that the 1984 federal budget resolution adopted by Congress bore an unmistakable print of the budget resolution adopted by the governors in March of 1983.

In a speech before The Brookings Institution on May 25, 1983, I noted that deficits that not long ago would have set the public howling draw barely a yawn today from even the most conservative quarters. As a result, too little thought is given to the devastating impact these budget overruns have on the future availability of private sector capital and on the treasuries of state and local governments. "Rhetoric about a balanced budget amendment was abundant last year, but it seems to have lost something in the translation from theory to practice," I said.

While not insensitive to the difficulties of reducing the federal budget deficit, I noted that state governments were forced, by constitutions and statutes, to balance their budgets. "Neither service cutbacks nor higher taxes are popular with the folks back home, but they are not unfamiliar to the nation's governors. Without 'budget resolutions' and $200 billion deficits to insulate us from political backlash, we've had to swallow hard and do whatever is necessary to balance our own state budgets," I said.

The Continuing Budget Debate

Governor James Thompson (R., Ill.) assumed chairmanship of the NGA at the August, 1983 meeting in Portland, Maine. I remained on the NGA executive committee and continued as lead governor on the federal budget. That issue would continue to dominate the attention of the governors through 1985.

Fiscal year 1983 ended on September 30 with a record deficit of $196 billion. When we opened our winter meeting in 1984, it was clear that a majority of governors wanted to take an even tougher stand on the federal budget than we had the previous year. In an article for the *Washington Post* on January 22, 1984, I joined with governors Lamm,

William Janklow (R., S.D.) and Snelling in arguing that "Federal deficits facing this country are a prescription for disaster. We are borrowing from our children to give ourselves tax relief, borrowing from our grandchildren to pay medical benefits that we really can't afford, borrowing from our great-grandchildren to get pensions that we know very well are chain letters to the future."

"We are four governors—two Democrats, two Republicans—who believe there is no higher priority in the American political scene than to form a bipartisan coalition to bring reality therapy to our disillusional belief that we can continue on this road to ruin," we wrote.

We then offered a "modest proposal as an agenda for a return to fiscal sanity." That agenda included limitations on increases in defense spending, reform of our health care systems and pensions, limiting the increases in Social Security to two percent below the rate of inflation, extending the retirement ages, pruning the tax deductions and credits granted to one group or another. We also proposed modification of the tax indexing law to provide for indexing at two percent below the inflation rate.

"Our thesis is that the current course of federal deficits is unsustainable and will lead this country into another recession and possibly into a depression. To finance deficits of the magnitude of $200 billion to $300 billion a year, every American worker would have to save $2,000 to $3,000 and loan it all to the federal government."

"In the end," we concluded, "we must find a way for our common interests as Americans to override our conflicting interests as retirees, doctors, military people, federal employees and so on. America's future is at stake, and we must be willing to make hard decisions."

As we approached the governors' winter meeting in 1984, we had five proposed policy positions from individual governors on the federal budget. Republican governors were urging support of a balanced budget amendment to the constitution and line-item veto power for the President. Democratic governors were decrying the President's cuts in low-income programs and urging an increase in federal tax revenues. The Democratic governors decided to adopt their own budget resolution prior to the NGA meeting as part of the Democratic governors' caucus, the language of which would be politically stronger than appropriate for the full governors' meeting.

On Saturday, February 25, the day before the opening of the governors' meeting, I had a special governors' work session on the federal budget. Nearly thirty of the nation's governors attended the afternoon workshop, which included presentations by Congressman Leon E. Panetta, chairman of the Budget Process Task Force, Martin Feldstein, chairman of the Council of Economic Advisors, Peter G. Peterson, founder of the bipartisan budget appeal, and Alice M. Rivlin, former director of the Congressional Budget Office and now director of economic studies programs at The Brookings Institution. Each urged us to continue our efforts on the federal budget deficit.

In a blunt statement adopted at the Plenary Session, we said that it was "critical that a federal deficit reduction program be enacted in 1984. While we support budget restraint and spending reductions in many areas, we have come to the conclusion that some tax increases are necessary to restore a proper balance between income and expenditures. Failure to address the problem this year will require stronger measures next year."

We urged Congress and the administration to agree on specific bipartisan deficit targets for each of the next five fiscal years. As a first step, the governors urged enactment of a three-year, $100 billion deficit "down payment." We also suggested that Congress adopt legislation to freeze the implementation of indexing income tax and COLAs on Social Security and other benefits, unless the budget adopted by Congress reached the deficit targets protected.

We were convinced that unless there was curtailment of automatic cost-of-living adjustments to benefits and to the income tax indexing that would force Congress to reduce the budget, we would continue to see "fiscal gridlock" — the inability of the administration and Congress to act. Unfortunately, that dilemma continued through 1984, an election year, and into 1985.

The Gramm-Rudman "Solution"

The action finally taken by the Congress and the President in December 1985 was not the result of a judicious compromise (as proposed by the governors in their budget resolution) over the growing federal debt — in 1986 approaching $2,000 billion ($2 trillion) — or the annual federal deficit of $200-plus billion a year. In fact, no "sacred cows" were sacrificed. President Reagan has kept his star wars strategic defense initiative; social security has remained inviolate; the legislation does not recognize the ugly word "taxes"; no one had to display any guts to vote for this bill and no blood was shed. Even so, its passage was significant.

During the four years since the passage of the tax cut of 1981 those who warned of rising federal deficits — the governors, Congressmen Jim Jones and Leon Panetta, Senators Pete Domenici and Robert Dole, among others — were voices lost in the wilderness. The congressional budget process was designed in 1974 as a more rational approach to federal spending and it may have worked under reasonable fiscal pressures. But it turned out to be useless in dealing with $200 billion deficits as the President and his followers in Congress blocked attempts to substantially reduce the defense budget buildup or to raise taxes. In addition, the House Democrats continued to ignore the President's pleas for cuts in domestic programs because of their perceived impacts on the poor and middle class.

Gramm-Rudman is an excuse rather than a solution. It creates an invisible force to magically balance the budget — not today — but in the future. One political columnist in discussing the "Rudman-Gramm Budget Balance Sham" suggests the President and Congress will try to outfox one another, creating a game of legislative-executive chicken with Congress appropriating lavishly and Reagan vetoing offhandedly.

Those who voted for the legislation suggest this is not so. They claim that the remedy for such legislative-executive abuse is so draconian (across-the-board cuts in everything not exempt) that both sides will have to play fair. Reasonableness, they say, will prevail as the President and Congress work towards a responsible solution.

The question remains, however: How tomorrow, if you couldn't do it today? Everything that the proponents of Gramm-Rudman hope for could have occurred without the Gramm-Rudman legislation. If the President remains committed to a no-reduction policy in his defense buildup, and the Congress refuses to sacrifice any of the major domestic programs and both ignore Social Security and other entitlements, the only answer is to increase taxes to meet the deficit targets. Yet Congress and the President have had that solution for several past years and have been unwilling to use it.

Some commentators have correctly pointed out that as an Act of Congress Gramm-Rudman can be amended and modified like any other piece of legislation. That, of course, is true. However, unlike a general resolution creating certain budget targets, this legislation creates a specific mechanism that cannot be ignored. To repeal the mechanism or substantially modify it requires passage by both houses of Congress and signature by the President. Thus it puts the potential modifiers at substantial political risk. It is inconceivable that the President or the Congress would take a leadership role in scuttling such legislation in 1986, an election year, or in 1987, just prior to the presidential campaign.

Major retreat from the direction set by Gramm-Rudman is unlikely. Yet the risks inherent in the legislation are profound. In its implementation the legislation will undoubtedly prove uneven, chaotic and in many cases counter-productive, as short-term savings may lead to long-term costs. Gramm-Rudman is a recognition that the President can't have it all: tax reduction, increased defense and a balanced budget. In placing the priority towards a balanced budget, this legislation necessarily portends that the defense buildup will suffer, that many domestic programs will receive further cuts and that a tax increase is a virtual certainty.

Conclusion

As the federal debt gets larger and as the size of the deficit grows, the measures needed to put the budget back on course become even more difficult and less politically feasible. The intransigence of President Reagan against accepting any tax increase as part of the solution merely disguises the fact that the continuing deficits create an increasing burden on the American public and place upward pressure on interest rates, creating an indirect tax on public and private borrowers and a continued drag on the economy. Shifts to the state and local governments are also likely to lead to local tax increases.

Admittedly, NGA did not solve the budget deficit problem, but, because we were able to present a united front, we did help to coalesce public opinion on the problem. However, a real solution or compromise between the President and Congress must occur sooner and not later.

CHAPTER 19

New Roles and Future Responsibilities

IN addition to the traditional role of managing state agencies, responding to disasters, putting together a budget and proposing agendas for state legislatures, the modern governor over the last fifteen years has had to cope with a more complicated and often altogether new set of priorities and responsibilities. They range from being the state's number one ambassador to teaching a class in federal-state relations at the local university to even preparing a budget for the Supreme Court.

The job description has certainly changed and will continue to expand in future years. I think the contrast between the historical and the emerging roles of the governor is best illustrated by two separate economic development events which occurred during my last term in office.

The first had to do with the traditional role of the governor in assisting economic development. Firms shopping for new locations are usually looking for tax incentives or special treatment of one kind or another for doing business within the state, even though those incentives are usually not the primary factors for the firm's location. I remember meeting with the corporate executives of a food processing firm considering locating a plant in central Utah. The company was down to a choice of four or five different sites, and several of their executive officers visited Utah. I met with them to discuss the advantages of Utah. The first question asked was, "What are you offering us to come to Utah?" I said, "The best working environment in the United States." They asked, in return, "You're not offering us any special tax exemptions?" I said, "No, I'm not offering you any of those short-term, carrot-type incentives. We'll offer you a work force that will stick with you and provide you a better profit over the long haul than any advantage you might receive from short-term incentives you have been offered or will be offered by other states. But if you're looking for tax exemptions and other kinds of special treatment, you should locate in another state."

The mayor of the community where the company was considering locating the plant went into a state of shock over my remarks. But it turned out that a week later the company decided to locate their plant in Utah. My comments simply reinforced the research they had already done about our state. They had determined that the work force they would hire and train in the Utah County area was of a higher caliber than the work force in any of the other states they were considering. Their research indicated that our people don't take extra long breaks, that they come to work on time every morning and have a strong work ethic. That translated into a higher bottom-line profit for the corporation. Although there are exceptions, special tax incentives do not normally determine siting decisions.

The role of the governor in developing business opportunities in the state has expanded dramatically in the last few years, particularly in the international arena, which provides my second economic development illustration.

In 1982, the states became embroiled in a major, international economic issue over the taxation of foreign multinational corporations. Because of the difficulty of estimating profits and losses of foreign corporations within the jurisdiction of an individual state, twelve states, including Utah, had determined to tax multinational corporations on a formula basis called the unitary tax. This approach takes into account the number of employees, property values and gross sales in the individual state compared to the worldwide employees, property value and sales of the international corporation. A number of the multinational corporations argued that the unitary tax was unfair because the company might well be profitable overall and yet unprofitable in a particular state. Even so, it was difficult for states to penetrate the maze of international corporate balance sheets in order to determine the profitability of a business within their jurisdictions. There was a feeling in the states that corporations could easily shift costs within their total operations, thereby making it appear that they were unprofitable in a given state where that might not be the actual case.

For some time the Common Market countries and Japan have been particularly strong opponents of this unitary tax approach. In response to that position the departments of State and Treasury negotiated a tax treaty with the United Kingdom in 1982 to remove the adverse impact of the unitary tax on foreign multinational corporations. However after fairly intense lobbying by the states, the United States Senate refused to ratify the treaty with the anti-unitary provision in it.

The unitary tax method was then judicially challenged. Ultimately, the United States Supreme Court upheld the constitutionality of the right of the states to tax on the unitary theory. Following the Court's decision an issue developed as to whether or not the Department of Justice should file a petition for rehearing on the side of the foreign multinationals or allow the states' position to prevail. After hearing lobbying from the governors, the President came down on the states' side and Justice did not file a petition for rehearing; however, as a part of that process, the states agreed to work with the President to try to negotiate a fair resolution of the unitary issue.

By chance, I happened to be in the White House on a different matter the day that the President came down on the side of the states. Needless to say, Treasury Secretary Regan was livid; but he met with Governor James Thompson (R., Ill.) and me on an ad hoc basis and agreed to work with us toward a solution.

Shortly thereafter, at the request of the President, Secretary Regan created a task force consisting of an equal number of individuals who supported the states' viewpoint and those who supported the position of the multinational corporations. Three governors — George Deukmejian (R., Cal.), Thompson and myself — were selected to represent the governors. Historically, California and Illinois have received the largest amount of state revenue from the unitary tax. In California alone, four multinationals have paid almost $500 million annually in state taxes under the unitary approach.

During the existence of the task force, I met with the ambassadors of the United Kingdom and Japan about the unitary issue. What impressed me most about the meetings was the fact that they came to Salt Lake City to visit me on the issue. In the past a matter of this level would have been solely the province of the federal government, particularly its departments of Treasury and State, and the Congress.

Both ambassadors were extremely knowledgeable. The ambassador from the United Kingdom took a soft-sell approach, arguing the issue of fairness, equity, good international feelings, and promotion of international trade — all positive reasons for changes in the unitary tax. In contrast, the ambassador from Japan was very aggressive during the briefing, indicating quite bluntly that Japan's multinational corporations were simply not going to do business or locate in any state that continued the unitary method of taxation.

All three governors on the task force were anxious to solve the unitary issue in a cooperative fashion. However, we did not want a solution imposed on us by Congress. After extensive briefings and meetings during 1983 and 1984, a solution was reached which would remove the states from the worldwide unitary approach, replacing it with a pro rata taxation of foreign multinationals on their United States subsidiaries, according to the so-called "water's edge" approach. Water's edge is nothing more than the states retreating to our national boundaries in imposing the unitary tax.

This solution was basically accepted by the task force, although a strong minority report was filed by the business members. Thereafter, six of the unitary states adopted or are in the process of adopting the water's edge approach.

Part of the task force agreement included a commitment by Treasury to recommend to Congress an expanded budget for more audits of foreign multinational corporations, to provide more Internal Revenue Service agents to audit those companies and to regulate the method of corporate accounting to make sure the states had the appropriate information upon which to make an assessment of the proper taxes for that state.

The unitary issue is important, not simply because of the revenue impact on the states, but because governors are playing a key role in finding a solution to an international problem affecting the United States' foreign relations. In fact, when Prime Minister Margaret Thatcher of Great Britain visited the United States in 1983, the removal of the unitary tax on foreign multinationals was a very high priority on her agenda with President Reagan.

Emerging Roles for the Governors

During the 1970s and 1980s, several trends emerged which gave governors an increased opportunity to exhibit leadership in a number of areas where they had not previously been involved. The first area was the emergence of the governor as the worldwide ambassador for the state in tourism and economic development, dealing not only with major multinational corporations, but with foreign governments. The unitary tax issue is only one manifestation of that trend.

Second, governors have become the symbols of reform and reemergence efforts at the state and local levels. Current initiatives for educational reform, for example, while proposed by the national study launched by Secretary of Education T. H. Bell and the findings of *A Nation at Risk,*[1] have largely been led by governors. The efforts of Governor Lamar Alexander (R., Tenn.) to improve the quality of public education and to establish a career ladder for teachers in his state has achieved nationwide attention. Alexander was able to convince the legislators to impose a substantial sales tax increase to pay for these reforms. Bob Graham (D., Fla.) was the first governor to marshall a major reform and tax program through his legislature. Several governors have proposed legislation to provide stiffer graduation requirements, competency testing (both for students and teachers), longer school years and better pay for teachers.

The third emerging trend is the strong role governors have played in protecting the independence of the executive and judicial branches during state governmental reorganizations of the last twenty-five years. They have, out of necessity, maintained the ongoing check and balance structure within state government, often challenging the actions of the legislative branch as it encroaches upon the other two branches. Statutory requirements for legislative membership on executive branch entities is particularly flagrant. Delay in modernizing the judicial branch still plagues many states.

The fourth emerging responsibility has seen governors play a pivotal and personal role in the arbitration of the rights of individuals versus the rights of society. The increasing militancy of individuals who hold certain moral viewpoints will likely exacerbate this duty.

Finally, the increasing attention given private-public partnerships in economic development and in other *privatization* activities requires governors to play the role of negotiator, both in establishing and facilitating that partnership. The continuing efforts of the Reagan Administration to devolve programs from the federal government to state and local governments and to the private sector will make this role increasingly important.

While these five trends have increased gubernatorial responsibility, they also require a different kind of governor today than was necessary twenty years ago. Today's governors need skills in management, budgeting, language, computers, capital formation, banking, accounting, bonding, trading, mediating, lawyering, and a host of other tasks. But the greatest need today is not really new; leadership has not gone out of style. Emerging trends require the modern governor, on an ongoing basis, to make new and difficult decisions. While the political process is important, voters should take into consideration a candidate's courage to stand by his values and convictions.

The John Singer Case

Governors have always had to weigh the rights of individuals against those of society. The challenges in recent years seem to have increased. Issues such as the Equal Rights Amendment, abortion and censorship of cable television require a governor to weigh the rights of individual freedom, guaranteed by law or the constitution, and the rights of society to maintain the majority view concerning general mores. Sometimes, a governor has a constitutional basis from which he can make such a decision, sometimes not. Usually, the issue is complex, and the governor's decision not clear-cut. One of the most complex individual rights issues I had to face involved John Singer.

Singer attracted nationwide attention on January 18, 1979 when he was shot and killed while resisting arrest. There is a growing number of people in the country who as a group or as individuals take a very strong attitude toward the rights of individuals to govern their own affairs. Their militancy often leads them into conflicts with legal authorities. To some, John Singer was a symbol of a David against the monolithic, governmental Goliath. To others, he was an extremist, a person who openly violated the law, who took another man's wife and children and who established a course of action that led to tragedy.[2]

Singer had been raised in Nazi Germany and was a member of the Hitler Youth. His father was a staunch Nazi; his mother a Mormon who opposed Nazism. Violent arguments ensued between the mother and father, and divorce followed. John traveled to the United States with his mother and later became an active Mormon. As he grew older, he became more fundamentalist in his beliefs and rejected the authority of the Mormon Church.

He was a rugged individualist who lived apart from organized society; he built a log cabin home with his own hands. Although he had no formal education after the age of sixteen, he taught himself the skills of carpentry, plumbing, electronics and farming. His complex of buildings had an independent water system and power supply. He farmed the land and was, in most respects, self-sufficient.

The problems between Singer and the state began in 1973 with his decision to take his children out of the public school system in Summit County. He objected to one of the books in the schools which praised Martin Luther King, Jr., whom Singer called a communist and traitor to his own people. He said that by showing mixed races together, the school system was teaching that it was all right for them to associate, which would lead to intermarriage — in Singer's mind, a racial disaster that was contrary to his religious beliefs. Accordingly, on March 29, 1973, Singer withdrew his children from the South Summit Elementary School.

Utah law requires attendance at a public school system or the development of an approved alternative method of education in the home. Over the next four years, repeated efforts were made to meet Singer's request that he educate his own children. Several attempts failed. Testing of the children in 1977 determined that their education and academic levels were below their intellectual abilities.

On November 15, 1977, Juvenile Judge Kent Bachman met with Singer and gave him three options: enroll the children in public schools, enroll the children in a registered private school or accept a certified tutor at the High Uintah Academy, which Singer had created and incorporated for his children's home education. Singer refused to cooperate with any of the alternatives and informed the judge that he was completely inflexible.

On December 16, Judge Bachman set a trial date for charges of neglect and habitual truancy against John Singer and his wife, Vickie. They failed to appear, and Judge Bachman issued a bench warrant for their arrest. In January and February, Judge Bachman attempted to draft another compromise plan calling for an in-house tutor at the Singer's home, to be paid for by the Summit County Board of Education. Singer, however, told Summit County Sheriff Ron Robinson that he would not allow his children to be tutored and would not appear at any hearing about the matter.

On March 14, 1978, a hearing date was set for contempt charges against Singer. Again he failed to appear. On April 6, 1978, Juvenile Judge John Farr Larsen, who had replaced Bachman, ordered Sheriff Robinson to arrest Singer. Singer told members of the news media that he would not allow the sheriff to arrest him and, if necessary, would resist with force. The sheriff made several attempts in the summer of 1978 to arrest Singer peacefully, but all efforts were rebuffed.

On July 17, 1978, Singer decided to take a second wife and married Shirley Black, wife of Dean Black. Mrs. Black did not inform her husband of her marriage to Singer at the time, but on October 4, 1978, she left her first husband and moved into the Singer home with her children. Dean Black was concerned for the safety and welfare of his children; he therefore petitioned the court and was awarded custody of the children. Third District Court Judge Bryant Croft ordered Sheriff Robinson to take the Black children out of the Singer home.

Two courts had now ordered action. After several additional, unsuccessful attempts by the sheriff to arrest Singer peacefully, Summit County attorney Terry Christiansen asked Judge Larsen to remove the provision that Singer be arrested in a manner that would not cause harm, indicating that the sheriff might not be able to exercise his responsibility with such a provision.

While I had followed the case since my election in 1976 and had received several phone calls and letters from people who were concerned about it, I did not officially get involved until October 1978, when Summit County Sheriff Ron Robinson came to Public Safety Commissioner Larry Lunnen to ask for state assistance in arresting Singer.

I did not make the decision to assist hastily. It came about only after considerable discussion with Judge Larsen about the case and a determination that Mr. Singer had been given the benefit of every reasonable consideration. Both the administrative proceedings and the process in the courts had been properly handled. While I had no difficulty in allowing Singer the right to teach his children in his home, Utah has a state requirement that a minimum standard of education must be met, and the state had determined that level was not being met. Singer had essentially rejected the state's authority over his children. His taking of a second wife and the children of another man into his house further aggravated the legal situation.

The first attempt to arrest Singer was an embarrassing fiasco. A plan was devised using law enforcement officers posing as reporters. While the officers had firearms, they intended to arrest Singer without any show of force. However, when they identified themselves as police officers, Singer put up a greater struggle than anticipated, and his wife, Vickie, and the children also jumped into the fray. Singer was armed, and he was able to break free and pull his gun. The police officers backed off and left.

The immediate public reaction was that the law enforcement officers had blown it. The news media naturally objected strongly to the officers pretending to be reporters, and they accused the state of approaching Singer under false pretenses. Frankly, they had a very good point. I told Lunnen that I wanted to be informed in advance of any future plans for Singer's arrest. One of many proposals they considered was to use an armored weapons carrier to crash through Singer's front gate and then tear gas his home. I rejected that alternative and others because of the high likelihood of injury to Singer's wives and the children.

The real challenge at that point was to devise a plan that would allow a high probability of arresting Singer without harm to him, under circumstances that did not pose unreasonable risk to the women and children. That was difficult. Singer's brother, Harald, came to see me in November 1978. Larry Lunnen was also present at the meeting when Harald said, "My brother is not going to be taken without violence. I'm in here to plead with you to instruct your people and all of the public law enforcement people to withdraw from the scene. Just let him alone. Let him live his life up there and teach his children any way he pleases. Public interest will be served best if we step aside. It's not serving anybody to go ahead with this effort to arrest the man."

I told Harald that I appreciated his concern for his brother, and that there were some legitimate points to his argument. But in this particular case, I didn't have any power as governor to substitute my views for those of the juvenile court. The judges of the court were the ones who had issued the warrants of arrest. It was a judicial decision; I felt the decision was not arbitrary or capricious, and that Singer had received ample and reasonable opportunity to comply.

I also felt that the Singer case was an important test of how we run our system. I understood there was some risk in arresting the man, but I felt that the public interest in enforcing the rules was sufficient to take that risk. We are a nation of laws, and Singer had set himself apart and above those laws. While the use of violence is of great concern to me, that is a risk that I think sometimes has to be taken if society is going to have a set of rules.

By January 1979, a surveillance team of Utah Public Safety and Summit County sheriff personnel had noticed a routine wherein Singer made a trip to the mailbox once a day. They devised a plan to come in on snowmobiles and isolate him from the house. They had hoped that an overwhelming show of force would cause Singer to yield. On January 18, uniformed sheriff's deputies and officers of the Department of Public Safety initiated the plan. Five snowmobiles, each containing a driver and an officer with a double-barreled shotgun moved in to surround Singer. He started to move back toward the house, pulled a pistol from his belt and aimed the pistol at one of the officers. That officer felled him with a single shot. He was dead on arrival at a local hospital.

The grievous nature of the arrest was a sad occasion for me. I felt very badly about the man losing his life. We made the choice, and though I don't regret that choice I do feel badly about the result.

Singer's death was an emotional event. I had to travel to Washington, D.C. the day of the shooting, and the governor's office received threatening calls throughout the day. Law enforcement people were sufficiently concerned about the safety of my family to take our children out of school that day and put them into seclusion. When I arrived in Washington, special security guards were assigned to sleep across the hall from me at my hotel that night.

Mrs. Singer later filed suit against the state of Utah, Commissioner Lunnen, Sheriff Robinson, the officers involved, and me personally, alleging, among other things, that Singer had been denied due process and that the force used had been unnecessary. Those allegations were rejected by the trial court and by the Tenth Circuit Court of Appeals.[3] After reviewing the case, I personally think that the officers did everything they could to effectuate a peaceful arrest and that the officer who shot Singer legitimately felt that his life was threatened.

People have suggested that the issues involved were not worth Singer's death. But what kind of precedent would we have set by turning our backs on the situation? That clearly would not be in the public interest. We live under a system of laws. If such a system espouses values, those values must be protected. I firmly believed we were protecting society's values.

Advocating for the Judiciary

As a lawyer, one of the reasons I wanted to be governor was because of my interest in the judicial branch of government. I viewed the governor's power to appoint judges as the key to the judicial system fulfilling its proper, modern role as an equal branch of state government. In state reorganization efforts during the past several years, the judicial branch had also lagged far behind.

The judicial branch in Utah had been very backward in terms of supporting its own budget and resource needs. Judges have barely survived economically. When I was elected their salaries ranked forty-ninth out of the fifty states. Historically, Utah judges have felt they should be aloof from the political process affecting their branch of state government. As governor, I was determined to find ways to bring them along into the major reorganization process. Getting the right people on bench was the way to begin.

In 1977, despite an explosive increase in cases, the five justices of the Utah Supreme Court had only one full-time law clerk each. Cases were still logged-in by hand. The court had no computer or word processing capability. They were slowly sinking into a quagmire. The budget for the entire judicial branch of government was less than one percent of the state's budget. I remember the Supreme Court's budget presentation my first year in office. It was basically a carbon copy of the prior year and failed to follow our new guidelines. My irritation evaporated when I discovered that no one was capable of preparing the documents as we had requested. We actually prepared their budget that year and added funds for a second law clerk for each judge as well as for badly needed word processing capability.

Several early opportunities for judicial appointments occurred, and by the end of my first term I had appointed the entire membership of the Utah Supreme Court. The new judges did assume a greater role in improving the quality of the judiciary, including vigorous support for the new circuit court system which upgraded the old city courts into courts of record with expanded jurisdiction — the first major court reorganization in Utah in over sixty years. In my third year in office, the judges received a twenty-four percent salary increase, the highest in the state's history. Several new judgeships were created at the district and juvenile court levels. New consolidated calendaring in the largest judicial district reduced trial delays substantially. The system was beginning to function efficiently.

In spite of substantial progress and streamlining procedures, however, the judicial branch of the state of Utah remained one major critical step away from providing efficient, quality judicial service. Our state constitution was originally designed to allow only one appeal from the trial court's decision. Over the years, the backlog in the Supreme Court has increased to the point where the five justices, even with substantial staff support, simply cannot keep up.

The problem was recognized in the late 1970s by Justice Richard L. Maughan. He championed the cause of an intermediate appellate court as the long-term solution rather than an expansion of the number of justices on the Supreme Court. His research was convincing and eventually attracted widespread support from other judges, legislators and the Utah State Bar. I was a supporter of his proposal early in the debate.

The matter was referred to the Utah Constitutional Revision Committee where a careful redrafting of the Judicial Articles of the

Constitution, allowing the legislative creation of an intermediate appellate court, was prepared and finally submitted to the voters in the 1984 election. It passed comfortably. Implementing legislation was adopted by the 1986 Utah legislature. The basic structure of final change is now in place. If we will only pay our judges decent salaries in the future, we can reasonably expect the quality to continue to improve.

The Philosophy of Selecting Judges

The impression that people have about the judiciary is almost always set by a single appearance in court. How the judge handles the experience usually determines how that person will feel about the judicial system for his lifetime. Therefore, I wanted to select judges who would make the commitment to provide the proper, personal environment in the courtroom.

I had no great concern about the politics of my appointees. One of my rules was to interview all of the candidates selected by the Judicial Nominating Commission. Three candidates were submitted to me, and I always interviewed them personally to find out about their work habits, their willingness to assume responsibility, to make decisions promptly, to work diligently and to be available to lawyers at odd hours. I often read examples of their written work. I never asked their political allegiance. I recognized that we demanded a lot of judicial officials, and in Utah their salaries are pathetic.

Occasionally, I actively encouraged individuals to apply for positions on the bench. Normally, I would get a small group of leaders of the Utah Bar together on an ad hoc basis to ask them to encourage good members of the Bar to submit applications. I insisted on only top-quality lawyers for the bench. Occasionally, I did intercede and ask individuals to apply for a position. For example, I asked Dallin Oaks, former president of Brigham Young University, to submit his name for a position on the Utah Supreme Court and was delighted to appoint him after he emerged as one of the three candidates from the nominating commission.

Matheson v. Ferry

Legislators have been increasingly intrusive into the executive branch of government. In Utah, there are many manifestations of this, such as the creation of oversight committees to monitor executive branch agencies and the creation of more detailed line-items to prevent the executive branch from having flexibility in the expenditures of funds. Many of these efforts are counterproductive and make it more difficult for the executive branch to function efficiently. But my greatest concern was the attempt of the Utah legislature to usurp the appointment of judges.

Utah had a Democratic governor for twelve years before I was elected. During that twelve years and the eight years I was in office, many judges were appointed. The record shows that I appointed about an equal number of Democrats and Republicans, but that was not the perception of the legislature. Accordingly, they passed legislation providing that the Senate had the right to advise and consent on judicial appointments.

Utah already had substantial checks and balances to assure the independence of the judicial branch. Judges were required to submit their applications to a nominating committee composed of appointees of the governor and appointees of the legislature. The committee submitted three names to the governor. Once selected by the governor, a judge had to run for reelection at the next general election for the balance of the remaining term. Of course, the legislature controlled the setting of judicial salaries and had the constitutional power of impeachment. My feeling was that the addition of the advise and consent provision would make judicial appointments more difficult and unattractive to good lawyers. It placed too much power in the hands of the legislative branch, and injected politics into the selection process. Accordingly, without the support of the Republican attorney general, I took the issue to the Utah Supreme Court. In *Matheson v. Ferry,* the Supreme Court agreed that the legislature had gone too far in violating the check and balance system and the independence of the judiciary.[4]

I was gratified that the Supreme Court agreed with me. It's nice to be sustained and to have the opportunity to take on a very political legislature, without the help of the Republican attorney general, and whip them.

In the final analysis, though, the legislature found a way to achieve advise and consent. I had strongly advocated the need for an intermediate court of appeals between the Utah trial courts and the Supreme Court. Included in the constitutional change presented to the voters in 1984 was advise and consent of the Utah Senate on judges. The tradeoff was one which I found acceptable because instead of running for reelection and possibly facing another opponent, the judges would now run under the so-called "Missouri Plan," where the people would simply vote "yes" or "no" on whether the judge should be retained in office. While I personally disliked the advise and consent process, the need for the intermediate court of appeals was more critical, and I supported passage of the revised constitutional amendment.

Protecting the Executive Branch

Another of the new roles I assumed as governor was making certain that the system of checks and balances was protected. Legislators always want progressively more control of executive branch action. Several times in office, I had to veto legislation which I felt placed the legislature in a position of intruding upon the independence and prerogatives of the executive branch. Still, I had to compromise those beliefs on many occasions. While the Utah Supreme Court has clearly indicated that it is inappropriate for legislators to serve on executive-type agencies, I was only able to get legislation for the Energy Conservation and Development Council in 1977 by agreeing to appoint four legislative members to that council. Legislators continue to serve on the Constitutional Revision Committee and other bodies that, in my judgment, are not appropriately served by their participation.

I'm sure it's frustrating for a legislator who is in session for a relatively short time to sit on the sidelines and watch the executive branch operate. But that is exactly the design of the system. The legislature sets broad policy parameters, passes legislation, adopts a budget, and the executive branch is supposed to take it from there. Legislative suspicion of the executive branch is inherent regardless of which party holds the governorship and which party controls the legislature. Republican Norman Bangerter succeeded me, ending twenty years of Democratic control in the governor's office. Given a Republican legislature with over two-thirds majority in each house, you might expect a honeymoon. But Governor Bangerter, a former House Speaker, soon found that he too was at odds with the legislative branch regarding gubernatorial prerogatives.

Clearly the executive branch owes the legislature full disclosure and accountability. But day-to-day control violates the separation of powers. Governors must monitor that situation constantly in order to act in a responsible fashion without undue restriction and control.

Promoting Economic Development

I also felt I needed to be untraditionally aggressive in the area of economic development. Utah was one of the last states to get into the business of economic development. It was not until 1965 at the prodding of newly-elected Governor Calvin L. Rampton that the legislature funded the Utah Industrial Promotion Commission, the forerunner of today's Department of Community and Economic Development (DCED).

During the past twenty years, the state has carried out a full-fledged national advertising and promotional campaign extolling the advantages of our highly-educated, productive work force, abundant natural resources and positive business climate. Our goal has been to change Utah's image from a backward, isolated state to a vibrant, progressive one at the center of the rapidly expanding western states' market.

All states now are heavily involved in promoting their own economic development, and their approach has changed dramatically over the last twenty years. When Rampton was first elected governor, Utah's population was already exploding, and yet the poor economic environment was forcing many college graduates to leave the state for jobs. Previously, the state and its people had "the Lord will provide" attitude toward its economic development. But Rampton knew it was necessary to go out and compete with other states for industries.

In the early 1960s, over ten percent of the jobs in Utah were in three industries — copper, steel and aerospace. Today, less than four percent of our jobs are in those industries, making our overall economy less vulnerable to cyclical fluctuations in those sectors. During my term in office alone, two hundred firms announced new or major expansions in Utah.

Perhaps most significant is the maturing image of Utah. Salt Lake City is listed as "one of the ten cities of great opportunity" by futurist John Naisbitt in his book, *Megatrends*.[5] We have been host to the world conference of corporate facility planners, and the state has a good reputation for promoting and facilitating economic development.

A major approach that we adopted during my administration was to attempt to target specific industries for possible location in Utah. We contracted a number of comparative analyses of how Utah stacked up with other potential sites throughout the nation or the world for a particular industrial sector.

My role was seeing to it that relevant information reached the chief executive officer of companies we were courting, and many times when our industrial development people couldn't get through to a certain corporation, I was able to pick up the phone and call the CEO and make an initial contact. Then, when the company would come into Utah to assess a particular plant location, I would meet with their corporate executives and set the overall tone for the meeting, although our DCED people, headed by Dale Carpenter, would provide the detailed briefing on the attractiveness of the state for that particular corporation.

I've met with chief executive officers both in Utah and at their home offices, and those meetings help establish a solid relationship to let the chief executives know that the state desires their business. But I wanted to make sure that by the time I got involved, the economic development people had done all of the research and analyzed all of the major issues — transportation, taxes, environmental issues, labor market, educational quality, etc. By the time a Utah governor sits down with a CEO, that officer is down to a final choice between Salt Lake City and maybe three or four other sites, such as Phoenix or Denver. Then it's up to the governor to find that magic additional resource or ingredient that attracts the company into your state. Of course, you know the governors of the other states are doing the same thing. You win some, and you lose some. My belief is that we should facilitate an overall positive economic development climate within the state and not provide special benefits to any one business or industrial sector.

Kimberly Clark provides a good example of my approach to corporate locations. They may provide the softest, most absorbent diapers in the country, but they are a very tough, hard-nosed executive company in terms of dealing with the state on business matters. They involved my office in a number of issues affecting their plant location, including how much they were charged for a building permit in one of the state's counties, facilitating a quick permit process through the Clean Air Committee in our Division of Environmental Health, and a number of other issues.

Kimberly Clark had agreed to come into Weber County, Utah and put in one diaper assembly line and indicated they would be willing to put in a second line if I would support a sales tax exemption on new equipment used to produce goods. I listened carefully to the CEO argue for the tax exemption, and my response was that we could not do it for an individual industrial category, that it was a mistake to do tax policy piecemeal. If exempting the sales tax on new productive machinery made sense, then we ought to do it for everyone.

I indicated to him that I would examine the overall question and was certainly anxious to provide any reasonable incentive to attract his industry to Utah. As we examined that issue, over half of the states had that exemption already on their books. We hired a consultant to look at various options. If we exempted the sales tax on new equipment, the potential tax loss to the state was somewhere between $20 and $25 million, a substantial revenue drain. However, if we limited the exemption to new equipment which was used to expand plant capacity and not simply replacement equipment, the tax loss dropped to $4 or $5 million, which was an amount I felt we could handle. That would provide an incentive for the location of new business in the state and the expansion of businesses already within the state. That legislation was adopted by the 1984 legislature.

I also became a very strong advocate for promoting the economic climate for small business in the state of Utah. We determined that we needed roughly 25,000 new jobs every year to keep up with the increasing population of the state. Since there were 30,000 to 40,000 small businesses in the state, if each one of them added just one new job each year, we could more than meet our goal. Therefore I was very supportive of Dale Carpenter's efforts to get the state involved in the Small

Business Revitalization Program developed under the Reagan Administration.

In Search of High-Tech

Everyone is now aware of the profound change taking place in the American economy, characterized by a shift from an industrial to an "information-based" society. But the transition is not well understood. The transition from an agricultural to an industrial society at the turn of the century did not mean the end of agriculture — on the contrary, more is produced today by fewer hands. Likewise, most goods-producing industries will survive during the new information-based age, but fewer and fewer people will bring home a paycheck from those industries.

The dwindling number of workers in manufacturing is a direct result of advanced technology. The current generation of robots may replace millions of existing factory jobs, perhaps as much as one-third of all manufacturing employment in the United States. Jobs that do survive in traditional industries will require more sophisticated training.

Effects of high technology are inescapable. Everyone's life will be touched, and every business and industry affected. In Utah during the first part of my administration, I banked upon natural resource development as the essential component of the state's economic future. Plunging oil prices and environmental and production problems have greatly changed our thinking.

I began to be swept up in the economic change as a result of an effort called the "Agenda for the 80s," which I put together to analyze the state's future. One of the areas examined was economic growth potential. *Megatrends* was on the bestseller list during this period and because I knew the author, I had a chance to read early drafts of some of the chapters. It became readily apparent that we were moving from a local to an international economy, and there was a change in the nature of how we earned our living from traditional jobs.

I also think my involvement with the National Governors' Association made me aware of what other states were doing to respond to new economic challenges. In the second term of my administration, I attempted to cope with these dynamic changes and develop new approaches to economic development.

It is naive to stake Utah's future economic growth on those industries characterized as purely "high-tech." Not every state can have a Silicon Valley, a Route 129 or a Research Triangle. But states can take a look at their technological resources, such as bioengineering skills and the capabilities of their universities, and thereafter begin to carve out a niche for themselves in the high-tech market.

I also think it is desirable to consider a broader definition of "high-tech," which includes the application of state-of-the-art technology in all industries. In that sense, almost every industry is potentially high-tech. Firms that fail to apply advanced technology will wither and die in the face of domestic or foreign competition.

States need to develop a strategy for competing in an advanced technology era. In Utah, the three elements which I believe are essential to our ability to compete are investing in human resources (education and training), developing working partnerships between the public and private sectors and creating an environment which nourishes technological innovation.

Governor's Future Responsibilities

It is foolhardy to predict the future, even ten or fifteen years ahead. Ten years ago we had not heard of personal computers. Today we can't do without them. Fifteen years ago President Richard Nixon was successfully persuading the Congress to share revenues with state and local governments. Today it is the costs of federal programs, not the revenues, that are being shared.

However, as I have watched the intergovernmental system change over the last fifteen years, with its fits and starts, strains and dynamic change, I have concluded that the post-Ronald Reagan intergovernmental era will be far different than many of us ever suspected. My prognostications are in no way inevitable and clearly some specifics are highly speculative. But the trends that I see are present and strong. If I am right about the coming reduction of the federal role in domestic programs (because of the President, Gramm-Rudman and the inevitable need to deal with the budget deficits), then the next ten to fifteen years will be a turbulent time for political leaders at all levels of government. Governors, especially, will face a number of new problems that will stretch their ability to cooperate and adapt to the changing dynamics of our intergovernmental system.

The Need for Interstate Cooperation

As the federal government sheds itself of major program responsibilities in the next five years, governors will need to find new vehicles for interstate cooperation and program responsibility. The end of federal involvement does not end the need to deal with problems on a multistate basis.

For example, the marketing of state goods and services to foreign nations is now highly fragmented. States are scrambling to open foreign trade offices to encourage investment from overseas and to market local products in foreign markets. A more efficient way to handle such efforts is through regional trade associations, multistate agreements or compacts. While a formal compact would require multistate legislative approval and the ratification by Congress, states could adopt less formal agreements through such groups as the Western Governors' Association and other regional associations.

Similarly, regional governors' associations could emerge with major program functions that the federal government has provided. Drug and Immigration Law enforcement, environmental protection, financial assistance and monitoring, water storage projects, international tourism, and other development and regulatory efforts could all be efficiently handled by regional associations. States could fund those efforts, just as they now fund existing compacts and other multistate efforts.

The Problem of Fiscal Disparities

Solving the federal budget deficit will likely entail a funding shift to the state level of programs helping the poor. The federal role in maintaining senior citizens, through Social Security and Medicare, is not likely to change dramatically over the next ten years. The senior lobby and commitments of both parties will keep that part of the "safety net" intact. The remainder, however, is likely to become a shadow of the current program. By the mid-1990s, or before, I expect federal support for public housing and Food Stamps to be terminated. And federal participation in welfare payments (now averaging fifty percent) will drop year by year.

Under those circumstances, many resource-poor states will not have the revenue base to pick up the loss of federal dollars. Many states may forego limited federal support and develop their own programs. Two results are likely. In 1984 the combined AFDC and Food Stamp grant averaged seventy-three percent of the census bureau's "poverty threshold." I expect that to drop to less than sixty percent as the states adjust to lower federal funds during the late 1980s and 1990s. Perhaps as many as a dozen states will have grant levels of fifty percent or less of the poverty level. These states will have low per capita income and high populations in poverty. No amount of tax effort in those states will improve those statistics.

A national outcry against the disparity of programs for the poor will inevitably occur. This may happen after a renewal of migration from poor states to wealthier communities. Even the richer states will recognize their no-win position. Some kind of national grants to equalize the fiscal disparities will be necessary.

Unlike the old revenue sharing which went to forty thousand individual states and local jurisdictions, thus diluting its impact, new fiscal capacity grants should only go to about fifteen states with the lowest per capita income and greatest percentage of population below the poverty level. The governors themselves may have to initiate the drive for such a program and be willing to support a national consumption or sales tax to finance it.

State-Local Relations

The major action in the domestic arena will be at the state level during the next fifteen years. We may even see political leaders giving up their U.S. Senate seats and running for governor — the reverse of the trends of previous years. With the end of federal fiscal largesse, it just may not be as much fun to be a senator.

Because of the devolution of federal programs to the states, by the year 2000 states will be stronger than at any time since the founding of our Republic. Local governments, which used to rely on federal grants for a large share of their budgets will be heavily dependent upon state aid and loan assistance.

Mayors will petition the governors for an increase in the state aid to local government. They will battle with state government over mandates without funding, home-rule issues and greater taxing authority.

By 2000 the mayors will lobby the governors for the same delegation of authority and responsibility that the governors had themselves asked of the federal government in the federalism debates in 1981.

Governors need to respond to local government needs and provide the fiscal resources (new tax sources or revenue sharing) to allow them to handle their own local problems; just as the states are now prepared to handle state problems.

Conclusion

Clearly the next ten to fifteen years will be stimulating and challenging for the nation's governors and for our intergovernmental, federal-state-local system. I am optimistic that new relationships and improved coordination will occur. The success of our federal system of government has been its ability to change to meet new needs and circumstances. I welcome a return of power and responsibility to state government. The system has been out of balance. The transformation is likely to cause pain but will inevitably lead to a healthier national economy, new responsibilities for state and local government and a significant, but more focused, federal role in domestic affairs.

Inaugural Address—
January 3, 1977

THANK you ladies and gentlemen.

Before I begin let me take a moment to express my thanks to Calvin L. Rampton and convey the respect and appreciation he so deserves. The people of the state of Utah have been very fortunate. Cal Rampton has led us ably. He has heard us with his energy, his intelligence, his foresight and his dedication. Cal and Lucybeth promised us bread to feed our bodies and hyacinths to feed our souls. They have kept their promise. The last twelve years have been our best. But even the governor will admit that it seems like yesterday.

We stay only a moment, and then we're gone. While we're here, we should do what we can to protect the past and secure the future. It is our time. There is much to do.

We must work to guarantee that the opportunities of the present and the challenges of the future are blended. We must design present goals to complement the goals of future generations.

Public life is something we move into . . . then out of. It is not an occupation. It is a fragile moment in a person's life when trust and confidence is placed. When honesty, integrity, foresight and energy is demanded . . . and must be given. Our lives are tied to the decisions we make. Our lives are inexorably structured by the environment we create. Our lives must be safe. Our lives must be free. Our lives must not be compromised.

We must assure our children a good life, unhampered by our mistakes. What we decide here must not adversely affect unborn generations. What we decide must create the base for future decision. It is a challenge. It is a contest in which there can be no losers. Each step must be taken deliberately, aware that yet another must follow. We cannot worry that the first step seems too small, if it is the largest step possible at the moment.

Our state borders encompass vast amounts of potential energy. Not only oil, tar sands, shale and coal, but human energy. I plan to use the human energy to determine the most appropriate use of the natural energy. Utah cannot afford to abuse either.

If we fail to move swiftly to meet our present needs and those of the nation, we are remiss. If we move too quickly and foresake the heritage of our children, we are shortsighted and selfish. We must temper the imperative needs of the whole society with the knowledge of past mistakes, made elsewhere, from which we can learn. The environment

must be a voting member of every committee, every group, every department which proposes development. We Utahns are fortunate that we
have not yet been exploited. Time is on our side, time to properly blend
our natural and human resources . . . to achieve a better life. But we've
been found.

We must also meet the demands imposed on us by a rapidly growing
state population. I do not consider this a crisis, because we have the
ability to harness the valuable human energy resource, which is the
essence of this state's creation. Working together, with common goals,
our increasing population can solve its own problems, it can develop its
own future. It must only be understood that we will provide it a theme,
and we will provide it a forum.

Utah cannot afford to give away everything of value. We must not
shortchange future generations. The current needs are obvious. Our
moral obligations, while clear, are onerous. The task is immense, but
the rewards are great. I believe we are on the threshold of decisions
which will not only determine the course of life as we live it . . . but,
life as it will be lived. Our verdict has lasting effect. The repercussions
are unending, and there may be no appeal. We cannot make these
decisions lightly.

We have been successful thus far, getting to where we are. Our parents gave us our chance. They placed a roof of experience over our
heads and protected us with walls of knowledge and human kindness.
We will not forget. There should be more to life than memory. The
winter years do not have to be frightening. As a state, as a government,
we will act to assure our older citizens a better life. We can do that. We
will do that. And, we will ask their help. Our older citizens are a part
of the human resource of which I speak. Their lasting energy and willingness to work will not be lost.

Youth must be promised an effort to maintain the principles of challenge. The opportunities that engage youthful minds and exuberance
must remain solid. The quick frustration and disappointment of growing can be tempered if the goals are meaningful and clear. There is great
sadness in promising youth, frustrated too quickly, disappointed too
frequently, who grow to adulthood thinking there is nothing else, nothing better, no hope. The human energy of youth must be involved in the
structuring the environment it will face. We need youthful input. The
climate we create today will control tomorrow's weather as well.

All people must have opportunity. But human tolerance cannot be
administered. The Constitution says, "All men are created equal." It
does not say all men *must* be equal. Even the country's founders understood the difference between legislation and compassion. I believe much

can be done to change attitudes by example. My administration will act as an example.

In speeches, I can talk of the future – how we must plan for it. And the past – how we must not forget it. All the while, I know that decisions are made in the present. I'm learning quickly that it is easier to make the speeches than it is to finally make the judgments. In the coming months, there are many critical decisions to be made. There are few tasks that can be done alone. There have been some tasks ignored – possibly because government was unaware. I plan to bring everyone into government and government to everyone.

I will react to the requests of special interest groups, but a different kind of special interest group. The miner is as much a part of our society as a mining corporation. A switchman as significant as the railroad. A teacher as important as the education system. I believe in the individuality of man, who is at his best when he stands alone – accountable to his family, to his neighbors, to his employers and, ultimately, to his God. But I believe we will need help in what we do, in what we accomplish, in our relationship to one another. If a government cannot be responsive to its citizens, if the citizens do not relate to their government, then the idealism of democracy will be lost, and we will have failed.

There is an important theme which has often been expressed but frequently forgotten or overlooked. We all own the air. The water belongs to each of us. This is our land. And this is our government. But all this is transitory if we do not protect it.

I plan to bring these elements into perspective, to cause involvement. Decisions will be made when all elements are considered. Judgments will be made after all views are heard. We are fortunate people. We have the quality of life most of us require. We have the ability to alter the quality of life for those less fortunate. We can be in charge of human events. Together, utilizing this vast human resource I speak of, we can define and direct. We can encourage the citizens, because the citizens will help.

These words are not new. In 431 B.C., Pericles said, "We do not separate the citizen from the statesman; when a man has not time to give to state affairs, we do not merely say that he is minding his own business, but we call him an unprofitable servant."

I know what you can do. I am well aware of what happens when the human energy of the state sets its sights on a goal.

I was a citizen candidate. I will be a citizen governor. My administration will be a citizen administration. My strength comes from people concerned with their government. It comes from the laborer, the businessman, the farmer, the cleric, the teacher, the housewife and the retired. My strength comes from the wide range of people we have in this state. My strength comes from you. You are the human resource I talk about. You have the talent and the courage and the desire we need. You will be part of this government. It is your government.

Thank you.

Inaugural Address— January 5, 1981

THANK you ladies and gentlemen.

Four years ago, we met together in this place. I stood before you as a freshman governor, crossing the bridge from the private sector to public life. We have gone through much since then, and we come together once again — all of us to celebrate the way of life we share and cherish, and I to renew my oath to serve our state as best I can.

An inauguration is by tradition a symbolic time of passage — between the season of elections past, and the new administration soon to come. Today, more than ever, it is a time to take a measure of our promise, of what we ask of one another, and of ourselves.

Seldom before have the voters spoken so loudly or questioned so forcefully the conduct of our public life, from the nation to the towns. And seldom have elected officials had better cause to reflect on their capacity to serve the public interest well.

As the nation and the state begin the governing process anew, I can think of no more appropriate occasion for a thought or two on the character of our public life. For serious questions have arisen that go to the heart of our democratic tradition; questions about our capacity and our willingness to govern the forces that control our lives, doubts about tolerance and respect for diversity in our society, and fears of a loss of civility in our public discourse.

The first principle of our political tradition is that, as citizens of a democracy, we must govern ourselves, sometimes by direct participation, other times through institutions and public servants responsive to our needs.

But today we have the sense that our system is not as responsive as it once was, that government has grown too distant, and that our lives are governed less by us and more by forces beyond our control.

We have come to realize that reliance on centralized power reaches frustrating limits, that the federal government cannot do it all, and should not do it all.

The democratic ideals to which we are committed require that we seek to revitalize the federal system, to return to the states and communities a greater hand in deciding our future, to bring government back home. For the heart of our political experience is to see ourselves as shapers of our own destiny, and we have found that a sense of membership as a large national community grows best when it is rooted in membership in a small one.

Federalism with new direction may give us the capacity for self-government, but we must also have the will. The powers of the community cannot be restored simply by trading the power of big government for the power of big business. So, we can shake our sagebrush at government from afar, but we must prepare to meet the challenges here at home. We are summoned at once to be innovative, pragmatic and progressive.

A progressive federalism must answer those who call for uninhibited development of our land, our water and our way of life. It is one of the day's greatest ironies that many who label themselves "conservative" in all respects would impose upon us all the radical consequences of uncontrolled growth.

Rapid growth is upon us, but it must be managed in a way that preserves the purity of our air, the cleanliness of our water, the quality of our schools, the beauty of our parks and all the best that we already have.

Only by restoring to states and localities a strong hand in shaping their future and only by exercising these powers creatively can we hope to progress in a way that preserves rather than disrupts the way of life we cherish and the sense of community that brings us together and carries our values from one generation to the next.

If we would renew our democratic ideals through a revitalized federal system, we must at the same time affirm the principles of toleration and mutual respect that make democratic government both possible and desirable.

Some see in the current public mood a resolve to elevate the moral character of our public life, and I for one can only hope that they are right. But it is well-known that morality in politics is one of those things that no one is against but that few can agree on. And so the issue of the day is not whether our politics and politicians should be moral, but what the moral responsibilities of citizens and public officials are or should be, and how best they can be realized.

Surely one of the basic principles of any political morality — and certainly of our own — is an appreciation of diversity and a healthy respect for the unique practices and beliefs that give individuals and communities their distinctive identities.

But despite all the recent talk about morality in politics, sadly little has been said about this fundamental value.

Instead, we find our traditions of toleration threatened most by those who preach the loudest, by those who confuse government by consent with a tyranny of the majority.

A self-appointed "moral majority" would suggest that questions of right and wrong can be settled by force of numbers. But our constitution, as well as our deepest moral and religious convictions, say that they are wrong: Where matters of conscience are concerned, even the majority cannot rule.

Finally, much as the moral character of our public life depends on the ideals of self-government and mutual respect, there is one further ingredient without which no political ethic can be complete. And this concerns the tone and spirit of our public debate.

Lively disagreement and vigorous dialogue are in the nature of a democratic society. And the way those disagreements and debates are conducted is one vital measure of the health and well-being of the community that sustains them. Political discussion is not only about public life: It forms a vital part of our public life. The way we advance our cause, as much as the cause itself, reflects our character, and conveys our esteem for those we would persuade.

In this state, perhaps more than most, we have long taken pride in the decency and civility of our political debate. We have insisted that our public discourse reflect the same qualities of integrity and self-restraint we so prize in our individual and family lives.

But here again, there is disturbing evidence in our recent experience that this crucial dimension of our public life is being eroded as well, sometimes, ironically enough, in the name of those very values – of family and community and moral decency – we seek, above all, to preserve.

Meanness of spirit can have no place in our public life, for it works to dissolve the moral fabric on which a sense of community and shared values depend. Those who seek public office, as much as those who hold it, have a responsibility to set a tone consistent with the values they defend, for when civility and self-restraint are removed from a democratic society, something basic to self-government is lost as well.

For me, such a loss would be deeply troubling. The ideal of self-government – that citizens will serve the community and work for the common good in a spirit of respect for one another – this is what attracted me to public life, and that is why I am standing here today.

I pledged four years ago to be a citizen candidate, and then promised to provide a citizen administration. Today I am a little older and, I hope, a little wiser, but I make the same commitment. And, there is still much to do.

I sense a strong commitment from the people of our state to be a part of this state government as we confidently accept the challenges of the 80s, and beyond, on behalf of our posterity. Together, it is time to be about our work.

Thank you.

Last Lecture Series, University of Utah— February 10, 1984

LADIES and Gentlemen:
It is a great pleasure to be with you today.
I have come today as a part of this lecture series to share some reflections and make an announcement. The reflections come first. I hope you will listen carefully, because they are about politics and public service, as best I understand them.

Eight years ago, I was a relatively unknown railroad attorney, and if I may indulge myself a bit, a pretty good one. And more than that, I thought of myself as a father, a husband, and committed citizen of this country and this state.

I had never sought political office, never harbored political ambitions. But, like most of us, I did hold political convictions. I had taught my children, as my parents taught me, that we owe our community public service, that paying our taxes is not enough, and that when public responsibilities beckon, we owe it to our fellow citizens and to ourselves to take our turn.

And so when public duties called, I took my turn and took my chances. From an unknown lawyer, I became an unknown candidate for the office of governor. My political advisors told me to shave my moustache, to improve my wardrobe and to change my speech. Of course, I refused. I had to be myself.

I offered myself in the tradition of Thomas Jefferson as a "citizen candidate," not as a career politician, as a public-minded citizen hoping to do something for the next generation.

I freely acknowledge the good fortune we had in winning that campaign. But it was exhilarating to think that our democratic politics would allow an unknown candidate who sought public service, who campaigned long and hard, and who tried to present ideas that "made sense," to obtain his party's nomination and be elected governor.

I remember well that election night of November in 1976 as if it were yesterday. We were assembled, family and friends, for a dinner to commemorate the end of the campaign. I recall saying to the others, "We knew at the beginning that it would be difficult, but now what do we do if we win?"

It was a good question then, and I often find myself asking the same question. The answer, I am convinced, has everything to do with the reasons for seeking public office in the first place, and with the spirit of that first campaign—to bring to state government a concern for the longer view—for the investment in the education of our children, for the aggressive development of our economy and our physical resources and for the protection of our environment.

As I explained in my first inaugural address in 1977, "We stay only a moment, and then we're gone. While we're here, we should do what we can to protect the past and secure the future . . . elective public life is something we move into . . . then out of. It is not an occupation. It is a fragile moment in a person's life when trust and confidence are placed. When honesty, integrity, foresight and energy are demanded . . . and must be given . . . I was a citizen candidate. I will be a citizen governor."

But beyond even these important concerns of governing, I have tried, as a "citizen candidate" and a "citizen governor," to reserve in our public debate those qualities of decency and civility that are at the heart of democratic citizenship and which are today, in our state, and elsewhere, in sadly diminishing supply.

That is why I found the 1980 election to be as disturbing as the 1976 election was exhilarating. In my second inaugural address, I expressed my concern that the decency and self-restraint we have long prized in this state are in danger of being eroded, "sometimes, ironically enough, in the name of those very values—of family and community and moral decency—we seek, above all, to preserve."

I believe now what I said then, that "meanness of spirit can have no place in our public life, for it works to dissolve the moral fabric on which a sense of community and shared values depend. Those who seek public office, as much as those who hold it, have a responsibility to set a tone consistent with the values they defend. For when civility and self-restraint are removed from a democratic society, something basic to self-government is lost as well."

Eight years ago, I was not a politician. Today, like it or not, I am. Eight years in politics have no doubt changed me—I hope, for the better. But some things have not changed, including my convictions about democratic citizenship and the ideal of self-government.

In recent weeks and months, many have urged me to seek reelection as governor on the grounds that no one else could do the job. Everyone likes to hear that he or she is indispensable—governors no less than most—and I enjoyed the compliment so much that I began to worry I might actually believe it. But the decision I announce today reflects the same ideals of citizenship and self-government that inspired my decision eight years ago.

I came of the private sector as a citizen candidate seeking public service, knowing it would be only part of my career, feeling that many competent citizens could handle the job and believing that democratic government should work that way. I have not changed my mind.

And so I am stepping back, not necessarily from public life and certainly not from public service, but from another term as state's governor. Much remains to be done, and there always will be—that is the promise and the hope of democratic government. I will not be a candidate for governor in 1984.

Now that you have my reflections and also my announcement, I hope you will bear with me for a few personal thoughts about those who have meant so much.

Last year, a student newspaper reporter from Brigham Young University asked if I had any advice for someone who is thinking of going into politics. I answered, "Yes, you must have the support of your family. If you don't have that support, don't go into politics."

I have had that support through two campaigns and two terms in office. As Norma and I have explained on many occasions, the decision to seek public office in 1976 was a family decision, a decision supported, to be sure, by family loyalty, but inspired even more by a shared family commitment to public service.

My family has assured me of their continued support and sacrifice had I decided to seek a third term, and for that I am deeply grateful, as I am grateful for all they have done to make my public service possible.

In particularly, Norma's good judgment and advice, her tireless service to the people of this state (especially senior citizens) and, most of all, her love and support have made me a better governor and this state a better place in ways that cannot be expressed adequately and that most will never know. I want her to know that she has my love and appreciation for all she has done, today and always.

I hope this announcement will be remembered for two things. In the short run, it will be chronicled as an announcement of immediate political intentions. In the long run, however, it is my wish that my comments be remembered as one person's statement of how our political actors should think and how our politics should work, a statement, I hope, that is worthy of further thought and consideration.

Before concluding this lecture, I want you to know that I love being governor and have done my best to serve. Working hard to fulfill the promise of this calling is the best that public service has to offer. I am proud and grateful to have had an opportunity for a brief time to be part of it.

I said eight years ago that "We need a governor who knows the difference between running a government and leading a state. That difference is purpose. That purpose is what our common commitment is all about." I will let you and history judge whether I have understood that purpose and have led this state accordingly.

Thank you very much.

Notes

IN order to limit the number of notes, the authors have not noted certain historical data or sources which are clearly identifiable in the text. All dated letters, speeches, testimony and memoranda, by, to and from Matheson, are contained in the *Records of Governor Scott M. Matheson,* Utah State Archives, Salt Lake City. Messages of the Presidents are contained in the *Public Papers of the Presidents,* National Archives and Records Service, Washington, D.C. Public laws and public media accounts are not cited where appropriately identified in the text. A copy of major source material for the book and interviews with Matheson Administration aides are contained in the *Scott M. Matheson Archives,* University of Utah, Salt Lake City.

In citing works in the notes, short titles have been used in frequently cited sources and are identified by the following abbreviations:

SMM Records   Records of Governor Scott M. Matheson, Utah State Archives, Salt Lake City.

SMM Speeches   Speeches and Testimony File, Records of Governor Scott M. Matheson, Utah State Archives, Salt Lake City.

CHAPTER 1

Fiscal Crisis: The Challenge to the States

1. David Broder, "The Rudman-Gramm Balanced Budget Sham," *Washington Post* (December 11, 1985).

2. The Report of the Committee on Federalism and National Purpose, *To Form a More Perfect Union* (Washington, D.C.: National Conference on Social Welfare, 1985).

3. David Stockman, *The Triumph of Politics* (New York City: Harper and Row, 1986): 8.

4. From President Reagan's Fiscal Year 1987 Budget, *Special Analysis.* The National Governors' Association has estimated the potential lost revenue at $16 billion from expected levels before enactment of Gramm-Rudman.

5. Spencer Rich, "States May Face $10 Billion Cut Under Budget Law, Study Says," *Washington Post* (February 4, 1986). Study by Fiscal Planning Services of Washington, D.C.

6. Estimates were prepared by authors from data of the National Association of State Budget Officers. They are estimated Fiscal Year 1987 obligations if Gramm-Rudman had not been enacted.

CHAPTER 2

Changing State Roles in a Federal System

1. Scott M. Matheson, "Scott M. Matheson Makes Sense on Intergovernmental Relations" (Salt Lake City: 1976 mimeographed).

2. "Suggested Goals of Matheson Administration," 1977, SMM Records.

3. Adlai Stevenson, "Reorganization from the State's Point of View," *Public Administration Review* 10, No. 5 (1950).

4. See, e.g., *Truax v. Corrigan,* 257 U.S. 312 (1921), dissent of Justice Holmes.

5. Woodrow Wilson, *Constitutional Government of the United States* (New York City: Columbia University Press, 1908): 173.

6. Terry Sanford, *Storm Over the States* (New York City: McGraw Hill, 1967).

7. *The States: Current Conditions, Future Directions* (Lexington: The Council of State Governments, 1985).

CHAPTER 3

Ronald Reagan and New Federalism

1. *The Federal Role in the Federal System: The Dynamics of Growth, An Agenda for American Federalism: Restoring Confidence and Competence* (Washington, D.C.: Advisory Commission on Intergovernmental Relations, 1981).

2. The origin of this quote has proven elusive; however, it was frequently cited during the 1982 New Federalism negotiations; e.g., Eugene Methuin, "Old Case for New Federalism," *Readers Digest* (June 1982).

3. Editorial, *Wall Street Journal* (January 29, 1982).

4. "Governors Vote to Oppose Welfare, Medicaid Shift to States," *Governors' Bulletin*, 81-33 (August 14, 1981).

5. WESTPO Resolution 81-029, adopted November 6, 1981, Scottsdale, Arizona.

6. Governor Richard Snelling to President Ronald Reagan, December 4, 1981, copy of letter, SMM Records.

7. "Reagan Changes Focus with Federalism Plan," *Congressional Quarterly* (January 30, 1982): 147-154, at 148.

8. Ibid.

9. Ibid. at 150.

10. "New Federalism or Feudalism," *Time* (February 8, 1982): 19.

11. *U.S. News & World Report* (March 8, 1982): 31.

12. Ibid.

13. "NGA Finds 1983 Budget Plan May Weaken New Federalism," *Governors' Bulletin,* 82-7 (February 12, 1982).

14. Governor Bruce Babbitt to Governor Richard Snelling, February 3, 1982, copy of letter, SMM Records.

15. David Broder and Herbert Denton, "Reagan's Aides Push Program Swap," *Washington Post* (January 29, 1982).

CHAPTER 4

The Governors Negotiate

1. "NGA Federalism Policy," adopted February 23, 1982, National Governors' Association, Washington, D.C.

2. David Broder and Herbert Denton, "Huge 'Sorting-Out' of Federal Role," *Washington Post* (January 27, 1982).

3. "Governors, White House to Negotiate Details of New Federalism Plan," *Governors' Bulletin,* 82-9, (February 26, 1982).

4. Herbert Denton, "White House Offers 'Federalism Deal,' " *Washington Post* (March 13, 1982).

CHAPTER 5

The Future of Federalism

1. "An Agenda for the Eighties: ACIR's Recommendations to Restore Balance and Discipline," *Intergovernmental Perspective,* 7 (Winter 1981): 6-7.

2. *The States: Current Conditions, Future Directions,* at 45.

3. Dennis P. Doyle and Terry W. Hartle, *Excellence in Education* (Washington, D.C.: American Enterprise Institute, 1985).

4. State efforts contained in *The States: Current Conditions, Future Directions,* and in a 1986 study by the National Governors' Association, *Revitalizing State Economies* (scheduled for publication in 1986).

CHAPTER 6

Confronting MX Deployment

1. For a complete discussion of the strategic and technical aspects of the current TRIAD and proposed MX Missile System, see Office of the Secretary, *Final Environmental Impact Statement: Milestone II* (Washington, D.C.: U.S. Department of the Air Force, 1978).

2. Scott M. Matheson to Secretary Harold Brown, telegram, May 2, 1979, SMM Records; Scott M. Matheson to President Jimmy Carter, telegram, May 2, 1979, SMM Records.

3. Office of Information, "M-X Quick Facts" (Washington, D.C.: U.S. Department of the Air Force, September 7, 1979, mimeographed): 1.

4. Office of the Secretary of Defense (Public Affairs), "Statement by Dr. William J. Perry, Under Secretary of Defense for Research and Engineering," News Release No. 439-79 (Washington, D.C.: U.S. Department of Defense, September 7, 1979, mimeographed): 2.

5. U.S. Department of the Air Force, "Notice of Intent to Prepare an Environmental Impact Statement," *Federal Register* 44, No. 229 (November 27, 1979): 67702.

6. Scott M. Matheson, Remarks Given to Yale Environmental Law Association at Yale University, November 26, 1979, SMM Speeches.

7. Scott M. Matheson to Chairman of the Council on Environmental Quality Gus Speth, December 24, 1979, SMM Records, and Speth to Matheson, January 16, 1980, SMM Records.

8. For a more complete discussion of the Kitsap County, Washington "front-end" method of impact mitigation financing, see testimony of Director of the Office of Economic Adjustment William J. Sheenan, in U.S. Congress, House Committee on Appropriations, *Military Construction Appropriations for 1980: Hearings Before the Subcommittee on Military Construction Appropriations,* 96th Cong. 1st sess., 1980.

CHAPTER 7

Deciding Against the MX

1. For further discussion of Dr. Van Cleave's proposals, see U.S. Congress, Senate Appropriation's Committee, *MX Missile Basing System: Hearings Before the Subcommittee on Military Construction Appropriations,* 96th Cong., 2d sess., 1980, 192-223.

2. For further discussion of Drs. Drell and Garwin's proposals, see U.S. Congress, House Committee on Interior and Insular Affairs, *MX Missile System: Oversight Hearings Before the Subcommittee on Public Lands,* 96th Cong., 1st and 2d sess., 1980, 451-87.

3. Brigadier General James P. McCarthy to Scott M. Matheson, August 20, 1980, SMM Records.

4. McCarthy to Matheson, June 24, 1980, SMM Records.

5. McCarthy to Matheson, August 20, 1980, SMM Records.

6. Matheson to McCarthy, July 17, 1980, SMM Records.

7. U.S. Department of the Air Force, Office of the Secretary, *MX Weapons System Deployment Area Selection/Land Withdrawal Draft Environmental Impact Statement* (Washington, D.C.: U.S. Department of the Air Force, 1980).

8. Scott M. Matheson to Undersecretary Antonia Chayes, December 24, 1980, SMM Records.

9. Chayes to Matheson, January 19, 1981, SMM Records.

10. Secretary Caspar Weinberger to Scott M. Matheson, April 6, 1981, SMM Records.

11. For state of Utah's comments, see Scott M. Matheson to Secretary Vernon Orr, April 23, 1981, SMM Records.

12. First Presidency, "Statement of the First Presidency of the Church of Jesus Christ of Latter-Day Saints on Basing of the MX Missile" (Salt Lake City: Church of Jesus Christ of Latter-Day Saints, May 5, 1981).

13. See, for example, Carl T. Rowan, "Mormon MX Stand Looks Convenient," *Salt Lake Tribune,* (May 14, 1981).

14. Steven Roberts, "Senate Supports MX Fund to Make 21 More Missiles," *New York Times* (March 20, 1985) and Steven Roberts, "House Vote Gives Final Approval for Purchase of 21 MX Missiles," *New York Times* (March 29, 1985).

CHAPTER 8

The Tragedy of Atomic Testing

1. For the state record of this incident, see Dr. Monroe Holmes to Dr. James Steele, "Radiation Health Effects Study," memo regarding Compiled Report on Cooperative Field Survey of Sheep Deaths in S.W. Utah, precise date unknown, Utah State Archives, Salt Lake City, Utah.

2. For a thorough discussion of the AEC's radiation study, see John G. Fuller, *The Day We Bombed Utah: America's Most Lethal Secret* (New York City: New American Library, 1984).

3. *Bulloch v. U.S.,* 145 F.Supp. 824 (1956).

4. For a discussion of AEC actions in 1950-51, see Charles Duncan, *Health Effects of Low-Level Radiation,* Joint Hearings before the Subcommittee on Oversight and Investigations, (Washington, D.C.: 1979). Also See Howard Ball, *Justice Downwind: The Story of America's Atomic Testing Program* (New York City: Oxford Press, 1986).

5. AEC minutes, meeting No. 141, December 13, 1950.

6. Charles Peterson, "Atomic Explosion at Yucca Flats, Nevada: Were You There? If So, the Government Wants to Hear From You!" *Parade* (June 17, 1977): 6.

7. Bill Lord, "Clouds of Doubt," KUTV "Extra" (October 26, 1977).

8. Joseph L. Lyon et al., "Childhood Leukemias Associated With Fallout From Nuclear Testing," *New England Journal of Medicine* 300, No. 8 (February 22, 1979): 397-402.

9. Dr. Edward S. Weiss, U.S. Public Health Service, "Leukemia Mortality Studies in Southwest Utah" (Atomic Energy Commission, unpublished, 1965).

10. "Statement of Joseph Califano Jr., Secretary of Health, Education and Welfare," News Release (Washington, D.C.: U.S. Department of Health, Education and Welfare, February 27, 1979, mimeographed).

11. Chase N. Peterson to Scott M. Matheson, November 21, 1979, SMM Records; and U.S. National Institute of Health, Interagency Radiation Research Committee, *Consideration of Three Proposals to Conduct Research on Possible Health Effects of Radiation From Nuclear Weapons Testing in Arizona, Nevada and Utah and Nuclear Weapons*

Testing and Studies Related to Health Effects: A Historical Summary (Responding to Recommendations by the Panel of Experts on the Archive of PHS Documents) (Washington, D.C.: U.S. Department of Health and Human Services, October 1980).

12. Director of the National Institutes of Health Dr. Donald Fredrickson to Scott M. Matheson, November 25, 1979, SMM Records.

13. U.S. Department of Health and Human Services, National Institute of Health, "HHS News," News Release (Washington, D.C.: September 22, 1980, mimeographed).

14. George Raine, "With $4 Million Aid, Utah Starts Rating Effects of N-Fallout," *Salt Lake Tribune* (September 28, 1980).

15. "Way Cleared for U. Fallout Studies," *Deseret News* (January 14, 1981).

CHAPTER 9

The Politics of Nerve Gas

1. See Rocky Mountain Arsenal and Army Materials and Mechanics Research Center, "Investigation of Leaking Weteye Bombs: Report of the Weteye Reassessment Inspection Task Group" (Colorado: U.S. Department of the Army, Rocky Mountain Arsenal, October 1979): III-1.

2. U.S. Army Material Development and Readiness Command, *Transportation of Chemical Material Operation RMT Final Environmental Impact Statement* (Alexandria, Virginia: U.S. Department of the Army, 1977).

3. *Utah v. Brown, et al.,* C79-0288, U.S. District Court for Utah (May 17, 1979).

4. Scott M. Matheson to Secretary Joseph Califano, May 19, 1978, SMM Records; and Scott M. Matheson to Assistant Secretary of Defense Thomas B. Ross, May 19, 1978, SMM Records.

5. "Technicians' Ills Not Tied to Nerve Gas," *Salt Lake Tribune* (May 25, 1979).

6. U.S. Army Material Development and Readiness Command, *Supplement to Final Environmental Impact Statement Transportation of Chemical Material Operation RMT (1977)* (Alexandria, Virginia: U.S. Department of the Army, 1978).

7. "Chemical War," *Washington Post* (October 1, 1980).

8. "Weteye Transfer Block Stunting TAD Future?" *Salt Lake Tribune* (November 19, 1978).

9. Section 809, Military Construction Authorization Act of 1981, Public Law 96-418.

CHAPTER 10

Public Lands: Rebellion or Cooperation

1. Dee Tranter, "Bulldozer 'Parade' Protests BLM Plan," *Salt Lake Tribune* (July 5, 1980) and Joe Bauman, "250 Watch 'Rebellion' Dozer Cut BLM Land," *Deseret News* (July 5, 1980).

2. For a thorough discussion of public land grants to the states and the evolution of public land policies in general, see U.S. Public Land Law Review Commission (Paul W. Gates), *History of Public Land Law Development* (Washington, D.C.: Government Printing Office, 1968); and U.S. Public Land Law Review Commission, *One Third of the Nation's Land: A Report to the President and the Congress by the Public Land Law Review Commission* (Washington, D.C.: Government Printing Office, 1970).

3. National Environmental Policy Act, 42 *U.S.C.* 4321 et seq. (1982 ed.).

4. See General Indemnity Act of February 28, 1981, 43 *U.S.C.* 851-52 (1982 ed.).

5. *Andrus v. Utah,* 446 U.S. 500 (1980).

6. See Office of Surface Mining, *Southern Utah Petition Evaluation Document Final 522 SMCRA Evaluation and Environmental Impact Statement* (Washington, D.C.: U.S. Department of the Interior, 1980).

7. See John G. Francis, "Environmental Politics, Intergovernmental Politics, and the Sagebrush Rebellion," in John Francis and Richard Gannzel, ed. *Western Public Lands* (Totowa, New Jersey: Rowman and Allenheld, 1984): 25-46.

8. Jones, Waldo, Holbrook and McDonough, "State Control of Energy Development in the West" (Salt Lake City: 1976, unpublished), SMM Records.

9. See, e.g., Utah Attorney General Robert Hansen to Solicitor Leo Krulitz, July 28, 1978, copy of letter, SMM Records.

10. Ch. 633 *Statutes of Nevada* (1979), 2:1362-67.

11. Richard L. Dewsnup to Robert B. Hansen, memo regarding Equal Footing and Federal Lands, July 23 1979, SMM Records.

12. Frank Gregg, "The Sagebrush Rebellion," Annual Gustavson Lecture at the University of Arizona, February 28, 1980.

13. For text of testimony on behalf of James G. Watt's nomination, see U.S. Congress, Senate Energy and Natural Resources Committee, *James G. Watt Nomination: Hearings Before the Energy and Natural Resources Committee,* pt. 1, 97th Cong., 1st sess., 1981, 204-18.

14. Scott M. Matheson, "The Sagebrush Rebellion and a Proposed Solution," Remarks delivered to Arizona State Law School Alumni, February 18, 1981, SMM Speeches.

15. Utah Department of Natural Resources, *Project BOLD: Alternatives for Utah Land Consolidation and Exchange* (Salt Lake City: State of Utah, 1982).

16. Ch. 324, *Laws of Utah* (1983), 2:1332-36; 65-111-1 et seq., *Utah Code Annotated,* 1953.

CHAPTER 11

Wilderness: Who is to Say

1. 16 *U.S.C.* 1134(c) (1982 ed.).

2. This was RARE II because RARE I was struck down by the courts in *Wyoming Outdoor Coordinating Council v. Butz,* 484 F.2d 1244 (10th Cir. 1973).

3. Minutes, State Wilderness Committee Meeting, January 27, 1978.

4. State Wilderness Committee, "Additional Information on Recommendations for Wilderness and Further Study Areas in Utah," (Salt Lake City: State of Utah, September 1978 unpublished).

5. See, for example, Clair Accord (Utah Wool Growers' Association) to Scott M. Matheson, copy of Wool Growers Comments on RARE DEIS, September 18, 1978, SMM Records.

6. Beth Jarman to Scott M. Matheson, memo regarding Wilderness Resolution Adopted by the Governor's Advisory Committee on Community Affairs, October 2, 1978, SMM Records.

7. Senator Jake Garn to Regional Forester Vern Hamre, March 8, 1979, copy of letter, SMM Records.

8. Gordon Harmston to Scott M. Matheson, memo regarding Wilderness Committee Recommendations, March 9, 1979, SMM Records.

9. Forest Service, *Summary - Final Environmental Statement: Roadless Area Review and Evaluation II* FS 324 (Washington, D.C.: U.S. Department of Agriculture, January 1979): 48-9.

10. Jim Butler to State Planning Coordinator Kent Briggs, memo "Ode to Utah Wilderness," March 9, 1979, SMM Records.

11. Washington County Commission Chairman Murray Webb to Scott M. Matheson, March 19, 1979, SMM Records.

12. U.S. Department of Agriculture, Forest Service, Proposed Rule, "National Forest Management System Land and Resource Management Planning," *Federal Register* 48, No. 75 (April 18, 1983): 16505.

13. Utah Wilderness Act of 1984, Public Law 98-428, 98 Stat. 1657-63.

CHAPTER 12

Water: Federal Preemption or Partnership

1. President Jimmy Carter, Press Release (Washington, D.C.: Office of the White House Press Secretary, February 21, 1977): 2.

2. Phillip Shabecoff, "Citizen's Support is Sought for Plan to Cut Dam Funds," *New York Times* (March 1, 1977).

3. *Sierra Club v. Stramm,* 507 F.2d 788 (10th Cir. 1975).

4. Bureau of Reclamation, *Central Utah Project - Bonneville Unit: Final Environmental Statement,* FES 73-42 (Washington, D.C.: Department of the Interior, August 1973).

5. See Scott M. Matheson, "President Carter's Water Policy: Partnership or Preemption?" *Rocky Mountain Mineral Law Institute* 25, No. 1 (1979): 1-25. The article is the basis for the historical perspective and the preemption issues.

6. National Governors' Association, *Policy Positions 1978-79* (Washington, D.C.: National Governors' Association, 1978): 102.

7. 73-10a-1 et seq., *Utah Code Annotated* 1953.

8. Utah Department of Natural Resources and Energy, Division of Water Resources, *State of Utah Water - 1985* (Salt Lake City: State of Utah, 1985): 1.

9. Henry Eason, "The Approaching Water-Supply Crisis," *Nation's Business* (August 1983): 22.

10. Ibid. at 23.

11. Ibid.

12. Ibid.

CHAPTER 13

Natural Resource Development and Environmental Quality

1. Quoted in Francis Leydet, "Coal vs. Parklands," *National Geographic* 138, No. 6 (December 1980): 782.

2. U.S. Bureau of Land Management, *Kaiparowits: Final Environmental Impact Statement* (Washington, D.C.: U.S. Department of Interior, 1976).

3. Christian Hill, "A Replay of Kaiparowitz?" *Wall Street Journal* (October 20, 1977).

4. Scott M. Matheson, "Scott Matheson Makes Sense on Energy and the Environment" (Salt Lake City, 1976, mimeographed).

5. See Note (George S. Young), "Prevention of Significant Deterioration of Air Quality: The Clean Air Act Amendments of 1977 and Utah's Power Generating Industry," *University of Utah Law Review* 4, (1977).

6. *Sierra Club v. Ruckelshaus,* 412 U.S. 541 (1973).

7. Scott M. Matheson, "On Energy and the Environment," at 1.

8. Intermountain Power Project, "Intermountain Power Project and the Clean Air Act Amendments of 1977" (Salt Lake City: July 11, 1979, mimeographed information bulletin).

9. 123 *Congressional Record S 9*, 272-3 (daily ed. June 9, 1977).

10. See 42 *U.S.C.A.* 7475(d)(2)(D)(iii).

11. 123 *Congressional Record H 5*, 013-52 (daily ed. May 25, 1977); and 123 *Congressional Record S 9*, 237-77 (daily ed. June 9, 1977).

12. Secretary Cecil B. Andrus to Joseph Fackrell, August 2, 1977, copy of letter, SMM Records.

13. See Energy Conservation and Development Council, *Report of the Interagency Task Force on Power Plan Siting: Intermountain Power Project* (Salt Lake City: State of Utah, 1977).

14. U.S. Department of the Interior, Bureau of Land Management, *Draft Environmental Impact Statement: Intermountain Power Project,* 3 Vols. (Salt Lake City: U.S. Department of the Interior, 1979).

15. President Jimmy Carter to Scott M. Matheson, December 19, 1979, SMM Records.

16. Robert S. Halliday, "Andrus Gives Go-Ahead on IPP," *Salt Lake Tribune* (December 20, 1979).

17. In 1982, the Community Impact Account was abolished and replaced with the Permanent Community Impact Fund and the Natural Resources Community Impact Board was terminated and replaced with the Permanent Community Impact Board. In addition to these changes, the statute was clarified as to the intent of the legislature as to the use of funds obtained from federal mineral leasing royalties. See 63-52-1 et seq., *Utah Code Annotated,* 1953.

18. Utah State Legislature, House, *Utah Major Facility Siting Act,* 44th Leg., gen. sess., 1981, H.B. 302.

19. 40 *CFR* 1500-1508.

20. For a good overview of major court decisions relating to the National Environmental Policy Act, see Council on Environmental Quality, *Annual Report* (Washington, D.C.: Government Printing Office, 1970-82).

CHAPTER 14

Becoming Governor

Material in this chapter is primarily from interviews of Scott M. Matheson by James Kee and interviews of Matheson aides, *Scott M. Matheson Archives,* University of Utah, Salt Lake City.

CHAPTER 15

Managing Crisis

1. For a good summary of the events of the coal strike and the state's response, see Michael R. Sibbert, *1977-78 Carbon County Coal Strike: A History and Review* (Salt Lake City: Department of Public Safety, Utah Highway Patrol, 1978, mimeographed).

2. The history of Utah flooding was compiled from notes kept by Public Safety Commissioner Larry Lunnen and his staff and newspaper accounts. A summary is con-

tained in *Hazard Mitigation Plan: Utah 1984* (Salt Lake City: Division of Comprehensive Emergency Management, Department of Public Safety, February 1984).

CHAPTER 16

Creating Excellence in Government

1. Thomas Peters and Robert Waterman, *In Search of Excellence: Lessons from America's Best Run Companies* (New York: Harper and Row, 1982).

2. See, e.g., Jed Kee and Roger Black, "Is Excellence in the Public Sector Possible?" *Public Productivity Review* 9, No. 1 (Summer 1985): 25-34. Several of the authors' concepts were first presented in this article.

3. Scott M. Matheson, Remarks to American Fork Area Lions Club, April 28, 1977, SMM Records.

4. Executive Order of the Governors, Executive Order of June 7, 1977, *Utah Administrative Rule Making Bulletin,* No. 77-8 (August 1977): 8.

5. Scott M. Matheson, Remarks at the Air Conservation Committee, January 5, 1977, Salt Lake City, SMM Records.

6. "Utah Majority Favors MX Construction," *Salt Lake Tribune* (October 28, 1979).

7. "MX Opposition Soars Since LDS Statement," *Deseret News* (May 25, 1981).

8. "By Design: Local Space Designers Describe How They Arrive at Eloquent Solutions to Tricky Problems," *Utah Holiday* (March 1983): 73.

9. Ibid.

CHAPTER 17

The Emergence of Regional and National Organizations

The historical background of events in this chapter comes from the notes of the authors and an interview with Kent Briggs, *Scott M. Matheson Archives,* University of Utah, Salt Lake City.

CHAPTER 18

The Governors Debate the Federal Budget

In addition to speeches and testimony of Scott M. Matheson, transcripts of minutes of the discussions and debate of the governors on the federal budget and policy positions are available at the National Governors' Association, Washington, D.C.

CHAPTER 19

New Roles and Future Responsibilities

1. National Commission on Excellence in Education, *A Nation at Risk* (Washington, D.C.: Government Printing Office, 1983).

2. For a detailed description of John Singer and his family, see Raye G. Ringholz, "Armageddon at Marion, Utah," Parts I and II, *Utah Holiday* (January 1979): 39-48 and (February 1979): 36-41.

3. *Singer v. Wadman,* 745 F.2d 606 (10th Cir. 1984), cert. den. March 4, 1985.

4. *Matheson v. Ferry,* 641 P.2d 674 (1982); the issues were reargued in a subsequent case with substantially the same results, *Matheson v. Ferry II,* 657 P.2d 240 (1982).

5. John Naisbitt, *Megatrends* (New York City: Warner Books, 1982): 225-226.

Index